AMERICA

AND THE

FOUNDING

OF ISRAEL

An Investigation of the Morality of America's Role

John W. Mulhall, CSP

Deshon Press
Los Angeles

Published by Deshon Press
Los Angeles

Printed and bound in the United States of America

Excerpts from *The Jerusalem Bible* copyright © 1966 by Darton, Longman & Todd, Ltd. and Doubleday, a division of Bantam Doubleday Dell Publishing Group, Inc. Reprinted by Permission.

Dedicated to Sr. Francis Mulhall, S.H., in gratitude for her constant encouragement

CONTENTS

INTRODUCTION

During the twenty-five years that I wrote and produced a nationally syndicated radio program, *Religion in the News*, and the twenty years that I was also director of Paulist Communications, I produced many radio programs dealing with social-justice issues. In most of these conflicts, such as apartheid, oppression in Latin America, poverty and racism in America, war and peace in the nuclear age, equality for women, right to life, and rights of Native Americans, I found a wide spectrum of Americans who vociferously shared my view that these were inherently burning moral issues. When it came to the morality of American involvement in the Israeli-Palestinian conflict, however, I did not find this to be the case; these same people did not seem to consider it a moral issue for Americans. At least they did not write about it very much.

Yet it was year-in-year-out American diplomacy and billions in American loans and/or outright grants voted for annually by Americans' representatives in Congress that were sustaining the Israeli-Palestinian conflict. It was American-made bombers, paid for, at least in part, by American taxpayers, that were pulverizing Beirut apartment houses and burying their occupants under the rubble. Rightly or wrongly, willingly or not, every American citizen, simply by his or her citizenship, was and is involved in the conflict. I therefore have had a long-standing desire to study this issue as a moral issue more fully.

In 1990, when my assignment to Paulist Communications was completed, I was assigned to a sabbatical year. I spent part of it researching the issue in the Holy Land. I have been able to continue this research as part of my current work. Being satisfied that one has cut through biased presentations, historical half-truths, oft-repeated myths, and exaggerations in order to reach the truth has not come easily. Many points of fact are disputed, and conclusions contested. I have briefly alluded to some of these but have not attempted exhaustively to air all of the arguments pro and con.

This volume explores the morality of American involvement in the Israeli-Palestinian conflict, particularly in the founding of the state of Israel. It does this within an historical context. For some readers the historical facts chronicled herein may speak for themselves. These readers will draw from the chronicles their own conclusions regarding the moral rightness or wrongness of American policy and actions. Other readers may desire an explicit moral evaluation which I believe flows from the facts. Therefore both are presented.

Wherever possible, the moral principles I use are those that transcend the world's major religious and cultural divisions. Most people recognize "is it fair," "do to others as you would have them do to you," "help those in need," "do not kill unjustly," and "do not steal" as universal moral values.

The book examines primarily the morality of *American* involvement in the conflict. However, the first few chapters present background which many readers may find useful in evaluating moral aspects of the conflict itself, and therefore helpful in evaluating the morality of American actions. The first two chapters briefly summarize thirty-six centuries of biblical portrayals and historical events. Added information on this background is given in Notes and in Appendix One.

This book treats only what I term the *objective* morality of a person's action, that is, the moral rightness or wrongness of the act considered just in itself, regardless of what the person doing the act thinks of its morality. The book in no way attempts to treat what I term *subjective* morality, that is, the moral rightness or wrongness of the act as perceived by the person doing it. Thus the book focuses solely on the objective morality of persons' actions, not on the subjective morality of the people who performed them. Moreover, the legality of the actions in terms of national or international law is outside the scope of this book. All of my statements should be understood within these contexts.

ACKNOWLEDGEMENTS

I thank the people who gave their time to read and critique manuscripts, especially Therese Andrysiak, Dr. Robert Bray, Marypat Doherty, Jan Honore', Sister Francis Mulhall of the Society of Helpers of the Holy Souls, and others who remain anonymous. The staffs of the UCLA Research Library, particularly its Public Affairs Section, and of the libraries of Hebrew Union College, Loyola-Marymount University and the University of Judaism, and of the Beverly Hills, Los Angeles and Santa Monica public libraries were always most helpful and courteous. I also thank Christine Coe, Joan Keenan, Eileen and Ted Martner, Anne Megowan and Enid Sevilla for their many hours of volunteer assistance. Anne also computerized and enhanced the maps.

I am very grateful to the many other people in Los Angeles and elsewhere who helped in their personal ways to make this project possible. John and Fran McQuade have been especially helpful in several ways. The final product is, of course, my own responsibility. It does not necessarily represent the thinking of those who have assisted me.

Los Angeles
August 1995

Chapter One

THE BIBLE: A "DEED OF OWNERSHIP" TO CANAAN?

1900 B.C.-722 B.C.

What is the morality of American involvement in the Israeli-Palestinian conflict? Discussing this question usually raises a second question: Who has a greater moral right to the land? How one answers the latter question greatly influences how one evaluates the morality of America's actions in the conflict. Palestinians maintain that until they either fled or were driven off their land during the 1947-49 war, they had owned the land either privately or in common and therefore still have a moral right to it.[1] Many Israelis, other Jews, and some non-Jews maintain that Jews have a prior and stronger moral right than do Palestinians to this same land. Their claims are based in part on (a) biblical stories of events they believe occurred between about 1800 and 500 B.C., and on (b) the history of the Jews between about 500 B.C. and A.D. 135. They maintain that the Bible is the Jews' "deed of ownership" to the land of Canaan. For instance, the Jewish National Fund uses the expression, "...the Bible, which is the Jewish People's 'Deed of Ownership' of the Land of Israel...."[2] This chapter explores the question: Does the Bible give today's Jewish people a "deed of ownership" to this land?

I. The Historical Accuracy in the Old Testament.

How one answers that last question depends greatly on how historically accurate one considers the pertinent books of the Jewish Scriptures, the Old Testament. We will look at three major positions: those of what may be coined the literalists, the moderate historicalists, and the reductionists.[3]

1. *Literalists* include Jewish and Christian fundamentalists. Some theologically very conservative Jews and Christians also

embrace literalism. Typical literalists believe that each word of the Bible is literally true and historically accurate. Literalists tend to equate both God's inspiration of the human biblical authors and God's own authorship of the Bible with historical accuracy. Moreover, they tend to equate all parts of the Bible that are expressed in narrative style with history as history is understood in a modern western sense. Therefore narratives which at first glance *seem* to be historical are understood by literalists as *certainly* historically accurate. To question this would be, for literalists, to question God's authorship of the Bible and God's inspiration of the human biblical authors. Some literalists may occasionally bend their own rules. For instance, some believe that the universe was created not in six days of twenty-four hours each but in six periods of time according to the sequence outlined in the Book of Genesis. Usually, however, literalists hold that "if the Bible says it, it says it; end of discussion." Therefore the promises that God is portrayed as making to Abraham regarding Canaan are to be understood literally. For typical literalists the Bible is for Jews a "deed of ownership" to that land.

2. *Moderate historicalists* include many mainline Protestant, Jewish and Catholic scripture scholars, many archaeologists, and people who consider their interpretations of events portrayed in the Bible as reasonable. They do not equate either God's inspiration of the Bible's human authors or God's own authorship of the Bible with its historical accuracy. Nor do they equate biblical concepts of history with modern western ideas of history. Thus they feel free to question the historical accuracy of some biblical passages, if they judge that this is warranted, without compromising their own faith either in the Bible itself or in God as its author. Moderate historicalists do not think that their present conclusions are necessarily fully accurate or the final word but rather the most plausible in the light of information they now have. They extensively use data that has come to light in Mideast archaeological excavations during the past 150 years. This includes a vast amount of information regarding ancient literature, cultures, trade, migration patterns, farming methods, livestock production, weather patterns (including periods of drought and plentiful

rainfall), military expeditions, development of tool making and housing construction, and religious beliefs and practices.

Moderate historicalists try to synthesize this data with the Bible. From this synthesis they attempt to reconstruct, insofar as they can, a history of the Hebrews from the nineteenth century B.C. through the first century A.D. Moderate historicalists maintain that the Bible's portrayals of events have varying degrees of historical value and must at least be considered part of the data when one is trying to reconstruct Hebrew history. As noted below, moderate historicalists hold positions that raise serious problems for those who claim that the Bible is a "deed of ownership" to Canaan.

3. *Reductionists* are similar to moderate historicalists but tend to assign less historical value to the Bible's portrayals of events. They rely more heavily, if not exclusively, on non-biblical data in trying to construct a history of Palestine's people. Reductionists have become more prominent since the mid-1970s. They do not hold identical positions among themselves. Reductionists agree that there are literary *sources* for the Pentateuch (the Bible's first five books), for the Old Testament's "historical" books from Joshua through Kings II, and for the books of the older prophets. However, reductionists tend to think that these sources were developed much later than moderate historicalists think. Reductionists hold other positions that raise even more serious problems than those raised by moderate historicalists for those who claim that the Bible is today's Jewish people's "deed of ownership" to Canaan.

Examining these positions more fully can help one understand how they relate to that claim of a "deed." First, at the risk of oversimplifying, these are some representative positions of *moderate historicalists*:[4]

II. Abram and His World, 2000-1750 B.C.

Abram (Abraham), a central character in the claim that the Bible is the Jews' "deed of ownership" to Canaan, is portrayed in Genesis as the Hebrews' key ancestor. To the extent that he may be historical he is thought to have lived between 2000 and 1750 B.C. According to Genesis, Abram was from Ur in southern

Mesopotamia but moved to Haran, a city in what is now southern Turkey. (Cf. Map One, p. 227.) Members of Abram's immediate ethnic group, the Arameans, were perhaps part of a larger group, the Amorites. Arameans lived in and near Haran. Some moderate historicalists think that between 2000 and 1750 B.C. many Arameans migrated southwest from there to Canaan. Archaeological evidence suggests that Canaan may have suffered greatly from marauders and had lost much of its population shortly before Abram's time. The Bible depicts God as calling him to migrate from Haran to Canaan.

How historical are Abram, his son, Isaac, and his grandson, Jacob - the Patriarchs - and the events which the Bible depicts about them? Our only accounts of them are in Genesis, probably written in its final form in the sixth or fifth century B.C.[5] However, many of these stories are thought to have been taken from two older pieces of literature, or at least from two traditions, which moderate historicalists *think* must have existed. If they did exist, moderate historicalists think they were probably shaped and perhaps even written between the tenth and eighth centuries B.C. These two traditions in turn would have incorporated much older traditions, either written or oral or both.[6] Therefore our lack of written documents dating back to the Patriarchs does not *necessarily* invalidate the factualness of the traditions about them. However, the passage of nearly one thousand years between the depicted events and the shaping of the two hypothesized traditions leaves room for doubt. The passage of another 300-500 years between the possible writing down of these traditions and the final draft of Genesis increases that room for doubt.

A similar caution applies to later events portrayed in the Pentateuch and in the books of Joshua and Judges regarding the Hebrew flight from Egypt, the promises God made to Moses, and the Hebrew entry into Canaan. According to scripture scholar Richard Clifford, "authentic stories of 2d-millennium ancestors have been revised and added to in the long course of their transmission; recovery of the 'original' stories is impossible because of the lack of extrabiblical sources."[7] Scholar Roland Murphy notes: "history is to be found in the book of Kings, rather than in the Pentateuch, although some kind of historical memory is preserved in the patriarchal and exodus narratives. "[8]

Artifacts that tell about the era in which the Patriarchs supposedly lived neither confirm nor deny their existence but do indicate that some of what Genesis depicts about them *could* have taken place. However, the stories in Genesis and the other Pentateuch books, insofar as they may reflect real people and events, are thought to be highly simplified. Some or all of the events attributed to the three Patriarchs and their families may have happened to other people but were combined and simplified as happening to members of these three families. Moderate historicalists think that the author or authors of Genesis were not trying to write history as we think of it. They were trying to explain to sixth or fifth century B.C. Jews how, from a religious viewpoint, the devastating Babylonian Captivity, 597/587-539, could have happened. They freely adapted existing traditions to meet their pedagogical needs.[9] Thus the *purpose* for which Genesis was written greatly increases the doubts about historical accuracy which were already created by the passage of time.

All of these factors make it impossible today to know how factual are the promises about the land, which God is portrayed as making to the Patriarchs.[10]

Genesis[11] depicts Abraham and his family as seminomads, sometimes moving in search of grazing land, sometimes settling down for a while on the edge of towns. The family enjoyed, with few exceptions, a peaceful existence; it used Canaan's less populated regions. Here seminomadic livestock producers could live peaceably with their townsfolk neighbors, supplying them with meat, wool and other products. Abraham and Isaac are not depicted as displacing the natives. The same is generally true of Genesis' portrayal of Jacob (Israel) and his twelve sons.[12] This pastoral backdrop may suggest that if God promised anything it was only a *share* in the land's *use*, not exclusive ownership of it.

III. Abraham's Descendants.

Typical moderate historicalists think that some of the stories about Abraham's sons and grandsons are probably not factual but a way of portraying the relationship between the Hebrews and their neighbors. According to this theory the story about the problems between the half brothers, Isaac and Ishmael, may express the troubled relationship between the Hebrews and the Arab tribes around them.[13] If Ishmael and the incident are factual, which moderate historicalists think unlikely, his descendants are presumably still among the Arabs in the area. Because *literalist* Jews and Christians accept the incident as factual, they believe it strengthens Jewish claims that God promised Canaan exclusively to Isaac's descendants. Genesis also portrays God as renewing to Isaac God's promise of the land.[14]

According to the same theory that moderate historicalists apply to the portrayal of the relationship between Isaac and Ishmael, the hostile relationship between Isaac's twin sons, Jacob and Esau, also is probably not factual. Instead it may represent the relationship between the Hebrews and the Edomites, their southeastern neighbors.[15] Genesis portrays the disinherited Esau as going to his banished uncle, Ishmael, and choosing one of his daughters as a wife, in addition to the wives he had. Thus she was his first cousin and their child was a descendant of Abraham on both of his parents' sides. If Esau and his disinheritance are factual, which moderate historicalists think unlikely, he lost his legal rights. But did Esau and his descendants, which presumably include Arabs in today's Holy Land, also lose their share in the promise made to Esau's grandfather, Abraham? This share would have been more than a legal right. Jews and Arabs disagree on the issue. It is relevant only to those who hold that the story is factual.

Thus, for the moderate historicalists the promises that God is portrayed as making to Abraham and Isaac, and the blessings which Isaac is portrayed as giving to Jacob rather than to Esau, are shrouded in doubt. Did they really take place, and if so, did they grant what they are depicted as granting? Or were they invented as symbols of some deeper reality? If one believes that in these particular passages (as in many others) the Bible perhaps teaches a deeper truth instead of the literal meaning, these promises and blessings lose any value as a basis for claiming that the Bible is the modern Jews' "deed of ownership" to the Holy Land. But if one holds with the literalists that every word of the Bible is literally and historically true, one has no choice but to conclude that these promises and blessings are historically factual.

IV. Hebrews' Migration to Egypt and Settlement in Canaan.

Those who maintain that the Bible gives the Jews a moral right to Canaan also point, in support of this, to the Bible's portrayal of God as aiding the Hebrews' conquest of Canaan forty years after their flight from Egypt. By way of background: According to Genesis, eleven of Jacob's sons had sold their brother, Joseph, into slavery. He became Egypt's prime minister. During a famine in Canaan, probably shortly before 1700 B.C., he forgivingly arranged for his father, brothers and their families to migrate to Egypt. Genesis indicates that it was 215 years after Abraham migrated to Canaan. The Book of Exodus, which continues the story after Genesis, says Jacob's descendants ("Hebrews" or "Israelites") remained in Egypt 430 years. However, the Septuagint, a Greek translation of the Bible from Hebrew, says the Hebrews were in Egypt only 215 years. This discrepancy may indicate that there was more than one Israelite migration both to Egypt and back to Canaan. In about 1550 B.C., a pharaoh virtually enslaved the Hebrews to work on state-owned projects. According to Exodus, Moses, under God's guidance and urging, led the Hebrews out of Egypt and into Sinai (probably between 1300 and 1280 B.C.). More than 600,000 men, plus women and children, are portrayed as taking part in the flight. On several occasions during the Hebrews' forty years in Sinai, God is depicted as promising them possession of Canaan. At the end of the forty years Moses died. According to the Book of Joshua, Moses' first assistant, Joshua, led the Hebrews west across the Jordan River. Through a series of military conquests they subdued part, but not all, of Canaan. God is portrayed as intervening on several occasions to help the Hebrews gain military victories.

From their present store of archaeological data, moderate historicalists think that some type of migration from Canaan into

Egypt and some type of exodus from Egypt into Sinai occurred. After a time in Sinai, Hebrews in some way entered Canaan. However, whatever happened was much more complex than Exodus and Joshua portray. Some moderate historicalists conjecture that:

1. The Hebrews who participated in Moses' flight had to be many fewer than the 600,000 men plus women and children stated in the books of Exodus and Numbers - an estimated total of 2.5 million people.[16] It is unlikely that the eleven families - seventy people - who moved to Egypt at Joseph's invitation multiplied within 430 years - some eleven generations - to about 2.5 million people, even if later migrations from Canaan greatly increased Egypt's Hebrew population. A. Lucas estimates that "the original seventy Israelites would have become 10,363 at the end of 430 years."[17] Lucas's projected figures are very unlikely but he could still be correct in arguing that a relatively small number of people could have fled Egypt and entered a land that was then sparsely settled. There may have been slightly more than 200,000 people in Canaan in the fourteenth century, about a century before Joshua supposedly entered it.[18]

2. Archaeological data suggests that during the time leading up to Joshua's era, Canaan had palatial villas owned by the very rich next to the hovels of their oppressed serfs. Perhaps at that time Canaan had virtually no middle class. Contemporary documents speak of "rootless" people with no place in the economic system, people who lived as outlaws. Canaan was seemingly ripe for revolution. Its city-states were under the loose control of Egypt's increasingly weak government. When the lords of these cities asked Egypt for military help to maintain order, their urgent requests went unanswered. Thus the political and military situation would have worked to the advantage of invading Hebrews *and* of rebels who may have allied themselves with them. Archaeologists have found several Canaanite cities that were destroyed at about the time Joshua would have entered Canaan. Some of the cities may have been torched either by natives rebelling against their overlords, or by rebels working in tandem with Hebrews attacking from outside.

3. The Book of Judges and the Book of Joshua itself frequently contradict the portrayal of the destruction of Canaan's inhabitants depicted in Joshua. According to Catholic scripture scholar Michael Coogan:

Archaeological evidence confirms the literary analysis of the book: few if any of the major episodes in Joshua can be shown to be historical. Thus, neither Jericho nor Ai nor Gibeon [cities portrayed in Joshua as destroyed by invading Israelites] was occupied in the period in which most scholars would date the emergence of Israel in Canaan (*ca.* 1200). Although some of the cities said to have been destroyed by Joshua show evidence of destruction in this period, the dates vary considerably; Hazor, for example, was destroyed a century before Lachish.[19]

4. Many native Canaanites were perhaps Amorites,[20] the large ethnic group of which Abram's Arameans were perhaps a subgroup. These Amorites would perhaps have been ethnically related to the incoming Hebrews.[21] If some of the natives were Jacob's descendants who had never left Canaan for Egypt or who had immigrated back to Canaan at various times during the 430 years before Moses' flight, they would have been even more closely related to the incoming Hebrews. When Moses' people arrived, they would have had relatives already there. The Bible portrays some natives as allying themselves with incoming Hebrews. There is no biblical or non-biblical evidence that Hebrews ever killed or expelled *these* natives.[22]

5. The Bible states that not only Amorites but other ethnic groups lived in Canaan in Joshua's era. He did not conquer all of them. Judges 1 states that Hebrews enslaved many natives rather than expel or kill them. Judges 3:5-6 also relates: "The Israelites lived among the Canaanites and Hittites and Amorites, the Perizzites, Hivites and Jebusites; they married the daughters of these peoples, gave their own daughters in marriage to their sons, and served their gods." According to this, extensive genetic, religious and cultural blending occurred. Large ethnic groups remained free. Some, including Hittites and Edomites, were noted in David's reign, more than two hundred years later. David vastly

extended Hebrew rule by both assimilation and conquest *within* Canaan. This shows how incomplete Hebrew rule was when he began to reign about 1000 B.C.[23] The Philistines, in Canaan's central and southern coastal area, became David's vassals but kept their identity until the second century B.C. or later.[24]

In light of these five points, many moderate historicalists maintain that what appears from a quick reading of Exodus and Joshua as primarily a military conquest may in fact have been much more of a gradual assimilation of the indigenous and the incoming populations under the control or leadership of the Israelites. What emerged as the Israelites in the early centuries of the first millennium B.C. was in reality a blend of Canaanite and Hebrew ancestry, with most of the ancestry having been Canaanite. Thus the Canaanites were not driven out but lived on as Israelites.

These conjectures greatly change the picture one gets from reading Exodus, Deuteronomy, Joshua and other Old Testament books about the type of migration that God is pictured as urging and assisting. However, the *impression* given in these books is that God promised a group of several million people that they and their descendants would receive exclusive, perpetual ownership of a land from which the natives should be completely either driven out or destroyed. It is this blood-soaked picture that has been handed down within the Judeo-Christian tradition at least since these books were written in the sixth and fifth centuries B.C. In the last 150 years the validity of that picture has been seriously questioned.

V. The Conquest of Land.

With regard to the area's *land*: The Bible indicates that during the 150-year era of Judges - the period after Joshua and before the first king, Saul - land *claimed* by the twelve tribes included all of Palestine west of the Jordan River and the Dead Sea, and southwest from the Dead Sea to the Mediterranean, well south of the present-day Gaza Strip.[25] The tribes did not claim the southern Negev[26] Desert. At that time tribes also claimed land northwest of the Sea of Galilee to a point slightly above Tyre, in modern Lebanon. Two and a half tribes also claimed land east of the

Jordan River and the Dead Sea, in the biblical Trans-Jordan region, now part of modern Jordan and Syria.

Although the Bible portrays the twelve tribes as claiming all of this land during the era of Judges, they did not control all of it, as David's wars with various groups also portray. Philistines ruled much of the coastal plain, including the modern Gaza Strip. They also may have controlled the Plain of Esdraelon, a long northwest-to-southeast valley south of Galilee. If they did, they would have virtually cut Hebrews' holdings into a northern and a southern region. The modern Gaza Strip was inhabited primarily by Philistines for most of the time between the twelfth and fifth centuries B.C. Therefore it was inhabited to a lesser extent by Hebrews than were other parts of Palestine. This helps explain why some modern Israelis are more willing, ideologically, to relinquish Gaza than they are West Bank - biblical Judea and Samaria - which was more often extensively inhabited by Hebrews.

VI. The Twelve Tribes' Relationship: an Alternate Theory.

The Bible fairly consistently portrays ancient Israel as composed of twelve tribes descended from Jacob's twelve sons. However, the lists vary. According to Old Testament scholar Lawrence Boadt: "As with so many biblical genealogies in the Book of Genesis, we must reckon that each 'son' really represents a whole tribe or clan, and that the twelve-tribe family understood themselves as equals ('brother') in some form of federation."[27] Father Boadt adds that differences in the lists of tribes may indicate that it took many decades for all twelve tribes to unite. Differences in the lists and what led to them "let us know that the simple stories of Jacob and his sons mask a long history of groups and individuals coming together to form what emerges at the end of the period of the judges as the nation of Israel."[28] If the theory is correct, perhaps the "Promised Land" was not so much a land conquered by outsiders as a land united by people already there.

The story of the Hebrew entry into Canaan is a major factor in modern attitudes toward Jewish claims to it. Any position regarding that account must be approached cautiously. Father

Boadt notes:

In studying the historical remembrances of the early period in Joshua and Judges we are faced with their claims that Israel took the land of Palestine by violent assault. Many scholars today offer other possible means by which Israel gained possession of its land. The evidence is complex and difficult to use because there is so little on which to base a conclusion. The newer theories point out the problems with a military conquest of the land, but their own counter proposals are even less certain.[29]

VII. Israel's Expansion Under David.

According to the Bible,[30] through many wars (of aggression), David expanded Israel's territory farther south into the Negev, into southwestern Syria, and somewhat farther east into Trans-Jordan than had been true during the Judges' era. Conflicting statements in the Bible present a confused picture of the actual size of the David-Solomon empire. David's son, Solomon, may also have gained some economic control of the area north of his Syrian holdings. Significantly, not all of the land under David and Solomon's military and political control became inhabited by Israelites, who remained within their traditional home areas. Lands beyond these claims were more like David and Solomon's personal possessions; they continued to be populated by their native ethnic groups. After Solomon died in 931, the ten northern tribes rebelled against the House of David and formed the Kingdom of Israel. Its capital was the city of Samaria. David's tribe of Judah, the tribe of Benjamin and part of the tribe of Simeon supported the kings descended from David and formed the southern Kingdom of Judah. The two kingdoms, weakened by their division, lost most of David's non-tribal conquests. They were regained briefly but were soon lost again permanently until the Negev was allotted to modern Israel in 1947. Many Jews today do not consider David's acquisitions outside of Palestine and tribal Trans-Jordan part of the true Israel of old - *Eretz Israel*. Therefore they are not part of the land they want to claim. But the former existence of that expanded empire worries modern Arab states whose areas include parts of that empire: If Jews have a moral right to the biblical land of Israel, will the distinction between the tribal land and the non-tribal Davidic additions always be recognized in the future?

Moderate historicalists may not unanimously accept the positions concerning the Old Testament exactly as stated above but many of them hold either these or similar positions. These positions seriously question the validity of claiming that the Bible is the Jews' "deed of ownership" to the Holy Land.[31]

VIII. Positions of Reductionists.

Although reductionists vary in their positions, they tend to carry the historical method of moderate historicalists further and therefore draw different conclusions. They tend to be more doubtful of the historical value of the pertinent books of the Bible. They see them more as fiction than as history. They think these books reflect very late written traditions, some as late as the sixth and fifth centuries B.C. Relying largely or solely on archaeological evidence reductionists tend to think that:

1. There was no Amorite-Aramean migration into Canaan between 2000 and 1750 B.C.

2. There was no *major* Hebrew invasion of Canaan in the thirteenth or any other century B.C. - perhaps no invasion at all. Instead, the movements of people in Canaan during the thirteenth century are better explained by: (a) natives moving from farming to grazing areas and back, due to long droughts followed by periods of plentiful rainfall; (b) serfs escaping from lowland city-states into relatively uninhabited highlands, where they began agricultural villages; (c) perhaps some gradual immigration by Amorites and by slaves escaping from Egypt; and (d) a variety of other possible causes. Each of the above causes is conjectural.

3. We have *no evidence* to indicate that the Hebrews were immigrants or invaders rather than simply, or at least primarily, descendants of the area's natives, whom the Bible calls Canaanites. On the contrary there is positive evidence indicating that the He-

brews are simply or at least primarily descendants of these Canaanites, rather than a blend of Canaanites and incoming Hebrews.

4. We have a single Egyptian reference to "Israel" about 1230
B.C., and several references to *Hapiru* (Hebrews?) in the Amarna
letters in the late fifteenth and early fourteenth centuries. Aside
from these we have only a fragmentary non-biblical history of the
region which the Bible calls Canaan, before the reign of King
Omri of Samaria in the mid-ninth century. However, we have
some archaeological evidence of what happened and what probably
did not happen. We have no non-biblical evidence that the
Patriarchs or Moses existed or that God made any promises to
anyone about the land of Canaan.[32]

5. According to at least one reductionist, archaeological data
indicates that Jerusalem was not an important city until the late
eighth century B.C., after Assyria captured Samaria and destroyed
the Kingdom of Israel, the "northern kingdom." Therefore, he
maintains, Jerusalem was developed much later than was the city
of Samaria. Jerusalem could not have been the capital of a
monarchy uniting Judea and Samaria under David and Solomon
during the tenth century. Moreover, there was no united monarchy
before Assyria destroyed the Kingdom of Israel in 722 B.C. (And
there could have been none afterward until the Maccabean period
in the second and first centuries B.C.) Thus the historical factualness of Saul, David and Solomon, their wars of conquest, and the
size of their empires would seem to be seriously questioned by this
reductionist.[33]

Another reductionist, J.M. Miller, thinks that many, perhaps
most, traditions about David and Solomon are based on actual
historical persons and events. But he thinks that their empire was
much smaller than some moderate historicalists believe. Miller
maintains that it extended only some fifteen miles north of Lake
Hulah and some twenty-five miles east into Syria. It did not
include the Bakaa Valley, Damascus, or lands nearer to the
Euphrates River, as some Bible passages seem to indicate.[34]

The reductionist group of archaeologists and biblical scholars
has grown in the past twenty years. Its scholarship, especially its

conclusions, have met with moderate-historicalist criticism. For what they are worth, reductionists' conclusions even more seriously call into question the claim that the Bible is the Jewish people's "deed of ownership" to the Holy Land.

IX. Positions of Fundamentalists and Other Biblical Literalists.

As noted above, fundamentalists and other biblical literalists assert that the Bible is such a deed. They contend that every word of the Bible, including God's promises to Abraham and Moses, must be understood exactly as stated. Fundamentalists' God of fire and brimstone has Its own terrifying code of justice unfettered by human concepts of human rights or of justice between humans. God can therefore authorize human beings to destroy other human beings - soldiers, civilians, little children - and take over their land. Some fundamentalists are also premillennialists. They believe that one condition for the second coming of Christ and for the Millennium to follow is the "ingathering" of all Jews into the Promised Land. Therefore they strongly support the state of Israel and Jewish immigration to the Holy Land. There are perhaps thirty million American fundamentalists. Many of them regularly watch premillennialism being preached by leading TV evangelists.[35] To deal adequately with biblical literalism as it relates to the morality of American involvement in the Israeli-Palestinian conflict would require a tangent beyond the scope of this study. The moral principles used herein should speak to all people, including biblical literalists.[36]

X. Doubtful Rights Versus Definite Rights.

Whether or not the historical factualness of God's promises to Abraham, Isaac and Moses can be proved, they still may have taken place. They may still be factual although unprovable to anyone but literalists. (Provability is not only in the evidence but also in the minds and hearts of those weighing it.) It would seem that the most that can be stated with certainty is that the Bible may reflect either (a) a non-historical literary devise, or (b) the existence of a deed of ownership to the land of Canaan, or (c) something between these two extremes. With the evidence we now have, this deed's existence seemingly cannot be proved to the satisfaction of anyone but biblical literalists. Its existence is at best doubtful not only to many people in general but to many non-fundamentalist Jews in particular. Therefore the moral rights which depend solely on the existence of a biblical deed of ownership either do not exist or are at best doubtful. Moreover, doubts exist about what the promises meant when they were supposedly made, and - if they were made - what they mean today. At the time of Abraham did they refer to real estate or to spiritual values? Today do they still refer to inherited real estate or to inherited spiritual values? Palestinians who had definite possession of that land for countless generations had a definite, clear right to it. Thus it is a case of weighing the definite right of the Palestinians against the at-best doubtful right of the Zionists. To take away a definite right from one person to make way for at best a doubtful right of another person does not seem morally just.

XI. Perspectives of Church Personnel in the Holy Land.

When I was in the Holy Land in 1991 I interviewed several people, including an Arab leader of a mainline Protestant church. He told me that the most difficult questions he faced regarding religious faith among his Palestinian Arab church members were these: Are the Jews really the People of God? Is this land theirs or ours? If it's theirs, how can God do such a thing? Does God love the Jews more than He loves the Palestinians? Is there any justice from God or don't we have justice from God either? This Protestant leader told me he would reply to his Arab students: Some churches, such as the Baptist Church and the new evangelical churches, interpret literally the portrayal of God taking the land away from the Canaanites and giving it to the Israelites; however, it is not our theology as non-fundamentalist Palestinians to take it literally.

His Beatitude, Msgr. Michel Sabbah, is the first Arab appointed Latin Catholic Patriarch of Jerusalem. He was the only one I interviewed who did not request anonymity. When I asked him if the covenants portrayed in the Old Testament give Jews today any special claim to the Holy Land, he replied in part: "God loves every human without discrimination....No injustice at all can be committed in the name of God's love. That is the criteria to judge whether the Jews have a religious right to the land or not....God's love cannot admit any injustice by one people against another."[37]

I spoke with several "third party" Catholic church personnel, that is, non-Jewish and non-Palestinian residents of the Holy Land. They are not a party to the Palestinian-Israeli conflict but live with its consequences and are forced to reflect on it. To the same question about whether the Old Testament covenants give Jews today any special claim to the Holy Land, a priest from Europe replied: This is a question not about morality but about how one interprets biblical passages. The answer would be different for a Christian, for a Jew and for a non-believer. The Bible is a religious book. Maybe it's also a cultural history, at least a cultural heritage for the Jewish people and also for Christians in a certain sense. But it's not a juridical book; it's not a code of law. The Bible, he said, does not in itself give any rights.

Jewish people, this priest continued, feel very attached to this land and consider it given to them by God, or at least linked to their destiny by God's will. But someone who does not believe as Jews believe, who is not a Jew, is not obliged to have the same conviction. Some Christians say the covenant is still valid; the promise of the land is still valid. However, we have the New Testament and the fact that now all the peoples are elected. Now the Covenant is with all the peoples of the earth. There is no one special people any more. The barrier between Jews and Gentiles has been abolished in Christ.

As a people, the Catholic priest said, the Jews are attached to this land for historical, cultural or religious reasons; the Bible and what it says to the Jewish people are one element of this attachment. The Palestinian people are attached to the same land for historical, social, cultural and sometimes religious reasons. But the religious reasons, whether held by Jews or Palestinians, are not absolute. Why? Because for someone who does not have the same faith, these religious reasons, and the rights based on them, are only on the same level as cultural, historical or social reasons. Moreover, both believer and non-believer can recognize Palestinians' and Jews' attachment to the land. But the question of whether this attachment creates rights to the land depends on whether or not the implementation of these rights can be realized without creating injustice for other people. Then we pass from the religious field to a completely different one - the field of international law. Again, the Bible does not give rights.

Another European Catholic priest and longtime Holy Land resident replied to my question about rights to the land being conveyed by the Old Testament covenants: Political rights, he said, are based on the rule of the civilization we live in, not on the Bible. He added: I do not believe that the Bible is to be strictly implemented today as it is written, because the framework is very different. Did Abraham have the *boundaries* of the country promised to him? No. National boundaries at that time were not known in the world. Even Assyria and Egypt did not have boundaries. Egypt consisted politically of its towns and in some way of the countryside. This was the concept of the state at that time. We cannot apply the manner of living of four millennia ago to the framework of the political family, of the human family, today. It's quite different. We cannot do it; it would be unjust.

The human race is a family, this second priest added. This family has grown during the intervening four thousand years. We must accept the political realities resulting from these changes if we're to see the current situation correctly. We cannot take a spiritual book written several millennia ago for a nation's *spiritual* destiny and apply it, just as it was written, to a political reality now. Such an attempt is not being true to the Bible.

My attempts to obtain Greek Catholic, Greek Orthodox and Jewish interviews in the Holy Land were unsuccessful. Several books by Jews at least touch on the moral dimensions of the conflict.[38] The basic principle among the Catholic and mainline Protestant church personnel I interviewed is that God could not be a party to an injustice, let alone promote it. Therefore God promised the Israelites nothing that would have been unjust to the Canaanite inhabitants. God promised nothing that would have violated Canaanites' rights to the land they called home. God would not have helped the Israelites capture Jericho from its rightful inhabitants. God would not have ordered the Israelites to slay soldiers and civilians captured in whatever cities they may have conquered. By the same line of reasoning, these Catholic and mainline Protestant church personnel maintain that God could not be a party to injustices against twentieth century Palestinians. They therefore deny that the Bible is the Jewish people's "deed of ownership" to the Holy Land.

Chapter Two

THE MORAL HEREDITARY RIGHT TO RETURN

721 B.C.-A.D. 1800

The assertion that the Bible is the Jews' "deed of ownership" to the land of Canaan is not the only basis for Zionists' claims to the Holy Land. They also cite Jews' long *history* there and maintain that it precedes that of the Palestinians. Zionists assert: "We were here first!"[1] This, they argue, gives Jews today a greater moral right to the Holy Land than Palestinians possess. They also maintain that after some Jews were driven out in 587 B.C. and in A.D. 135, they never gave up their *desire to return* there and have their own independent state. Zionists contend that this historical involvement and the desire to return created a *moral hereditary right* to the Holy Land that in itself outweighs any moral right of the Palestinians. (A moral right may be one which its possessor has independently of any legal basis. Such a moral right, for instance the right to life or to religion, is inherent and thus does not depend on human legislation or decree for its existence. A second type of moral right may flow partly from one or more primary moral rights and partly from legislation or other type of legal action - for instance, some inheritance rights and political rights.)

Chapter One looked at Hebrews' involvement in the Holy Land between 1900 B.C. and 722 B.C. In the next year that involvement changed radically. Chapter Two looks at (a) the Jews' ensuing involvement with the Holy Land and at (b) Diaspora Jews' desire to return there. It examines whether in the light of history these two factors created a true *moral hereditary right* that outweighs the Palestinians' moral rights.

I. Assyria, Babylon, Post-exilic Life, 721-168 B.C.[2]

In 721 the Assyrian Empire, helped by the Kingdom of Judah,

completed its conquest of the Kingdom of Israel, the "northern kingdom."[3] (Judah was then probably a vassal state of Assyria.) Assyria deported many, perhaps most, of Israel's people to upper Mesopotamia, and to Media in the eastern part of the empire. These deportees, the "ten lost tribes of Israel," vanished as an identifiable ethnic group. Assyria imported non-Israelites into the former kingdom. These importees intermarried with Israelites who had not been deported. These families were the origin of the Samaritans, who have lived in Samaria ever since. In A.D. 1990 about 550 Samaritans lived in and around Nablus, and Holon, near Tel Aviv.[4] In 597 B.C. Babylon defeated the Kingdom of Judah and deported some of its people, called Jews, to southern Mesopotamia. In 587 Babylon crushed a revolt among the remnant in Judah. Babylon destroyed Jerusalem, including Solomon's magnificent Temple, and deported many of Judah's remaining inhabitants to Babylon. Some farm workers and others were allowed to stay. Some Jews from Judah fled to Egypt and joined or began Diaspora colonies there.

Forty-eight years after the second deportation, in 539, Cyrus, a Persian king, conquered Babylon. According to the Bible he allowed Jews to return to Jerusalem, and helped finance their return. The initial group of returnees apparently was small. The noted archaeologist and scripture scholar, W.F. Albright, estimated that the Persian district of Judah had some twenty thousand people by 522 B.C. This included those who had never left it.[5] A second group was larger. Ezra, one of the Bible's books treating this period, says this group contained 42,360 free people, 7,337 slaves and two hundred singers.[6] According to Father Boadt: "This may be many more than actually made the journey itself, and may include the people already living in the Jerusalem area."[7]

Judah's territory, about forty miles wide and twenty-five miles deep in 440 B.C., was much smaller than the former Kingdom of Judah. Now it was essentially the area around Jerusalem, which Jews were rebuilding. As part of the Persian Empire Judah enjoyed extensive religious and cultural freedom. But many, perhaps most, Jews did not choose to return there.[8] They had sunk roots in the Babylonian - then Persian - Empire. Many were prospering. They preferred to stay where they were rather than undertake the long, difficult and somewhat dangerous trip back to the ruins of Jerusalem and to the hostile environment that other ethnic groups in the area provided. Their decision continued the Diaspora - Jewish life outside Palestine. The Diaspora has been the experience of most Jews ever since. Understandable as was the decision *not* to return, what effect, if any, should that decision have on the moral right of *those* Jews' descendants to immigrate to the Holy Land twenty-four centuries later? This will be examined in Section VI of this chapter.

In 332 Macedonia's King Alexander took over Judah from Persia. After his death in 323 his empire was divided among his generals. Following a power struggle Palestine was ruled first by the Ptolemies, based in Egypt, then, after 198 B.C., by other Greeks, the Seleucids, based in Antioch, in Syria.

During this time non-Samaritan descendants of the Israelites left behind when Assyria deported much of the Kingdom of Israel in 721 were living outside of Judah, in other parts of Palestine such as Galilee, and in Trans-Jordan. Some of them were probably at least nominally Yahwists, at least nominally believers in the God of the Jews. According to biblical scholar John Bright, some of them "came to reckon themselves to be the Jewish community. At least this was true by the second century [B.C.] and was probably the case much sooner."[9] Thus people who were ethnically Israelites and other people who were converts to Judaism or their descendants lived both in Judah and throughout Palestine and in Trans-Jordan. However, non-Jews also lived there, including Greek colonists, Samaritans in Samaria, and Philistines or their descendants along the coast.

II. Maccabean War, Roman Take-over, 168 B.C.-A.D. 65.

In 168 B.C.[10] some Judean Jews, led by the family later known as the Maccabees and then as the Hasmoneans, revolted against the Seleucid Empire. They repeatedly defeated the

Seleucids in protracted warfare. By 141 B.C. the Palestinian Jews emerged *de facto* as a virtually independent nation although they remained nominally subject to the Seleucids. The area controlled by the Maccabees was approximately that perhaps claimed by the Twelve Tribes during the era of the Judges. Conversion to Judaism was forced on Idumeans living in Maccabean-conquered areas. This increased the Jewish population.

By 63 B.C. the Jewish leaders were fighting among themselves. The Roman Empire, which was exercising increasing influence in the eastern Mediterranean, was invited to intervene. As a result, Rome's Pompey marched into Jerusalem and ended some seventy-eight years of Jewish independence. Rome allowed Jews to practice their religion and follow their customs. In 40 B.C. Parthians invaded the neighborhood of Palestine - the name Greeks had given to the area because of its Philistines. A Hasmonean, Antigonus, took advantage of the war to reassert Jewish independence. He ruled part of Palestine for three years until defeated by Rome in 37 B.C. With this brief exception, the seventy-eight-year period of virtual independence under the Maccabees (141-63 B.C.) was the only virtual political independence that Palestinian Jews had between the time that Judah became a vassal state of Assyria in 732 B.C. and Israel's founding in A.D. 1948.

Between 37 B.C. and A.D. 65, Rome ruled different parts of Palestine in various ways, such as through puppet kings and procurators. Jews continued to live in Judea, Galilee and part of Trans-Jordan. Samaritans inhabited Samaria, where Jewish travelers were usually tolerated but not very welcome. Southern Phoenicia, including Tyre and Sidon, was primarily non-Jewish.

It is impossible to reconstruct Jewish populations of past centuries accurately. But estimates that have been made give us a useful though very rough profile of the fluctuating Jewish population in Palestine. Estimates of the worldwide Jewish population in A.D. 65, on the eve of the first Jewish-Roman war, go as high as 7.5 to eight million. The Diaspora has been estimated at five million. Three or four million of these Diaspora Jews were scattered about the Roman Empire, where they received special status and privileges; most of the rest of the Diaspora were in the Persian Empire. If these figures are somewhat accurate, the vast majority of Jews, even before the Jewish-Roman wars, did not choose to live in Palestine. Even during the seventy-eight years of Maccabean independence most Diaspora Jews did not choose to return.[11]

III. Jewish Revolts and Dispersals, A.D. 66-135.

In A.D. 66 many Palestinian Jews, especially in Jerusalem, revolted against the Romans. Some Jews, including many Christian Jews, did not join the revolt but fled Jerusalem. It was conquered; Herod's Temple and much of the city was destroyed. This war ended what Jews call the Second Jewish Commonwealth (even though Rome had ruled the area - with a three-year partial interruption - since 63 B.C.). According to Werner Keller, a modern historian, in this first Jewish-Roman war more than half of the Jews in Palestine were either killed or left the country as slaves, prisoners or fugitives.[12] Of the remainder, a small group stayed on in Jerusalem. Many other Jerusalem Jews moved to Galilee, which had neither been as involved in the revolt nor as devastated by it. Jews remained a majority in Palestine.[13] Within sixty years, some of those who left during the war, or their children, returned.

In A.D. 132 Palestinian Jews, especially in Judea, again revolted. By 135 Rome again defeated them. During the war Rome destroyed many villages and reportedly killed more than 500,000 Jewish men. Perhaps another 200,000 Jews left; they either fled to the Diaspora, or were sold into slavery, or were otherwise dispersed in the empire. Virtually no Jews remained in Judea. The area around Jerusalem was repopulated by retired Roman soldiers and other non-Jews from Syria and other neighboring regions. Jews, including Jewish Christians, were forbidden to enter Jerusalem except on the ninth of Ab, the anniversary of the Temple's destruction, to mourn. Except for a brief period this rule was enforced perhaps until Persians captured the city in 614.[14]

"In 135 the Romans drove the Jews out of Palestine; until recently they were never allowed to return." This paraphrases a common, highly inaccurate perception[15] which still supports the Zionist argument that the Jews were unjustly expelled from their homeland in 135 and therefore have a moral hereditary right both to return to it and to reclaim it exclusively as their own. Moreover, Zionists maintain, this right is prior to and outweighs the rights of the people who have lived in Palestine allegedly only since some time after 135.

The question is not whether the Romans treated the Jews cruelly and unjustly. That is evident. However, an examination of Jewish migration to and from Palestine during the past two thousand years indicates that the perception quoted above substantially skews reality. The expulsion of Jews from *part* of Palestine in 135 did not exclude them from its other parts. Many Jews continued to live in Palestine, especially in Galilee; many expellees returned. Significantly, it was not only during the Jewish-Roman wars but during the succeeding centuries as well that the Jewish population of Palestine substantially decreased. Emigration - sometimes sporadic, sometimes gradual - was seemingly a major cause of this decrease. Therefore those who view the Diaspora as completely imposed on the Jews rather than as at least partly a result of *Jews'* own decisions both to leave Palestine and not to return, are looking at only part of the picture. Similarly, those who look to the Roman edicts of 135 as a basis for a right to claim the Holy Land may also have to look elsewhere to argue for their claim. A further look at history supports this conclusion.

IV. Palestine After the Second Revolt, 136-637.

Of the sixty-four Jewish villages in Galilee before the revolt of A.D. 132, fifty-six (88 percent) remained after it - inhabited by Jews. In 138, Hadrian, against whom the Jews had revolted, died. His successor, Antonius Pius, revoked many of Hadrian's edicts against Judean Jews. Not only expellees but some who had fled to the Diaspora returned. Some Jews sold as slaves also returned after other Jews bought their freedom. In Galilee several centers of Jewish studies sprang up, which attracted students from throughout Palestine. The Sanhedrin, the Jews' highest judicial and legislative body, moved to Usha, near Haifa. It had the authority, recognized by Rome, to rule Jews in intra-Jewish affairs not only in Palestine but throughout the Diaspora. This enabled widely scattered Jews, despite the temple's destruction, to continue sharing a religious life unified by a center in Palestine. Usha, and later Tiberias, on the Sea of Galilee, became the headquarters of the Jewish patriarch, who had the title of prince. Rome recognized him as the Jews' representative in their dealings with both the Roman governor in Caesarea, who ruled the region in civil matters, and the emperor.

The Jewish Sanhedrin enacted laws to encourage Jews to buy land in Palestine from non-Jews. It also forbade Jews to leave Palestine.[16] This indicates that Jews were then not being forced out of Palestine but leaving it freely. Moreover, Diaspora Jews were usually politically free to move into Palestine, though not into Jerusalem.

The third century was a mixed blessing for Jews in the Roman Empire. In 212 Rome extended citizenship to all free inhabitants of the empire, including Jews. (Some Jews were already citizens.) Emperor Alexander Severus (ruled 222-235) admired Judaism and granted many favors to Palestinian Jews. He increased their power to legislate regarding internal matters; he authorized Jewish judges to settle civil cases between Jews; he gave Jewish patriarchs the right to judge even in capital cases. In the third century the patriarch headed what in some ways resembled a national government.[17] Despite these political advances, Palestine, with the rest of the empire, suffered economically from frequent violent political coups and military revolts in Rome between 235 and 285. Many Jews emigrated from Palestine, not stopping until they had left the empire and had reached prospering Babylon. Palestinian rabbis tried to discourage this, using religious reasons to try to convince Jews not to desert the land they believed God had promised them.

Thus a substantial Jewish exodus from Palestine took place during the two centuries between A.D. 136 and the early fourth century, when imperial instructions legalized Christianity and the imperial government moved to Byzantium.

The next three centuries, those of Byzantine-Roman rule over Palestine, were darkened by emperors' attempts to subject religion to their concept of the all-powerful state. Some emperors were harsh, even ruthless, toward Christians who refused to bend to them. Emperors sometimes showed this same harshness toward Jews. This absolutism, coupled with some emperors' and bishops' anti-Semitism, resulted in Jews having restrictions imposed on them, especially in their relations with Christians. They were deprived of some rights and privileges they had enjoyed in the pre-Constantinian empire. This situation and attitude adversely affected Jews not only in Palestine but throughout the shrinking empire between 324 and 638.

Despite the emigration of many Jews from Palestine during the third century, a substantial Jewish population remained there into the fourth century - enough to revolt against the Romans, again unsuccessfully, in 352. Emperor Julian "the Apostate" befriended Jews and let them reenter Jerusalem during his eighteen-month reign (361-63). His successors, however, reimposed restrictions and many Palestinian Jews moved away. In the late fourth century Huns invaded southern Palestine and destroyed many villages, including Jewish towns. More Jews emigrated to Mesopotamia, where the Jewish communities "were experiencing a great efflorescence. Between A.D. 200 and 500 they may have increased...from one million to two; and before long their impressive educational centres eclipsed the scholarship of Palestine Jewry itself."[18]

St. Jerome, who lived in Bethlehem from 386 to 420, wrote that Palestine's Jewish population dropped to a tenth of its former level. Jews continued to be more numerous in northern Palestine, but even there they reportedly comprised only about 15 percent of the population.[19] In about 429 the emperor abolished the Jewish patriarchate but the Sanhedrin continued to function.

It was perhaps during the third or fourth century, if not before, that Jews ceased being Palestine's major ethnic group. Only in the twentieth century did Jews fully reverse the effects of these gradual emigrations of the second, third and fourth centuries.

Israeli demographer Roberto Bachi indicates that in the centuries before the Arabs conquered Palestine (634-640), conversions of Jews to Christianity helped to reduce the population that identified itself as Jewish.[20] The descendants of these converts are still perhaps among the Christian and Muslim Arabs of Palestine whose roots go back to the Canaanites. These Arabs' Palestinian roots would obviously be as old as those of the Jews. Except for perhaps a few Jews whose ancestors may have lived continuously in Palestine, these Arabs' Palestinian roots would be much more *continuous* than those of all Jews.

Life for Jews in Palestine during the Roman-Byzantine era had positive sides to it. Within at least one period, perhaps more Jews moved into Palestine than left it. During much of the fifth and sixth centuries Palestine prospered and was generally peaceful. According to demographer Bachi, around the fifth century Palestine probably had its largest population ever until the twentieth century:

> During the late Roman and Byzantine periods peace prevailed, agriculture was intensively developed and extended to southern areas and a considerable urban development occurred. The Negev served also for eastern trade, and some part of it was cultivated. The considerable flow of capital from the Imperial treasury and from abroad in the Byzantine period contributed to the relative prosperity of the country.[21]

In the sixth century an estimated 250,000 Jews lived in Palestine. In 555, hoping to found an independent state, they joined Samaritans in an unsuccessful revolt. During the sixth century Christians became the majority in Palestine. Arabs moved into it from surrounding areas.

By the beginning of the seventh century probably not more than 500,000 Jews lived in the shrunken Roman empire. However, there were enough Jews and Samaritans in Palestine to help the Persians conquer Jerusalem in 614. Jews and Samaritans, probably helped by Persians, "were said to have massacred nearly 100,000 Christians."[22] This may be an exaggeration; a contemporary, a monk of the Monastery of St. Sabas, said there were 62,455 corpses after the massacre, 24,000 of which were unarmed prisoners who were killed.[23] Many Christians were sold as slaves. The Jews and their Persian overlords soon had a falling out. After Constantinople defeated the Persians in 627-28, Jews faced the anger of the surviving Christians, who did not want them to live in the city. Hardships resulting from living near the unstable frontier between the two frequently warring empires motivated many Palestinian Jews to emigrate south into western Arabia. It was from them that the Arabian Mohammed (570-632) learned much about Judaism, which greatly influenced the religion he founded. By 638 Palestine was perhaps only one-tenth Jewish.[24]

V. Palestine Under Muslim and Crusader Rule, 638-1800.[25]

After Jerusalem Christians peacefully surrendered to Muslim Arabs in 638 the Muslims allowed Palestine's Jews and Christians to continue practicing their religion. Both groups were subject to a special tax, which usually was not heavy. Muslims removed many Roman restrictions. Jews could again pray regularly not only at the base of the Temple Mount, the Western or "Wailing" Wall, but also on the top of the area, the "Temple platform." Seventy Jewish families were permitted to move into Jerusalem. Jews also moved into Hebron in southern Judea. Throughout Muslim lands Jews were generally much better treated than they had been under Byzantine-Romans.

Palestine was slowly Arabized culturally, religiously and to some extent ethnically. Arab tribes gradually immigrated into Palestine from Arabia but the indigenous people were allowed to remain. Eventually many of these two groups presumably intermarried. Therefore many, if not virtually all, present-day Palestinian Arabs presumably include in their ancestry people who lived in Palestine *before* the arrival of the Arabs. This ancestry undoubtedly includes Arabized Jews who converted to Islam. Through them this ancestry probably reaches back into the Canaanites. To say that today's Palestinian Arabs have been there only since the seventh century is to oversimplify an ethnic blending that probably extends from pre-Abrahamic Canaanite times into the twentieth century.

Under Caliph Omar II (ruled 717-720), non-Muslims, especially Christians, lived under humiliating restrictions. To avoid these, many converted to Islam and blended into the Arabic culture.

It is estimated that in A.D. 1000 there were no more than 1-1.5 million Jews throughout the world - a small fraction of those in A.D. 65.[26] Some lived in the new nations of western Europe, where, for instance, they had been welcomed to the Frankish court of Charlemagne, who became the first Holy Roman Emperor in 800. Jews were also welcome in Islamic Spain. By 942 Palestine had become less significant than other centers for Jewish studies, which were flourishing in North Africa and Europe. Despite some Jewish migration into Palestine, Jews there remained few. It could not compete with opportunities offered to Jews elsewhere. During the reign of the perhaps psychotic ruler, al Hakim (996-1021), those who refused to recognize his divinity, especially non-Muslims, were severely persecuted. He reimposed laws against Christians and Jews and added new ones. Jews who refused to become Muslims were forced to wear bells and carry six-pound wooden blocks about their necks.[27] In 1009 he ordered that several churches, including the Church of the Holy Sepulcher, be destroyed.[28] Many Jews and Christians converted or emigrated. A Turkish invasion and intermittent warfare later in the eleventh century further reduced Palestine's Jewish population so that by the time of the barbaric Crusader arrival in 1099 only a few thousand Jews lived there.

This level would continue with some fluctuations, exacerbated by wars and massacres, until 1800, at which time Palestine had some 265,000-325,000 Arabs[29] and 5,000-6,500 Jews (1.47-2.36 percent of the population). During this 700-year period since the First Crusade, some Palestinian Jews prospered but many, especially the large proportion of life-long religious students and the elderly, depended on the charity of Diaspora Jews for their living.

VI. The Moral Hereditary Right to Return.

This brief survey indicates that Jews were never completely

excluded from Palestine; some have lived there continuously at least since Joshua's time. According to both moderate historicalists and reductionists, through Jews' Canaanite ancestry they have lived there much longer.

Since A.D. 135 it has been possible for Jews to move into at least some areas of Palestine. Whether this would have been permitted on a large scale was probably not fully tested until the late nineteenth century. Of course Jews who did immigrate there did not go to an independent Jewish country but to one under non-Jewish rule. However, that had been the case, with one three-year exception, since 63 B.C., 195 years before the second Jewish-Roman war.

Certainly that war was a disaster for Palestinian Jews at that time, especially those in Judea and Jerusalem. However, as the preceding sketch indicates, the *long-term* effect of keeping Jews out of Palestine, commonly attributed to the war's outcome, seems not to have existed. This is very significant with regard to the claim that twentieth century Jews have a moral hereditary right to repossess Palestine. Throughout the 1,665 years between the Jews' partial expulsion from Judea in 135, and 1800, some Diaspora Jews moved into Palestine. However, during those 1,665 years most Diaspora Jews did not choose to move back there. And during those years many - perhaps most - Palestinian Jews decided to move out of Palestine. Both groups had myriads of reasons: better educational and job opportunities elsewhere, religious persecution, danger from war and marauders, and natural disasters such as earthquakes and droughts - to mention a few. However, Jews, like Gentiles, faced these same problems elsewhere. The usual personal and family reasons for either leaving Palestine or not moving to it must also have been factors. These reasons were persuasive to them, and perhaps sometimes even "tied their hands," but they had little or nothing to do with the revolt of 132. As a result of the varying reasons Jews had for either leaving Palestine or not moving to it, after the fourth century, and perhaps before then, Jews were only a minority within Palestine. After perhaps the 700s they were a very small minority. Granted that Jews' decisions were sometimes made under varying degrees of duress, the *continuation* of the Diaspora resulting from the Babylonian Captivity and from the Jewish-Roman wars was probably the result sometimes of duress and sometimes of free choice.

Much of that duress has been the difficulty many Jews have experienced in making a living in Palestine. For the past several hundred years visitors have noted the extreme poverty of many Palestinian Jews, whose main income was the charity of Diaspora Jews. Even modern Israeli Jews receive an annual subsidy that averages about $750 for each man, woman and child from U.S. taxpayers (more if U.S. interest costs are included). Moreover, extensive additional subsidies come from Diaspora Jews, especially American Jews.

During most of the time between A.D. 135 and perhaps 614, the desire, "next year in Jerusalem," could not be fulfilled, even by a visit, except for one day each year. During most of the time since 638 it has been possible for Jews to fulfill that desire, both by visiting the city and, to a limited extent, by living there. However, it was only during the nineteenth and twentieth centuries that the nationalist movement called Zionism gave that desire the magnetic strength (and political power and organization) that it has today. The desire may have been common, but before 1800 relatively very few Jews acted on it.

The preceding sketch seemingly indicates that those who look to the results of the Roman edicts of 135 as a basis for Jews' moral hereditary right to the Holy Land have to look elsewhere for that basis.

As noted, the Jews who left Palestine in 135 did so under duress; those who emigrated since then did so either under varying degrees of duress or freely:

1. Regarding *those who left under serious duress* such as religious or political persecution or near famine, not simply for better job or educational opportunities: It would seem that long-term inhabitants such as citizens or their equivalents, *and their descendants born in forced exile*, together with their immediate families, *always have a refugee's moral right to return* even if they did not return to Palestine within a reasonably short time after

the factors prohibiting their return ceased. However, if they wished to reclaim property they might have had to have done this within a few years to avoid leaving the subsequent occupants "in limbo."

2. Regarding the *refugees' immediate descendants who were born into voluntary exile* - for example, the refugees who decided not to return to Palestine but remained in the Diaspora and then had children, and these children decided to return: It would seem that they had some *moral hereditary right* to return to Palestine as long as they did so within a reasonably short time after the factors prohibiting their ancestors' return ceased. It is hard to pinpoint, as a moral issue, what was "a reasonably short time," as this could have varied with circumstances. It would probably not have been more than a generation - about twenty-five years. Beyond that time the descendants would seem to have forfeited or at least seriously weakened their moral *hereditary* right to return. This weakening, if not forfeiture, would have increased with each succeeding generation to the point where the right ceased entirely.

3. Regarding the descendants of those who left Palestine *freely*: It would seem that their moral *hereditary* right to immigrate to Palestine was either non-existent or at least very weak, especially after a generation or two.

Why is it that in either forced or free emigration situations whatever moral right originally existed becomes weaker and eventually ceases with the passage of successive generations? One reason is the chaos that would result if the right continued to be valid indefinitely. The immigrant ancestors of many of today's Americans were political, economic or religious refugees, or expellees, from other countries. These emigrants left under varying degrees of duress. Chaos would result if their descendants still had a moral hereditary right to return to the lands of their ancestors and if enough people were to act on that right. Except under morally just limitations controlled by the current inhabitants of those lands, the returnees would violate the stronger rights of those inhabitants. Yet the post-A.D. 1600 migration to what is now America is much more recent than most of the migration from Palestine to the Diaspora.

With regard to the descendants of the Jews who chose not to return after the end of the Babylonian Captivity in 539 B.C.: Their claim to a moral hereditary right to immigrate to Palestine would seem to be even weaker than that of descendants of those who left, either freely or as refugees or expellees, after the Jewish-Roman wars in A.D. 65 and 135. The ancestors of the former were, according to the Bible, invited by the king of Persia to return to Judah but they declined the offer. Moreover, the time span since 539 B.C. is also up to 674 years longer than that since the Jewish-Roman wars. The distinction between the two groups is, of course, largely irrelevant both because the time frame for both groups spans so many generations and because the two groups have somewhat, if not entirely, intermingled.

The line of reasoning outlined above does not deny people's inherent right to immigrate and nations' duty to accept immigrants. But in the current issue regarding the Holy Land, whatever basis there may be for that right and duty, it seemingly is not heredity. The historical involvement of the Jews in Palestine before A.D. 135 and the desire of some Jews during the intervening centuries to return there and establish their own state seem at best very weak bases for a moral hereditary right today. Whatever moral hereditary right that might still exist would not outweigh the moral rights of the Palestinian Arabs to land they have not only inherited but possessed at least since the Canaanite share of their own ancestry lived there. Obviously this applies fully only to Arabs who have such an ancestry. Today it would presumably be difficult to identify these, just as it would be difficult to identify Jews who are biologically descended from the Jews of the Babylonian Captivity or from the exodus of A.D. 135.

It would seem that Native Americans whose lands were unjustly taken from their ancestors have a much stronger claim to a moral hereditary right to return to those lands than do Jews with regard to Palestine. Whatever argument Americans may make for Jewish hereditary rights to Palestine would perhaps apply with greater force to Native American rights to at least some property in America. However, the two cases are not fully parallel because of the low ratio of Native Americans to land at the time the lands were conquered by the European settlers.

VII. Moral Rights From Jews' 3200 Years in Canaan.

There has been an *uninterrupted presence* of some Jews in Palestine since about 1240 B.C. according to the Bible, and probably much earlier than that through Jews' at least partial Canaanite ancestry. This seemingly should be considered in weighing Jews' and Palestinian Arabs' relative rights to the Holy Land. However, many if not most Palestinian Arabs' ancestry also probably goes back in part to the Canaanites. Until after the State of Israel was formed in 1948 there were more Palestinian Arabs than Jews in the Holy Land. Thus the "long-term-presence" factor seemingly adds more weight to the Palestinian Arab side of the balance of moral rights than to the Jewish side.

VIII. An Independent Jewish State.

As to the issue of establishing a sovereign Jewish national state, an issue that is distinct from immigration: After the two Jewish-Roman wars and before modern Zionism, with the exceptions of the revolts of A.D. 352 and 555, there were no significant attempts by Jews to establish a sovereign Jewish state in Palestine or elsewhere. (The eighth-to-tenth century Khazar kingdom in what is now part of the Ukraine and Russia was comprised primarily of converts to Judaism and their descendants in an already-existing kingdom.) Given the small minority population of Jews in Palestine and the overpowering might of Palestine's rulers - Romans, Arabs, Crusaders, Turks - creating a Jewish state in Palestine would have been extremely hazardous if not impossible. Perhaps a Jewish state in part of Palestine proportionate in size to the percent of population that was Jewish might have been equitable then. However, as Jews became a diminishing component of Palestine's total population between the second and fifth centuries A.D., the rights of the non-Jewish component would have raised moral questions similar to those in the present conflict between Jews and Arabs over forming a specifically Jewish state in

Palestine.

After America's discovery, Jews made some efforts to establish colonies within the colonial empires of European nations. However, they did not try to establish a sovereign state before European powers had laid claim to all the coastlands of North America. Perhaps such a Jewish state would not have been recognized by the colonizing European nations, most of which had persecuted Jews. (Spain and Portugal claimed all of Latin America and ruthlessly pursued Jews who tried to hide there.) Moreover, there seems to have been little desire by Diaspora Jews or even by Palestinian Jews to form a state anywhere. Forming a sovereign Jewish state in the New World probably would have created the same justice problems regarding the rights of Native Americans that plagued the colonizing efforts of the European nations. Because Jews did not - perhaps could not - form their own nation then, they did not have a national homeland, which would have been of great value to them in the early and mid-twentieth century. But that is hindsight.

Chapter Three

THE RIGHT TO IMMIGRATE;
THE START OF POLITICAL ZIONISM

1800-1914

Chapter One examined whether the Bible is a "deed of owner-ship" to Canaan for modern Jews. Chapter Two examined modern Jews' "moral hereditary right to return." This chapter will examine the right to immigrate, limited by "the common good rightly understood." It will do this in the context of the history of Zionism between 1800 and 1914.

I. Jewish Immigration To Palestine Before 1882.[1]

In 1800 Palestine was somewhat feudal, with many large landowners - some of them absentee - and impoverished peasants working for them, as well as small, independent farmers, craftsmen and shopkeepers. Seminomadic Bedouin grazed sheep and goats. They also raided farms and villages, which had little police protection. This discouraged settling rural areas. Some land, especially in the Jordan valley and along the coast, was swampy, malarial and sparsely inhabited. Jews lived primarily in the four holy cities, Jerusalem, Hebron, Tiberias and Safed. They were mostly shopkeepers, artisans, and students of the Bible, the Talmud and other Jewish religious teachings. Virtually none were farmers. Since the late 1700s a few Jewish immigrants, including elderly wishing to die there, continued to enter Palestine. By 1850 Palestine's Jews had increased to about 10,000-13,000.[2] Jewish immigration also stemmed from the influence of several Jewish writers who advocated a type of Zionism, a return to Palestine. Some of these proto-Zionists urged forming Jewish colonies there, but not necessarily a separate Jewish state; that later movement would be called political Zionism.[3] The early writers did not think

43

Jews could or even should be fully assimilated into the predominantly Gentile societies in Europe and the Americas. Some early and middle nineteenth century writers advocated a religious and/or cultural Zionism. Palestine was seen as the fitting center of Jewish religious and cultural life, in some ways comparable to Rome's leadership role among Catholics.

Meanwhile many European and U.S. Jews thought that assimilation into the culture and society in which they found themselves was both possible and desirable. Many of these *assimilationists* saw their Judaism primarily as a religion rather than as an ethnic (or racial) or cultural factor to be dealt with. Before 1882 relatively few Jews embraced any form of Zionism. According to author Moshe Leshem, few, if any rabbinical authorities taught that Jews might be restored to *Eretz Israel* before the Messiah came. Only some time after 1850 did some rabbis consider Jewish immigration there a good preparation for redemption. "They undoubtedly did so," Leshem noted, "under the influence of the surge of nationalism in Europe, not out of any theological understandings."[4]

II. The First Immigration Wave (First Aliyah), 1882-1903.

Russia has a long history of anti-Semitism. Czars required most Jews to live within the Pale of Settlement, a wide strip of western Russia (which then included Lithuania and eastern pre-1772 Poland) and the Ukraine, between the Baltic and Black seas. In 1881 Czar Alexander II was murdered. A Jew was one of several people accused in his death. Alexander III, who succeeded his father, condoned pogroms - anti-Semitic rioting - which began in June 1881. When Jews tried physically to defend themselves, police moved against *them*. The brutality quickly spread throughout the Pale of Settlement, ending in 1884. Hundreds of Jews had been murdered. Thousands fled, mostly to western Europe and America. Many who remained were reduced to abject poverty and some were starving. The pogroms triggered the first large-scale immigration to Palestine - the First Aliyah - between 1882 and 1903.

The Ottoman sultan, 'Abdul Hamid II, (ruled 1876-1909), was

somewhat liberal toward Jews but opposed their moving to Palestine. He feared it would increase European governments' already extensive meddling in Palestine. He was especially wary of immigrants from Russia, his expansionist neighbor, because he feared they might be its agents. After the influx of Russian Jews in 1882 the sultan banned Jewish immigration and land purchase. This ban was soon withdrawn but reinstated in 1891. However, it was not strictly enforced; his officials could be bribed. During the First Aliyah some 25,000 Jews moved to Palestine. They founded several farming settlements, including some in malarial swamps. Russian shopkeepers and artisans were unaccustomed to the harsh life and work of reclaiming land; many left Palestine. Jews in Palestine increased to between 27,000 and 50,000 by 1904.[5]

Those in farm settlements often hired Arabs to work the fields. This forestalled much of the anti-Jewish feeling that later aliyahs created because many of the later newcomers did their own farm work and displaced Arab workers. Nevertheless some Arabs reacted negatively even to the First Aliyah. In 1891 Arab merchants and craftsmen in Jerusalem telegraphed the Ottoman grand vizier, noting that they expected more Jewish immigration. They called for a halt to this and to further Jewish purchase of land. Palestinian Arabs made this twofold demand four years before Theodor Herzl wrote *Der Judenstaat*, a book about an independent Jewish state. They would repeat their demand many times in the next fifty-six years as more immigrants came and acquired more land.[6]

A leading Russian "spiritual" or "cultural" Zionist, Ahad Ha'am - pen name of Asher Ginsberg (1856-1927) - visited Palestine in 1891, the year of the first Arab protest. He found the Arabs generally quiet but he warned: "If ever...we...develop...our life in Erez-Israel to the point where we shall be encroaching upon them...[we should not expect them] to yield their place easily."[7] Conor Cruise O'Brien, author of *The Siege*, points out:

That was not an insight shared (or at least acknowledged) by any other Zionist, either at that time or for long afterwards. Officially, the Zionist position was that there was no conflict of interest, but only a community of interest, between Arabs and Zionists. That long remained an article of faith to

Zionists in the Diaspora.[8]

O'Brien contends, however, that among Jews who lived in Palestine there was a growing realization that Ahad Ha'am was right about possible Arab reaction. Ha'am thought Jews should develop Palestine as a worldwide Jewish spiritual and cultural center. In some of his writings he did not see Palestine as a political magnet - a homeland to which masses of Jews should immigrate. He assumed that Jews would still live throughout the Diaspora. Although he actively promoted the development of Palestine as a spiritual and cultural center, he saw no urgency in it.[9] Despite his concern over possible Arab reaction to large-scale Jewish immigration, he maintained in 1903 that "Palestine will become our spiritual centre only when the Jews are a majority of the population and own most of the land."[10] Ha'am was setting forth his vision of cultural Zionism in 1896 and afterward. Meanwhile, political Zionism was rapidly surpassing his ideas in popularity among European, especially Russian, Jews.

III. The Beginning of Political Zionism.

Political Zionism included the desire to form in Palestine an independent Jewish state. A Russian Jewish immigrant, Ze'ev Dubnov, wrote in 1882 that his final purpose was "to take possession in due course of Palestine and to restore to the Jews the political independence of which they have now been deprived for 2,000 years."[11] He said this could be achieved by establishing colonies of farmers and various types of workshops and industries, and then gradually expanding them "to put all the land, all the industry, in the hands of the Jews."[12] Dubnov advocated teaching young Palestinian Jews how to use arms. "Then the Jews, if necessary with arms in their hands, will publicly proclaim themselves masters of their own, ancient fatherland."[13] Significantly, Dubnov does not mention the indigenous Arabs or their desires, unless the arms were to be used against Arab neighbors, not just Ottoman troops. This practice of ignoring or discounting the rights and feelings of the native Arabs would recur often in political Zionists' writings and actions.

Political Zionism won its first prominence when championed by Theodor Herzl (1860-1904), a Jewish Austrian playwright and journalist. He had seen virulent anti-Semitism in Vienna and Paris and was convinced that Jews could protect themselves from it only by moving from anti-Semitic countries to a land that would be their own. In 1896 he published *Der Judenstaat*.[14] Herzl opposed mere Jewish *immigration* into a country. He wanted an internationally recognized charter in which a country would cede to Jewish immigrants a political entity of their own. He considered both Palestine and part of Argentina desirable sites. He noted that Argentina was sparsely settled and had fertile land and a good climate, while Palestine had a strong historical attraction for Jews. *Der Judenstaat* was ridiculed by some non-Zionist Jews. Other Jews took it seriously but rejected it because they did not consider Jews a nation. Even Zionists considered the book unoriginal. Ha'am and his cultural Zionists thought it was not specifically Jewish enough. They felt that solely flight from anti-Semitism would not create a bond strong enough to build a state.[15]

Herzl, undeterred, organized the First Zionist Congress, in Basel, Switzerland, in 1897. It stated:

Zionism strives to create for the Jewish people a home in Palestine secured by public law. The congress contemplates the following means to gain this end: 1. The promotion on suitable lines of the colonization of Palestine by Jewish agricultural and industrial workers. 2. The organization and binding together of the whole of Jewry by means of appropriate institutions, local and international, in accordance with the laws of each country. 3. The strengthening and fostering of Jewish national sentiment and consciousness. 4. Preparatory steps toward gaining government consent where necessary to achieve the aim of Zionism.[16]

Herzl intended to form a state. This is clear from a diary entry he made soon after the Congress: "At Basel I founded the Jewish state."[17]

Herzl and his political Zionists from western Europe felt a much greater sense of urgency about enacting political Zionism than did Russian Ha'am about enacting his cultural and spiritual Zionism.

Ha'am was familiar with a type of anti-Semitism that Jews had long experienced in Europe. But Herzl and other western Europeans had experienced a new type of anti-Semitism that was secular, anti-Christian, and gaining strength. Herzl considered it very dangerous. Thus, as noted, he, unlike Ha'am, concluded that Jews needed not just a spiritual and cultural center they could look to for leadership but their own sovereign state to which they could immigrate *en masse* and which they could control politically. He preferred that this be Palestine but he was open to other sites.[18]

According to corrected Ottoman figures, in 1897 Palestine had 563,000 people, including 529,500 Arabs and 21,500 Jews.[19]

IV. Arab Reactions to Political Zionism, 1898-99.

As educated Arabs learned of Zionism and its goals some became concerned. A few months after the First Zionist Congress, a Lebanese writer, Rashid Rida, warned Arabs that the Jews "can take possession of your country, establish colonies in it, and reduce its masters to hired labourers and its rich to poor men."[20] Rida "thought that nothing prevented the Jews from becoming 'the mightiest nation on earth' except statehood, and they were well on their way to achieving that, through their powers of organization."[21]

Yusuf al-Khalidi was a member of a prominent Muslim family in Jerusalem. In 1899, while mayor of Jerusalem, he wrote to France's chief rabbi, Zadoc Kahn: "There are still uninhabited countries where one could settle millions of poor Jews who may perhaps become happy there and one day constitute a nation ....But...let Palestine be left in peace."[22]

Kahn sent the letter to Herzl, who wrote a reassuring reply to al-Khalidi. He predicted the Arabs would share in the prosperity that Jews would bring to Palestine. At least this part of Herzl's reply reflected reality at that time because during the First Aliyah Jewish farming settlers paid well for land and hired Arab workers. Herzl assured al-Khalidi that *no one was trying to remove Arabs.* O'Brien comments:

it is easy to see in retrospect that al-Khalidi was raising real difficulties, and Herzl, returning unreal answers. Did he simply have his tongue in his cheek?...he was saying how he hoped - and intended - things would turn out....What would happen, if the things he hoped would happen did not happen, was not something Herzl ever much cared to contemplate.[23]

It seems that Herzl's answers were not merely unreal but also not what he intended. He had written in his *Diary* four years earlier:

> We must expropriate gently the private property on the states assigned to us. We shall try to spirit the penniless population across the border by procuring employment for it in the transit countries, while denying it any employment in our own country. The property owners will come over to our side. Both the process of expropriation and the removal of the poor must be carried out discretely and circumspectly. Let the owners of immoveable property believe that they are cheating us, selling us things for more than they are worth. But we are not going to sell them anything back.[24]

Herzl also wrote to al-Khalidi that in the immigrants "the Sultan will acquire loyal and good subjects."[25] In saying this, contends O'Brien, Herzl "was saying what he knew to be untrue and intended to be untrue."[26] Herzl stipulated that his diary not be opened until twenty years after his death.[27] In it he stated that he always intended that the Jewish homeland would be an independent Jewish state but that he was not always open about this because of political problems such openness might cause. Thus Herzl must have intended that the Palestinian Arabs would be incorporated into a specifically Jewish state, not an Arab-Jewish state. This seems to be his assumption in *Altneuland*, a novel he wrote in 1902 to describe his vision of the Jewish state in Palestine. In the novel, relations with Arabs present no problems because they share in the riches that the Jews' introduction of modern irrigation and other modern technology has brought to all the people of Palestine. The Arabs appreciate what the Jews have done for them.[28]

Joseph Jeffries also criticizes Herzl's attitude: "He even visits Palestine, but seems to find nobody there but his fellow-Jews.

Arabs apparently vanish before him as in their own Arabian Nights."[29] The British historian's criticism may seem overdone but it points to a real problem. Herzl met Arabs and corresponded with a few of them, but historian Walter Zeev Laqueur notes that in Herzl's mind "the Arabs certainly did not figure prominently, though he did not ignore them altogether....He was aware of the rising national movement in Egypt and on various occasions stressed the close relationship between Jews and Muslims."[30]

V. The Movement for Alternative Areas to Palestine, 1902-14.

Herzl repeatedly tried to obtain a charter for an autonomous Jewish national home in Palestine. The sultan refused but offered to let Jews settle in small groups throughout the empire. They would have to become Turkish citizens; immigration to Palestine could be only minimal. Herzl rejected the offer and considered other sites. Because of increased Russian Jewish immigration to Britain since 1882, its Jewish population by 1902 exceeded 100,000. London wished to restrict further immigration and thus was open to considering Jewish settlements in British possessions. Zionists proposed the island of Cyprus - technically part of the Ottoman Empire but under British control. Britain rejected the plan; it would require evicting Greeks and Muslims.[31]

In 1902 Herzl proposed making a Jewish colony at Wadi El 'Arish, on the Mediterranean about thirty miles southwest of the Palestinian-Egyptian border. Egypt was technically an Ottoman vassal but Britain controlled it. Water for El 'Arish would have to come from the Nile, but Egypt objected to losing so much water. Britain, refusing to force that issue, rejected the idea in May, 1903. In 1906 some Zionists urged London to reconsider, but tension along the *de facto* Ottoman-British frontier in Sinai tabled the idea indefinitely.[32]

In April 1903 the British colonial secretary told Herzl that Uganda, then a British colony, seemed ideal for a Jewish homeland. The site tentatively offered, which is now in Kenya, had some 6,000 square miles. Because of tribal warfare it had few people. Britain suggested that a Jewish settlement in a British colony could at best be as politically independent and have as much authority as a British county council, with a Jewish governor and a Jewish administration. London did not want "an empire within an empire." Both Herzl and Britain pursued the idea. Herzl and some other Zionists thought it would offer Jews at least temporary refuge from Russian pogroms, which had again erupted. However, the Russian delegates to the Sixth Zionist Congress, held in Basel that August, bitterly opposed Uganda and would consider only Palestine.[33] They argued that accepting Uganda even as a temporary refuge would destroy any chance for a homeland in Palestine, for if Jews had another refuge the European powers would lose their motive to help Jews win a homeland there. Non-Russians at the Congress proposed at least forming a commission to study Uganda's feasibility. The resolution passed but the Russian delegates, including Chaim Weizmann (1874-1952), Zionism's future leader, walked out. They returned only after Herzl personally appealed for unity.[34]

The Russian attitude was forcefully expressed by Menachem Ussishkin (1863-1941), the leader of Russian political Zionism, who was in Palestine during that Sixth Congress: "Just as no majority in the world can cause me to apostatize from the faith of Israel or the law of Israel, so no numerical majority at the Congress will detach me from the Land of Israel."[35] According to O'Brien: "One thing the East Africa debate revealed was how thin the secular covering was over the sacred core of Zionism."[36] At that time many if not most Zionists were Russian. After the Congress Herzl realized that so many Russian Zionists would hear only of Palestine that proposing any other site was unrealistic. He died within a year but the battle continued at the Seventh Zionist Congress in 1905. The Congress, urged by Russian delegates, voted overwhelmingly "to reject all colonization programs other than those in Palestine and adjacent countries."[37]

For Russian Zionists this effectively killed Uganda. Britain also cooled to the project. Some government officials argued that it would be unfair to British taxpayers, who had paid for a road built to the area. They also feared antagonizing local Africans.

After the Seventh Congress's vote, forty delegates opposing it founded the Jewish Territorial Organization (ITO) in August 1905. It explored sites in East Africa, Cyrenaica (Libya), Angola, Mesopotamia (Iraq), Canada, Mexico, Honduras, Dutch Guiana (Suriname), Australia and Siberia. All were judged unusable because either local governments opposed their use or the inhabitants were expected to, or the sites lacked water or had other serious weather problems. Meanwhile, the Galveston Immigration Scheme (GIS) brought 10,000 Jews to Texas between 1906 and 1914; ITO ran GIS from 1907 until GIS ended at the start of World War I.[38] The decision of the Seventh Zionist Congress "to reject all colonization programs other than those in Palestine and adjacent countries," together with ITO's failure to find suitable alternate sites, has had fateful consequences for both Jews and Palestinian Arabs. Through hindsight one can ask: What if enough Zionists had been content to develop simply a spiritual and cultural center in Jerusalem, and Zionists had succeeded in forming a sovereign or almost sovereign state elsewhere? Then the refuge that Herzl foresaw the need of would have existed. In retrospect ITO's demise was very sad for humanity.

In either failing, neglecting or refusing adequately to acknowledge the presence of the Palestinian Arabs and their moral rights and aspirations did the "Palestine-or-nothing" Zionists unwittingly help seal the fate of several million European Jews thirty years later? Or would some or all have died anyway? Was there as a matter of fact no other place on this planet that was (a) vacant enough, (b) politically available enough, and (c) inhabitable enough to become a Jewish state? ITO searched but found nothing it judged feasible. Did it look hard enough? Did it reject sites that could have been developed? Were non-Jewish nations overly possessive of perhaps excess feasible sites?

These are post-Holocaust questions. It is unrealistic to ask them both of the people searching for sites and the people approached before that disaster, the enormity of which no one could foresee. This is not to imply that had they foreseen the disaster they would have been able to establish a Jewish state on some non-Palestinian site. Perhaps there simply was no livable place which was not also inhabited by people, people who had the same rights regarding their homeland as had - and have - the Palestinian Arabs regarding their homeland - moral rights which required respect. To raise the questions is not to "blame the victim"; it is not to imply that the "Palestine-only" Zionists of 1905 were partly responsible for European Jews not having anywhere to flee from the Nazis.

VI. The Second Aliyah, 1904-14.

In 1903, widespread Russian pogroms again erupted. Before the ensuing Second Aliyah was ended by World War I, some 40,000 more Jews - mostly Russian - came to Palestine. (The causal relationship between European anti-Semitism and Zionism generally, and Jewish immigration to Palestine in particular, manifests itself repeatedly. If Europeans had treated Jews justly there would probably have been no large-scale Zionist movement and no large aliyahs.) Many of the new immigrants left Palestine. However, by 1914, some forty-seven farming settlements with about 12,000 Jewish occupants had been founded.[39] Like many other Zionist projects, many of these were largely funded by Rothschild family members, some of whom had softened their anti-Zionism. Readers of some Zionist writings which extol Zionist pioneers who drained swamps and turned desert into farmland could get the impression that settlement founders bought only previously unused land. In fact, Arabs had already farmed some of these settlements.

According to an ancient custom recognized by Ottoman law, Palestinian villagers shared the use of grazing land around their village even if they did not hold individual title to the land. Some new Jewish landowners did not allow this. On the other hand, some settlers loaned their farm equipment to Arabs, and Jewish doctors did not always charge their poor Arab patients. Such neighborliness did not remove the bitterness felt by Arabs who were now hired laborers working the very fields they once tended either as owners or tenants. Second Aliyah immigrants seeking work on Jewish farms started during the First Aliyah often found it hard to convince their Jewish managers to hire them because Arabs worked for less and had more experience.[40] Second Aliyah immigrants who chose to live in newly purchased or developed farm settlements were more inclined to work the land themselves than had been First Aliyah immigrants. Therefore, if Second Aliyah immigrants bought a farm village from, for instance, an absentee Arab owner, its Arab peasants often were forcibly replaced with Jewish workers. Thus Arabs feared and resented the increasing Jewish settlements as a threat to their livelihood. Sometimes Arabs attacked immigrants. Displaced rural Arabs, lacking urban job and social skills, were nevertheless forced to move to towns and cities.[41] There they often could not find work and did not have their village social support system to sustain them physically and psychologically. Arab resentment therefore also simmered among urban dwellers, where most of Palestine's Jews lived.[42]

In the spring of 1908, Jewish and Arab workers in Jaffa clashed. S.D. Levontin, the Jewish director of the local Anglo-Palestine Bank, complained to David Wolffsohn, the head of the World Zionist executive, that young Jewish men were largely responsible. He said that they were armed with sticks, knives and guns, and behaved toward Arabs with arrogance and contempt. That same year Levontin also wrote to Wolffsohn that Zionist labor leaders were creating local ill will for Zionism by urging that jobs be given to Jews instead of to Arabs.[43]

Arabs also complained that immigrants did not bother to learn about Palestinian Arabs' customs or respect them. Regarding their economic standards, Laqueur maintains that Palestinian Arabs were no worse off than Arabs in neighboring countries:

> urbanization in Palestine did not proceed at a faster rate than in the neighbouring Arab countries...and the birth rate rose more quickly than in the neighbouring countries, as did the living standards of the Arabs in the neighborhood of the new Jewish settlements....[This was true] both for the prewar period and the 1920s. If some Arabs suffered as a result of Jewish settlement, the number of those who benefitted directly or indirectly was certainly greater. True, if Arab living standards improved, the Jewish settlers were still much better off, and the emergence of prosperous colonies must have caused considerable envy.[44]

Between 1890 and 1914, educated Christian *and* Muslim Arabs voiced worry that Zionism threatened their future *political independence*. Some Zionist leaders, primarily those in Palestine, recognized that this danger was felt by both Muslims and Christians. One non-Palestinian Zionist, Richard Lichtheim, a German who represented the Zionist central executive committee in Istanbul, wrote in 1913: "The Arabs are and will remain our natural opponents. They....want to preserve their nation and cultivate their culture....The Jew for them is a competitor who threatens their predominance in Palestine."[45] Later Lichtheim stated that even before 1914 it was clear that the national aspirations of Zionists and Palestinian Arabs were incompatible.[46] Some non-Palestinian Zionists mistakenly thought only *Christian* Palestinian Arabs worried about Zionism. Because they were a small minority of Arabs some Zionists thought they could be ignored.[47] In 1931 Weizmann, Zionism's international leader, stated: "If you look at prewar Zionist literature you will find hardly a word about the Arabs."[48] According to Laqueur, Weizmann's remark "implied that the Zionist leaders had been half aware of the existence of the Arabs but for reasons of their own had acted as if they did not exist. Or had it been a case of real, if astonishing blindness? The issue was in fact considerably more complex."[49]

Laqueur contends that "Zionists certainly paid little attention to the first stirrings of the Arab national movement and few envisaged the possibility of a clash of national interests."[50]

The political threat posed for the Arabs by the increasing number of Zionist settlements would be actualized within a few years. After Britain succeeded in engineering its mandate over Palestine, each settlement helped to increase Zionist political pressure on Britain, pressure which proved disastrous to Palestinian Arabs.

By 1914, some 56,000-60,000 Jews and some 659,000 Arabs lived in Palestine. Some Zionists assert that the increase in Arabs was due to many non-Palestinian Arabs moving into Palestine. Thus, these Zionists claim, Palestinian Arabs, like Jews, are primarily recent newcomers and cannot claim several centuries' residency. But demographer Justin McCarthy claims there is no evidence between the 1870s and 1914 of a significant Arab immigration. (Before the 1870s the Ottomans did little census work in Palestine.) He maintains that the increase was comparable to that throughout the Empire at that time and resulted from a high birth rate and a lowered mortality rate.[51] Israeli demographer Bachi's findings support McCarthy: "It is possible that some part of the growth of the Moslem population was due to immigration. However, it seems likely that the dominant determinant of this modest growth was the beginning of some natural increase."[52]

Bachi added that possible causes for this small improvement in life expectancy, which resulted in the population increase "are likely to be found in the apparent absence between 1840 and 1914 of major calamities (although various large-scale epidemic outbreaks did occur)."[53] Thus the Israeli demographer himself attests to the Arabs' long occupancy in Palestine.

VII. The Right to Immigrate Versus the Rights of Inhabitants.

In *Pacem in Terris*, Pope John XXIII stated in 1963:
when there are just reasons for it, [one has] the right to emigrate to other countries and take up residence there. The fact that one is a citizen of a particular state does not detract in any way from one's citizenship in the world community and one's common tie with all people....A person [has the right to] enter a political community where one hopes one can more fittingly provide a future for one's self and one's dependents.[54]

This right to immigrate, Pope John states in that encyclical, creates a corresponding duty: "Wherefore, as far as the common good rightly understood permits, it is the duty of that state to accept such immigrants and to help to integrate them as new members."[55] Thus the right to immigrate is both basic and yet limited by "the common good rightly understood." This common good includes especially the good of the people living in the country where the emigrants wish to live. When *Pacem in Terris* speaks of immigration, it presumably envisions (a) movement to an already-existing state and (b) the immigrants' intent to become part of the society *already there*. Pope John presumably was not considering a situation in which immigrants would revolt, establish their own state, supplant the indigenous people, or prevent the latter from exercising their right to self-determination.

In the late nineteenth and early twentieth centuries the small number of Jews entering Palestine, considered simply as immigrants, would have had a small impact, either positive or negative, on Palestinian Arabs. Therefore *considered simply in terms of immigration* it would seem that the balance of rights at that time could have been in the immigrants' favor. (This is not to say that the immigrants, especially in the Second Aliyah, who displaced Palestinian Arabs from their jobs and villages were acting justly, for that displacement certainly disrupted those peasants' "common good rightly understood." But that is a moral issue that is related to but not intrinsic to the immigration issue itself.)

In weighing the rights of the immigrants versus those of the inhabitants, the immigrants' *intent* is also a factor. Did they intend simply to purchase a limited amount of property and develop it in such a way that it would not unduly disrupt the Palestinian Arabs' "common good rightly understood" or did they intend (a) to displace the Palestinian Arabs from all or much of Palestine and also (b) to found a specifically Jewish state which by its nature would seriously harm the Palestinian Arabs' common good? The intent probably varied among the immigrants. But, as noted, the goal of at least some immigrants and their leaders was to form a state that was specifically Jewish, while other immigrants wanted it to be almost exclusively Jewish. As intended by Zionists, their state would radically harm Palestinian Arabs' right to self-determination. This state would seriously harm Arabs' society and culture, and, indeed, virtually every facet of their lives. This would inevitably constitute a serious violation of Palestinian Arabs' right to their common good. Thus, although it seems evident that a limited number of Jews would ordinarily have had a right to immigrate to Palestine simply as immigrants, that right was limited. For no one has a right to immigrate to a country with the intent of supplanting the indigenous people, preventing the exercise of their right to self-determination, or otherwise disrupting their common good. Therefore it would seem that Zionists with such intentions forfeited their moral right to immigrate to Palestine.

However, the same onus would not seem to fall on these immigrants' descendants who were born in the Holy Land. Seemingly a person ordinarily has a moral right to first-class citizenship in the land in which one is born, or, more accurately, in the land in which one's mother is a resident when one is born. Regardless of the legitimacy of one's parents' actions, the child should not be subject to banishment from the state of its birth. Nor should that child be relegated to second-class citizenship in that state. The argument for the right seemingly flows from what might be called appropriateness or fittingness: It is inappropriate to expel someone from the land of one's birth. A problem with this position is that one generation of aggressors can unjustly inundate an indigenous people's territory; then the aggressors' children, enjoying the moral right to first-class citizenship, might be able to politically, socially and culturally swamp the indigenous people. Like all other moral rights, this right must be weighed against competing moral rights. For this and other reasons it seems difficult to delineate how substantial this birth right is.

Many Israelis were born in what is now Israel. Seemingly their strongest basis for a moral right to live there does not depend on whether the Bible is a "deed of ownership" to the land of Canaan or whether there is a moral hereditary right of Jews to *Eretz Israel*. Their strongest basis seemingly flows from the fact that they are natives. Arabs should recognize that these Israelis especially may have a strong moral right to live there. Moreover, this moral right would seem to increase with the length of time, reaching back from the present, that these Israelis or their ancestors have actually been living in the Holy Land. Some Jewish families can trace their modern roots there back to the First Aliyah in the 1880s. A few families may be able to go back even further. It would seem that such people are in a real sense indigenous.

The moral-rights basis for political rights is different from the moral-rights basis for the right to own or use property. Thus the moral rights to political self-determination flowing from birth in the Holy Land and from *modern* ancestral presence would not establish a moral right to property confiscated as recently as 1948.

Of course these rights also apply to Palestinian Arabs, including refugees born in the Holy Land. Most of them have longer modern ancestral roots there than do the children of the Jewish immigrants. These rights also belong to the descendants of the Palestinian Arabs who were expelled in 1947-49 and barred from returning. These descendants should not be penalized because they were unjustly denied their right to be born in their ancestral homeland. (Cf. Ch. Two, Sec. VI.) But this is getting ahead of the story.

Some Palestinian Arabs in the early twentieth century knew of or at least suspected the Zionists' intent regarding statehood. Their response reflected their fear for their own future, which the intent threatened. History has shown that this fear was well founded. At least after the Second Aliyah began in 1904, immigration to Palestine became increasingly involved not simply in the moral issue of (a) immigration but also in the moral issues of (b) displacing workers and of (c) forming a state in which the indigenous people would be seriously disadvantaged. These three issues, which generated increasing violence after World War I, will be more fully examined in the following chapters.

Chapter Four

WILSON - PART 1; THE BALFOUR DECLARATION

1914-17

This chapter, within the context of the Balfour Declaration, continues to examine the moral right to immigrate. It also examines the moral right of a people to self-determination, and the morality of Woodrow Wilson's support of the Declaration.

World War I moved Zionism's center to London. Britain became much more immersed in Zionism because of Britain's Balfour Declaration and its postwar mandate over Palestine. The debate over Balfour initiated America into the Zionist-Palestinian conflict. Both the declaration and the mandate would create moral issues for Britain and America.

I. British Duplicity With Arabs, 1914-16.

When the war began, Britain tried to foment revolt among Arabs, who comprised most of the non-Turks in the Asiatic part of the Ottoman Empire. Fomenting revolt was difficult because the Ottoman sultan was also the religious leader of many of the largely Muslim Arabs; moreover, the Allies were non-Muslims, "infidels." Britain also wanted to win worldwide Jewish support for the Allies, especially in America. This too was difficult because Russia, abhorred by Jews because of its brutal anti-Semitism, was an Ally. Germany, despite much subtle and some open anti-Semitism, treated Jews much better. To win over both Arabs and Jews Britain made contradictory promises about Palestine to each. This helped create the problem that America still faced in 1995.

Britain promised Arabs that if they revolted and the Allies won, it would work to see that Arabs could form their own independent countries. In various documents Britain declared that Allied war aims included: (a) guaranteeing the liberation of the peoples subject to Germany and its allies, (b) establishing national governments which derive their authority from the initiative and free choice of the indigenous peoples, (c) recognizing Arab independence as soon as effectively established, (d) ensuring impartial and equal justice to all, and (e) facilitating economic development and education.[1]

Between July 1915 and March 1916, Sir Henry McMahon, British High Commissioner in Cairo, and Sherif Hussein of Mecca, an Arab leader in the Ottoman Empire, exchanged ten letters - the Hussein-McMahon Correspondence. They contain the two men's negotiations about Arab participation in the war and independence after it. The bargaining produced a conditioned British pledge of independence for Arabs. Arabs maintain that this included independence for Palestine. With the Allied victory, Britain contended that Palestine was not included. Arguments to back Britain's position are complex; their validity is disputed. Britain asserted that Sherif Hussein failed to create a widespread revolt and so did not fulfill his part of the bargain; therefore Britain was freed from its part.[2] However, even a *British* committee, appointed in 1939 to study the letters, rejected the British arguments. The committee concluded that it was

> evident from these statements that His Majesty's Government were[3] not free to dispose of Palestine without regard for the wishes and interests of the inhabitants of Palestine and that these statements must all be taken into account in any attempt to estimate the responsibilities which...His Majesty's Government have incurred towards these inhabitants as a result of the Correspondence.[4]

The inherent moral right of Palestine's inhabitants to determine their own future did not, of course, belong to Britain. It certainly had no moral right to grant or withhold independence. However, the Allies won the war and Britain engineered its own acquisition of the legal power to deny the inhabitants of Palestine the exercise of their moral right to self-determination.

While Britain bargained with Arabs it also secretly negotiated primarily with France and secondarily with Russia over the division among themselves of Ottoman lands in Asia. Their Sykes-

Picot Agreement of May 1916 provided independence for Saudi Arabia and Yemen; France was to get Lebanon and Syria, and Britain was to get Iraq and Trans-Jordan. Sykes-Picot said that in certain areas these two Allies were "to establish such direct or indirect administration or control as they desire and as they may think fit to arrange with the Arab State or Confederation of Arab States."[5] Part of Palestine was to be put under "an international administration, the form of which is to be decided upon after consultation with Russia and subsequently in consultation with the other Allies, and the representatives of the Shereef of Mecca."[6]

Despite the euphemisms, Arabs would have no real voice in the decisions. David Lloyd George (1863-1945), who became British prime minister in December 1916, approved Sykes-Picot even though he called it "a foolish document."[7] Britain did not tell Hussein of it because it basically undid Britain's agreement with him in the McMahon-Hussein Correspondence. After the war Britain and France implemented a modified version of Sykes-Picot; most of Palestine went under British control; its northern section went under French control.

Britain was also trying to coax America into the war. Many U.S. Jews had come from Russia; Britain hoped to offset their anti-Russian hostility so that they would not oppose this. Because of repeated German attacks on its merchant ships America entered the war in April 1917. This was six months before Britain adopted the Balfour Declaration, in which it pledged to support a Jewish homeland in Palestine. Nevertheless, in 1937 Lloyd George told the Palestine Royal (Peel) Commission: "Zionist leaders gave us a definite promise that, if the Allies committed themselves to giving facilities for the establishment of a national home for the Jews in Palestine, they would do their best to rally Jewish sentiment and support throughout the world to the Allied cause. They kept their word."[8]

II. The British Debate Over the Balfour Declaration, 1917.

The British War Cabinet's adoption of the Balfour Declaration on October 31, 1917, was a major development in the Zionist-

Palestinian conflict. It stated:

His Majesty's Government view with favour the establishment in Palestine of a national home for the Jewish people, and will use their best endeavours to facilitate the achievement of this object, it being clearly understood that nothing shall be done which may prejudice the civil and religious rights of existing non-Jewish communities in Palestine, or the rights and political status enjoyed by Jews in any other country.[9]

The political and diplomatic maneuvering preceding the declaration extended over several years and involved President Woodrow Wilson (1856-1924). It is briefly summarized here.

Prime Minister Herbert Asquith's Liberal government, which was in power during the first two years of the war, did not want to be solely responsible for Palestine after the war; nor did it want to form a Jewish national home there. In December 1916 Asquith was succeeded by Lloyd George, who thought that postwar British control of Palestine would help protect the nearby Suez Canal, which Britain controlled. British Zionists supported this idea, but stressed that the canal would be even safer if Palestine had a National Home populated by Jews sympathetic to Britain.[10] Chaim Weizmann, a chemist, lived in England and developed explosives for Britain. He and other European Zionists began negotiating with the new foreign minister, Arthur Balfour (1848-1930), about a British statement that would support a Jewish homeland in Palestine. Weizmann, a major author of the proposed declaration, was in frequent contact with Balfour. Lloyd George supported such a statement because of its potential wartime propaganda value among Jews, especially in America. He also thought it would help Britain gain sole postwar control of Palestine rather than share it with France, as Britain had recently agreed to do in Sykes-Picot. Lloyd George knew that Zionists wanted their homeland to be under Britain's initial protection rather than France's.

III. Wilson's Approval of the Proposed Declaration, 1917.

Despite support for Zionism within the Lloyd George War Cabinet, several of its members strongly opposed cabinet endorsement of a Jewish national home. Edwin Montagu, a cabinet member and an assimilated Jew, opposed the concept as "anti-Semitic." Lord George Curzon (1859-1925), chairman of the cabinet committee on Middle East acquisitions, thought such a homeland unfeasible because Palestine was already inhabited. Due to the controversy, the cabinet on September 3, 1917, voted to learn if Wilson approved of such a declaration. Lord Robert Cecil, a Foreign Office official, cabled Colonel Edward House, Wilson's chief foreign affairs adviser: "We are being pressed here for a declaration of sympathy with the Zionist movement and I should be very grateful if you felt able to ascertain unofficially if the President favours such a declaration."[11] House himself said he saw "many dangers lurking" in it. On September 10 House cabled Cecil that Wilson was reluctant to endorse it: "The time was not opportune for any definite statement further, perhaps, than one of sympathy, provided it can be made without conveying any real commitment."[12] Wilson's situation was delicate: America was not at war with Turkey but only with its allies. For him publicly to endorse the proposed statement, which would impinge on Ottoman sovereignty, would certainly worsen U.S.-Ottoman relations - relations already severely strained by the war. This Wilson did not want.

Weizmann soon learned of House's reply. On September 19 he cabled the draft declaration's text to a U.S. Supreme Court justice, Louis Brandeis (1856-1941), the preeminent Zionist leader in America and Wilson's close friend and confidant. Weizmann also cabled other U.S. Zionists urging them to change Wilson's mind. House later complained about the pressure put on himself: "The Jews...descended in force, and they seemed determined to break in with a jimmy, if they are not let in."[13] Despite his complaints, House met with Brandeis on September 23 and gave him what he wanted. O'Brien contends that "Brandeis...was an extremely impressive character, both intellectually and morally....But Wilson was a practical politician, and he knew that there was a political force behind Brandeis's argument."[14] After that meeting, Brandeis told Weizmann, "From talks I have had with President and from expressions of opinion given to closest advisers...I can answer that he is in entire sympathy with declaration."[15] Thus within two weeks Zionists got Wilson to reverse his position. O'Brien notes: "Brandeis's contribution to the securing of the Balfour Declaration had been second only to Weizmann's own."[16] O'Brien's statement indicates that he considers Wilson's approval vital to the passage of the declaration.

In mid-October Wilson more formally sent Britain his approval. However, he asked London not to make it known publicly, for after Britain would make the declaration itself public, American Jews would ask him for his approval of it and he would publicly give it.[17] Wilson therefore decided to risk harming U.S. relations with Turkey rather than alienate a powerful segment of his own political constituency. London saw his approval of the draft declaration both as support for the Jewish national home and as a strong sign that America would support Britain's postwar bid to gain Palestine as a protectorate. Thus Wilson strengthened the position of the pro-declaration members of the War Cabinet. In doing this he seriously undermined the fulfillment of the moral right of Palestinian Arabs to self-determination.

IV. The Balfour Declaration's Final Debate and Passage, 1917.

In late October Curzon told the cabinet that he would favor increased immigration of eastern European Jews to Palestine and letting them have the same religious and civic rights as Palestine's other inhabitants, but that he was still against the special privileges which would go with a homeland. Zionists considered his anti-homeland position unacceptable. However, Zionist leaders told Leopold Amery, whom Balfour had commissioned to help draft the declaration, that "the argument that the Jews wanted a state was 'wholly fallacious', that it was not in fact part of the Zionist programme."[18] If that were the case, these Zionists were stepping back from Herzl's stated goal of a Jewish state. Did Zionists in fact not want the national home to be an independent state but only a political entity with less independence? The goal perhaps varied among Zionists. Were some Zionists not sure at that point in time? Were some keeping their goal of an independent state hidden? At least some Zionists undoubtedly wanted a state; their position soon became very prominent at the postwar peace talks and in the jockeying over Britain's mandate over Palestine. Therefore, if "the argument that the Jews wanted a state was 'wholly fallacious'" in October 1917, it was clearly not wholly fallacious by July 1920, only thirty-three months later, by which time Britain had *de facto* obtained the mandate.

Meanwhile, bolstered by Wilson's mid-October approval of the proposed declaration, Lloyd George put his War Cabinet's own approval of it on the agenda of its next meeting, October 31, 1917. Curzon, chairman of the cabinet committee on Middle East acquisitions, again objected that Palestine was already inhabited by some half million Arabs who "will not be content either to be expropriated for Jewish immigrants or to act merely as hewers of wood and drawers of water for the latter."[19] Balfour, however, stressed three points:

1. Germany might make its own declaration in support of a Jewish national home in Palestine, and thus beat Britain to the punch and win Jewish support throughout the world, including America. According to Israeli historian Michael J. Cohen, "The British became convinced (thanks to an assiduous Jewish lobby that supplied the government with press clippings) that if they did not issue a pro-Zionist declaration, the Germans would preempt them."[20] Actually Balfour probably had no valid evidence that this would happen. He should have seriously doubted that it would happen. Although Germany had interceded with Turkey on behalf of Jews in Palestine, it was not apt to make a declaration offensive to its Ottoman ally.

2. Lord Balfour stressed that the British declaration would increase Russian Jews' support for the Allied war effort. This point, part of his argument that the statement would be good wartime propaganda, was already questionable. Russia's ability to fight had been seriously undermined for several months by its increasing political turmoil, which had already resulted in the October Revolution. The triumphant Bolsheviks, including Jewish Bolsheviks, wanted Russia to leave the war completely. British courting of Russian Jews' favor would have little hope of returning

Russia to the war as an effective fighting force. (Within two months Russia signed an armistice with Germany.)

3. Lord Balfour asserted that a British declaration favoring a Jewish national home in Palestine would increase U.S. Jews' support of the Allied war effort. According to O'Brien: "The point about America had great substance, and on that, Wilson's approval was decisive. Curzon did not press his objection, and the War Cabinet approved the Balfour Declaration."[21]

In saying that "Wilson's approval was decisive," O'Brien implies that Britain probably would not have adopted the statement without it. Wilson, as O'Brien notes above, would not have approved it if he had not been pressured by U.S. Zionists. Laqueur favors a similar conclusion. He states that Zionists considered Wilson's initial refusal to approve the declaration a disaster. But when he reversed himself within two weeks and approved it, Laqueur comments, the "Zionists had surmounted yet another major hurdle owing to the help received from American Jewry."[22] One can only speculate whether Britain would have adopted the declaration without the stated approval of America's president. The fact is that he did approve it. This approval probably aided its adoption by Britain. Wilson was undoubtedly a party to its adoption.

British papers soon printed the declaration. Britain had no sovereignty over Palestine when it was adopted and so it had no legal standing other than its being a commitment by Britain. Because it was a commitment, Arab leaders strongly objected. However, Sherif Hussein's son, Feisal, hoping Britain would make him King of Syria, allegedly signed two pledges to support a Jewish national home in Palestine. When the French took over Syria they expelled Feisal, who claimed the signatures on the pledges were forgeries.[23] Within a few months after Britain adopted Balfour, France, Italy, China, Japan, Greece and Siam at least implicitly endorsed it. Although Wilson had already approved a draft of Balfour, his government could not formally *endorse* it because it was at peace with Turkey. With Wilson approving Balfour and the War Cabinet passing it, both the British government and at least the White House in effect approved of Zionism itself. Many Jews concluded that Gentiles would no longer question their loyalty even if they were Zionists. Only then did many, but not all, British and U.S. Jews drop their anti-Zionism.

V. Moral Issues Surrounding the Balfour Declaration.

The declaration did not adequately safeguard the rights of Palestinian Arabs. It refers only to their "civil and religious rights," not to their political rights.[24] If Britain intended that "civil rights" include political rights, the document would have been stronger on Arab rights than it appears. This apparently was not the case, however; for Britain, in order to implement the declaration, violated Palestinian Arabs' *moral right* to the *political freedom* due to them. Specifically, if the establishment of the Jewish national home were to have been put to a popular vote in Palestine before Zionists became a majority there, it would have lost. Therefore this part of the declaration required that Britain forcibly withhold political freedom from Palestine's inhabitants.

Did Britain, by violating the Palestinian Arabs' right to political freedom, commit an injustice? It can be argued that if Britain had not developed the Balfour Declaration and the accompanying mandate, Palestinians still would probably not have experienced democracy but rather a monarchy. (*Palestinians* here means not only Arabs but all inhabitants of Palestine.) Most of the other Arab countries which were formed from the Ottoman Empire, and which achieved independence, became monarchies - either emirates, kingdoms or dictatorships. Therefore, one might argue, Britain did not take away Palestinians' rights because they would not have had them anyway. This argument presumes that if the Palestinians would not have had a democracy (which was not proven), they would have elected to live under a British mandate rather than under an Arab monarch. (The evidence indicates that king-designate Feisal would probably have been preferred.) The argument also presumes that because an Arab monarch *might* have violated Palestinians' political rights, Britain automatically had the moral right to violate those rights. The argument does not undo the fact that Palestinians' rights were violated by Britain. This must be construed as an injustice. To conclude otherwise would require that the moral rights of the British and Zionists outweighed the moral rights of Palestinians. That, of course, is a key moral issue regarding this crucial period in the Zionist-Palestinian conflict.

Both Britain, and Wilson in supporting Britain, seemingly were working out of a colonialist moral framework in which right was judged by might. During the preceding century England had conquered vast colonies around the world, and America had pushed its own frontier from eastern Illinois to Alaska. Numerous Native Americans, Puerto Ricans, Hawaiians, Filipinos and other Pacific islanders had come under the U.S. flag without being asked whether or not they wanted to. In 1917 Palestinians were being victimized by this colonialist moral framework.

In addition to the issue of violating Palestinians' right to political freedom the Balfour Declaration raises *a second moral issue*: Did it violate the moral rights of Palestine's indigenous people by making it possible for so many non-Palestinians to immigrate there that they would inevitably upset *"the common good rightly understood?"*[25] Would such a large influx of immigrants almost certainly unduly disrupt the lives of the indigenous people? The declaration (fully quoted at the top of the previous section) indicated that it would not let this happen: "...it being clearly understood that nothing shall be done which may prejudice the civil and religious rights of existing non-Jewish communities in Palestine." However, the declaration made no provision for these non-Jewish communities to be a judge of what might "prejudice" their "civil and religious rights." The policing of this clause would be under British, not Palestinian, control. The success or failure of the clause would depend partly on the number of immigrants that *Britain* would allow. In the following years Britain allowed so many non-Palestinians to immigrate that they did in fact upset "the common good rightly understood." The way in which the clause, "nothing shall be done...," would be implemented would also depend on how *Britain* would interpret the phrase, "the establishment in Palestine of a national home for the Jewish people." Britain would allow so many Zionists to immigrate that they would eventually be able to help force the establishment not only of a home but of a state.

Balfour had told the War Cabinet that the term, "'national home'....did not necessarily involve the *early* establishment of an independent Jewish state, which was a matter of gradual development in accordance with the ordinary laws of political evolution."[26] Thus Balfour himself foresaw the possibility of an *eventual* establishment of a Jewish state. However, the Balfour Declaration did not clarify when or perhaps even whether the homeland for Jews in Palestine should be an independent state. Nor did it set forth how this homeland could be established in such a way that, as it stated, "nothing shall be done which may prejudice the civil and religious rights of existing non-Jewish communities in Palestine." This ambiguity would be a factor exacerbating the extremely muddled diplomacy that would develop during the thirty-one years between the adoption of the declaration and the establishment of the state of Israel.

Therefore *a third issue* regarding the morality of the Balfour Declaration is this: *Did the proviso for this national home violate the rights of the indigenous people?* The phrase, "national home," is so deliberately vague that it could mean a large or small part of Palestine; it could mean a fully independent state or some entity with less independence. By crafting a deliberately vague declaration Britain gave its future governments a blank check regarding its enactment. The only restriction regarding Palestine was the proviso not to prejudice the civil and religious rights of non-Jews. However, as noted, interpreting this was a British prerogative. Eventually Britain technically answered to the League of Nations, but Britain dominated the League. The declaration was bound to cause dissention because it was virtually self-contradictory: If the clause about "the establishment in Palestine of a national home for the Jewish people" were to be fulfilled on a scale satisfactory to Zionists, this would "prejudice the civil and religious rights of the existing non-Jewish communities in Palestine." If, however, Britain made sure that "nothing shall be done which may prejudice" these rights, then the clause about the "national home" would be met on a scale unsatisfactory to Zionists. Reconciling these two poles may have been theoretically possible, but it would have required a much higher degree of sensitivity, cooperation, justice, and love for one's neighbor than is usually attained in stressful inter-ethnic relationships. The Balfour Declaration did nothing to create the just and compassionate atmosphere necessary for its own success.

Within a few months of its passage, some Zionists in Palestine were openly discussing the clash with their Arab neighbors that they thought would be inevitable. In 1918, Y. A. Wilkansky alluded to the moral reservations that some Jews were experiencing with regard to Jewish plans for Palestine. He told the Conference of the *Yishuv* (the Jews living in Palestine) that Jews who want a Palestinian national home but do not want to displace the Arabs are like people who oppose cruelty to animals and yet eat meat. He disparaged such Jews for maintaining that:

it was impossible to evict the fellahin (the Arabs), even if we wanted to....Nevertheless, if it were *possible*, I would commit an injustice towards the Arabs....There are those among us who are opposed to this from the point of view of supreme righteousness and morality. Gentlemen,...if one wants to be a 'preventer of cruelty to animals,' one must be an extremist in the matter. When you enter into the midst of the Arab nation and do not allow it to unite, here too you are taking its life. The Arabs are not salt-fish; they have blood, they live, and they feel pain with the entry of a 'foreign body' into their midst. Why don't our moralists dwell on *this* point? We must be either complete vegetarians or meat-eaters: not one-half, one-third, or one-quarter vegetarians.[27]

Apparently Wilkansky and Zionists who thought like him did not agree with the Balfour Declaration proviso that "nothing shall be done which may prejudice the civil and religious rights of existing non-Jewish communities in Palestine." Either that, or these Zionists did not consider displacing Arabs something that would "prejudice their civil...rights."

A fourth issue concerns *the morality of American involvement in the declaration* because of Wilson's approval of it.

1. As a party to Britain's adoption of the declaration, Wilson must have known that Britain intended to have some type of

postwar control over Palestine in order to implement the document. Otherwise it would have little meaning. Therefore America, through its president, was seemingly a party to the violation of Palestinians' moral right to political self-determination, to political independence.

2. America, through Wilson, was also a party to giving Britain a blank check with regard to both the number of immigrants and the size and nature of the national home. In doing this it would seem that America also violated the moral right of the Palestinians to determine these issues themselves.

If it was moral for America and Britain to take the actions they did regarding Palestinians' rights then it would be moral for a group of other nations to take similar actions regarding basic rights of the British and Americans. To argue otherwise requires that moral rights of people in Britain and America are more sacred than the moral rights of people in Palestine.

One may argue that America was not morally responsible for Wilson's acts, especially because the Senate did not ratify these. Most Americans, either then or since, were not even aware of Wilson's endorsement. How could they be morally responsible for what he did? They may not have been responsible but they can still be accountable and therefore morally responsible for correcting the violation in so far as they can. As will be noted in Chapter Six, Wilson's approval was seconded by the next two presidents, Harding and Coolidge, and by both the Senate and House during Harding's Administration and by the Senate in Coolidge's. Thus the approval was not an isolated action of one president acting alone but the work of a wide spectrum of the government. Moreover, the approval was expressed on several occasions. All of this increased America's involvement and therefore, it would seem, its corporate moral responsibility.

Chapter Five

WILSON - PART 2;
THE BRITISH MANDATE OVER PALESTINE

1918-21

The Balfour Declaration was useless to Zionists without British control of Palestine. Obtaining a mandate from the proposed League of Nations seemed the best way to gain this. Britain, together with British and U.S. Zionists, were the primary agents in this project. America itself, by what it did and did not do, also played a decisive role. This chapter shows that President Wilson repeatedly supported the Balfour Declaration for the remaining three and a half years of his presidency. He did this despite his repeated pronouncements of principles supporting Palestinians' right to self determination. Thus through repeated inconsistencies he turned what might have been an isolated action done under Zionist pressure - his original support of Balfour in the fall of 1917 - into presidential policy. The moral issues during this period when the mandate was being engineered were very similar to those in the earlier Balfour phase of the Zionist-Palestinian conflict.

I. British and French Promises to Arabs, 1918.

In January 1918, when Britain still needed Arab military help, it sent what is called the Hogarth Message to Sherif Hussein. It stated that "Jewish settlement in Palestine would only be allowed in so far as would be consistent with the political and economic freedom of the Arab population."[1] This statement went further than did the Balfour Declaration in supporting the political rights of the indigenous people, for it spoke of their "political and economic freedom" and not just of their "civil and religious rights."[2] Arabs argued from this that "political...freedom of the Arab population" meant independence. On February 8 Britain issued the Bassett Letter, which stated:

His Majesty's Government and their allies remain steadfast to the policy of helping any movement which aims at setting free those nations where are oppressed....The Government... repeats its previous promise in respect of the freedom and the emancipation of the Arab peoples.[3]

On June 16 Britain's Declaration to the Seven (seven Syrian leaders) stated, "the policy of His Majesty's Government towards the inhabitants...is that the future government...should be based upon the principle of the consent of the governed. This policy will always be that of His Majesty's Government."[4] During all of this time Arabs continued their efforts to overthrow Turkish rule.

On November 7, eight days after the Allied armistice with Turkey, and four days before the armistice with Germany ended the war, Britain and France released The Anglo-French Joint Declaration. It stated that France and Great Britain's goal

is the complete and definite emancipation of the peoples so long oppressed by the Turks, and the establishment of National Governments and administrations deriving their authority from the initiative and free choice of the indigenous populations.

...France and Great Britain are at one in encouraging and assisting the establishment of indigenous Governments and administrations in Syria [which included Palestine] and Mesopotamia [Iraq]....Far from wishing to impose on the populations of those regions any particular institutions, they are only concerned to secure...the regular working of Governments and administrations freely chosen by the populations themselves.[5]

This Anglo-French Declaration was perhaps sincere about Saudi Arabia and Yemen; it seems completely insincere about Mesopotamia, Syria, Lebanon, Trans-Jordan and Palestine because France and Britain already intended to take these. If enacted it would have canceled out Balfour. The Anglo-French Declaration was distributed by Britain in Jerusalem and led Palestinian Arabs to hope they would be allowed to choose their own future. Through Britain's numerous promises to Arabs *during* the war she took away from

Balfour as much as she had promised Jews in it. Despite these promises, *after* the war Britain did much more to fulfill Balfour's pro-Zionist part than to honor British promises to Arabs.

II. Wilson's Pro-democracy Statements, 1918.

The U.S. government, though much less involved with Palestine than was Britain, did not fully ignore the discussions concerning it. On January 8, 1918, Wilson proclaimed his Fourteen Peace Points. In Point Five he called for an "adjustment of colonial claims with concern for the wishes and interests of the inhabitants as well as for the titles of rival claimants."[6] In Point Twelve, devoted to the Ottoman Empire, Wilson urged that its non-Turkish nationalities "should be assured...an absolutely unmolested opportunity of autonomous development."[7] The people in Palestine were obviously part of these non-Turkish nationalities. On February 11, concerning future peace agreements, he stated: "Peoples are not to be handed about from one sovereignty to another by an international conference or an understanding between rivals and antagonists."[8] On July 4 he declared:

The settlement of every question, whether of territory, of sovereignty, of economic arrangement, or of political relationship, [should be] upon the basis of the free acceptance of that settlement by the people concerned and not upon the basis of the material interest or advantage of any other nation or people which may desire a different settlement for the sake of its own exterior influence or mastery.[9]

A Wilson theme was that "the world must be made safe for democracy."[10] In each of these statements Wilson set forth principles which seem to be diametrically opposed to both the Balfour Declaration's goal and Britain's efforts to get a mandate over Palestine. Yet Wilson did not withdraw his own approval of Balfour nor did he specifically oppose Britain's obtaining the mandate. Instead, in an August 31, 1918, letter he wrote:

I welcome an opportunity to express the satisfaction I have felt in the progress of the Zionist movement in the United States and in the allied countries since the declaration of Mr.

Balfour, on behalf of the British Government, of Great
Britain's approval of the establishment in Palestine of a
national home for the Jewish people and his promise that the
British Government would use its best endeavors to facilitate
the achievement of that object, with the understanding that
nothing would be done to prejudice the civil and religious
rights of non-Jewish people in Palestine....[11]

British-Arab forces occupied all of Palestine by October 1918.
British military ruled it until July 1920. In 1918 Jews owned 253
square miles of urban and farm land - some 2.5 percent of Palestine; this included fifty-one Jewish settlements.[12]

III. American Involvement, 1919.

As the Paris Peace Conference approached, lobbying increased
both for and against incorporating Balfour into the accords. At
first Zionists demanded that the *yishuv* be given majority rights in
Palestine even though they were definitely only a small minority
of the population. Eventually they toned down this demand.[13]
Some Palestinian Arabs wanted Palestine to be part of a greater
Syria, which Feisal, its king-designate, already ruled in a subordi-
nate way. Palestinian Arabs already held important positions within his new administration. An Arab delegation was formed to go
to Paris to propose this. Britain, however, kept it from travelling
because its proposal would thwart London's own desire to control
Palestine.[14] Thus Britain physically prevented these Palestinians
from attending the very conference that was to decide their future.
Feisal and Zionists were allowed to go to Paris, although they did
not have a delegation within the conference itself.

Protestant missionary groups running Mideast churches and
schools opposed Balfour and its U.S. support. Dr. Howard Bliss,
president of Beirut's Syrian Protestant College, went to Paris,
where he urged forming a commission to determine what the
native people of the Mideast wanted for themselves. This sugges-
tion was embraced by the U.S. diplomatic staff in Paris. They
hoped that Wilson, especially in light of the principles he had

enunciated, would also accept it.[15] Princeton's Professor Philip Brown, in Cairo for the YMCA, provided requested reports to the U.S. State Department on his assessment of Zionism's impact on Palestine. In several reports he asserted that Zionism would be a disaster for both Arabs and Jews. He also went to Paris to lobby against Zionist goals and U.S. efforts to support them.[16]

Wilson sent to the American Jewish community New Year's Day (1919) greetings endorsing the Zionist program, including Balfour. Brandeis responded by declaring that opposition to Zionism could henceforth be considered disloyalty to America.[17]

During the Paris Peace Conference, held primarily in early 1919, the U.S. delegation wrote an Outline of Recommendations regarding Palestine. It followed most of the Zionist goals, including the Balfour points and large boundaries for Palestine. The Outline also minimized Arab claims to the area. However, William Westermann, director of the State Department's Western Asia Division, made a study of the Zionist program in the light of American interests and Wilsonian principles. He concluded that America "could not afford to support" Balfour.[18] The most valid argument against it, he wrote, "is that it impinges upon the rights and desires of most of the Arab population of Palestine," who constitute 80 percent of its people, and "who do not want their country to be made into a 'homeland' for the Jews."[19] Westermann and others thought Arab claims were much more in accord with Wilson's own principles than was the Balfour Declaration. They circulated Arab material.[20]

Ignoring Arab rights and sensibilities was not limited to governments of the Allies. Melvin Urofsky, an historian of Zionism and very sympathetic to it, wrote in 1974:

most Zionists did not take the more than half million Arabs who lived there seriously. The Americans were as guilty of this as anyone else, and in the general celebrating over the Balfour Declaration, made only passing reference to the non-Jews in Palestine, glibly predicting future cooperation between Arab and Jew.[21]

Urofsky added that Felix Frankfurter, who was at the peace

conference, recognized the potential danger and sought out Feisal "to stress to him the American tradition opposing colonialism."[22] Frankfurter was then a prominent Harvard law professor, a Zionist leader, and a future U.S. Supreme Court justice. "The last thing the Jews wanted," he told Feisal, "was to triumph at the expense of the Arab people and Arab civilization."[23] Statements and actions around that time by other Zionists make one question how many of them shared the sentiments toward Arabs that he expressed. Moreover, "the American tradition opposing colonialism" must have surprised Feisal if he knew much about U.S. expansionism during the 130 years previous to his meeting with Frankfurter.

IV. The American King-Crane Commission, 1919.

In March 1919, during the peace conference, the four major Allies - Britain, France, Italy and America - agreed to form an Inter-Allied Commission to learn the wishes of those who had been under Ottoman rule. However, the commission was not formed. Wilson therefore sent an American team, the King-Crane Commission. It spent six weeks in June and July 1919 touring what would become Syria, Lebanon, Palestine, Trans-Jordan and south-central Turkey to learn people's wishes firsthand. In Palestine it met with both Jews and Arabs. The Commission reported that 1,350 petitions, comprising 72 percent of the 1,863 received from the whole of Syria were "against Zionist claims and purposes."[24] (The Allies then treated Lebanon and Palestine as temporarily part of Syria, from which they had been ruled by the Ottomans.) The commission said mandatory powers should follow these principles:

1. "The well-being and development" of the people involved form "a sacred trust." "Securities for the performance of this trust shall be embodied in the constitution of the League of Nations."[25]

2. The peoples so long oppressed by the Turks should become completely and definitively free.

3. The national governments and administrations to be established should derive their authority from the initiative and free choice of the native populations.[26]

For Palestine the King-Crane Commission recommended

"serious modification of the extreme Zionist Program for Palestine of unlimited immigration of Jews, [which looked]...finally to making Palestine distinctly a Jewish state."[27] The commission stated that its members "began their study of Zionism with minds predisposed in its favor, but the actual facts in Palestine, coupled with the force of the general principles proclaimed by the Allies and accepted by the Syrians have driven them to the recommendation here made."[28]

The Commissioners pointed out that the Balfour Declaration "favoring the establishment in Palestine of 'a national home for the Jewish people,' is not equivalent to making Palestine into a Jewish state."[29] They added that the erection of such a state could be accomplished only with "the gravest trespass upon the 'civil and religious rights of existing non-Jewish communities in Palestine.'"[30] The commissioners asserted that in their meetings with Jewish representatives it "came out repeatedly...that *the Zionists looked forward to a practically complete dispossession of the present non-Jewish inhabitants of Palestine*, by various forms of purchase."[31] The commission said that its surveys showed that there was no one thing upon which the Palestinian Arabs were more agreed upon than their opposition to the Zionist program. "To subject a people so minded to unlimited Jewish immigration, and to steady financial and social pressure to surrender the land, would be a gross violation of the principle [stated by Wilson on July 4, 1918] and of the peoples' rights, though it be kept within the forms of law."[32]

The King-Crane Commission added: "There is a further consideration that cannot justly be ignored, if the world is to look forward to Palestine becoming a definitely Jewish state....That consideration grows out of the fact that Palestine is 'the Holy Land' for Jews, Christians and Moslems alike."[33]

One effect of urging "the extreme Zionist program" would be an intensification of "anti-Jewish feeling both in Palestine and in all other portions of the world which look to Palestine as 'the Holy Land."[34] The commission recommended that "Jewish immigration should be definitely limited and...the project for making Palestine distinctly a Jewish commonwealth should be given up...(Palestine should be) included in a united Syrian state, just as other portions of the country."[35]

Thus the King-Krane Commission clearly maintained that for the vast majority of Palestine's people, Balfour did not reflect Wilson's Fourteen Points. The team therefore urged that postwar colonial adjustments be made with concern for the wishes and interests of the inhabitants as well as for the titles of rival claimants. The team's report foresaw that the adjustments, instead of being made in the light of the Fourteen Points, would be made at gun point. The team noted that "no British officer, consulted by the Commissioners, believed that the Zionist program could be carried out except by force of arms."[36] Most officers thought that Britain would need 50,000 soldiers to start it.

The King-Crane Commission Report went to the White House in the fall of 1919. By this time Wilson had met several major defeats in his efforts for a just peace. He was very ill. *The U.S. government kept the commission's recommendations secret until 1922.* Historian Urofsky notes: "Both the British and American leaders had gone too far in their support of Zionist aspirations to back down. With the burial of the King-Crane report, a major obstacle in the Zionist path disappeared."[37] The report's burial exemplified the type of maneuvering that surrounded the early history of the Balfour Declaration. Lord Balfour himself observed, "so far as Palestine is concerned, the powers [the major Allies] have made no statement of fact that is not admittedly wrong, and no declaration of policy which, at least in the letter, they have not always intended to violate."[38]

V. Palestine's Change to a British Mandate, 1920-22.

After the Paris conference temporarily adjourned in the spring of 1919, Wilson and the U.S. government became much less involved in the peace talks. There were several reasons: Wilson's defeats in Paris, his bad health, his failure to get the Republican Congress to vote for U.S. entry into the League of Nations, and the strong isolationism sweeping America. Because of U.S. reclusiveness, primarily Britain and secondarily France dominated the

Allied Supreme Council even more than they had.

Weizmann, working closely with the British government, drafted a document by which initially the Allied Supreme Council and subsequently the League of Nations would grant Palestine as a mandated territory to Britain. The Balfour Declaration was to be part of this mandate document. However, some members of Britain's cabinet opposed putting the Balfour Declaration in the document. When Lord Curzon, who followed Lord Balfour as foreign secretary, saw a draft of the mandate in March 1920, he stated:

I think the entire conception wrong. Here is a country with 580,000 Arabs and 30,000 or is it 60,000 Jews (by no means all Zionists). Acting upon the noble principles of self-determination and ending with a splendid appeal to the League of Nations, we then proceed to draw up a document which reeks of Judaism in every paragraph and is an avowed constitution for a Jewish State. Even the poor Arabs are only allowed to look through the keyhole as a non-Jewish community.

It is quite clear that this mandate has been drawn up by someone reeling under the fumes of Zionism. If we are all to submit to that intoxicant, this draft is all right. Perhaps there is no alternative. But I...should like to see something worded differently.[39]

One draft of the mandate document included the words, "Recognizing...the historical connection of the Jews with Palestine, and the claim which this gives them to reconstitute it as their national home."[40] Curzon later wrote: "I do not myself recognize that the connection of the Jews with Palestine, which terminated 1200 years ago (sic), gives them any claim whatsoever. On this principle we have a stronger claim to parts of France."[41] Curzon was able to get the wording slightly changed, but not to his satisfaction. However, as foreign secretary he then helped implement the mandate. Britain's military in Palestine warned London that enacting Balfour would lead to a Palestinian revolt and endanger Britain's position throughout the area. The army dissuaded London from promulgating the declaration in Palestine until after the San Remo Conference in April 1920.[42]

Meanwhile, Zionists worked with Allies' diplomats and politicians so that they would give Palestine the largest borders possible. Zionists especially wanted its northern border to be the Litani River in present-day southern Lebanon. This would have given the Jewish national home access to its water and maximized the home's northern area. U.S. Zionists began telegraphing the Allied leaders about the borders. Brandeis wrote to Wilson "suggesting that a denial of viable borders would be a betrayal of Christian promises....[He asked Wilson] 'to move the statesmen of Christian nations to keep their solemn promise to Israel.'"[43] Brandeis added that Wilson's word to Prime Minister Lloyd George and to French premier Alexandre Millerand "may be decisive." Wilson therefore told Secretary of State Robert Lansing to instruct the U.S. representative in Paris to support Zionists' border wishes. However, State was reluctant to do this because America had virtually pulled out of the peace negotiations. To intrude at that point seemed inappropriate. Lansing toned down Wilson's letter and had it delivered orally and informally.[44]

The Allied Supreme Council met in San Remo, Italy in April 1920 to finish peace treaty items unresolved at Paris. America was represented by its ambassador to Rome, who sat in only as an observer.[45] Urofsky notes that during this period "the Zionists kept up their pressure on different governments."[46] Palestine's final borders did not include the Litani River but generally met Zionist demands. Both the Council and the new League of Nations, also dominated by London, agreed to Britain gaining the mandate over Palestine. The League included the Balfour Declaration in the mandate's preamble and gave final confirmation of the mandate in July 1922. (Technically, the Treaty of Lausanne, which legalized the status of Palestine as a League of Nations mandate, did not come into force until August 1924. But the mandate took effect *de facto* in July 1920, after San Remo.)[47] The Zionists' *Encyclopedia of Zionism and Israel* stated, "The Balfour Declaration helped lay the foundations for the future State of Israel."[48]

The League recognized Saudi Arabia and Yemen as independent. Thus, regarding their promises of independence, France and

Britain partly kept their word to some of the Arabs in that they allowed certain leaders to become their monarchs. (No Arab country carved from the Ottoman Empire became a democracy at that time.) The League mandated Syria, including Lebanon, to France; Iraq and Trans-Jordan, along with Palestine, were mandated to Britain. Thus Paris and London did not keep their promises to the Arabs in these areas.

VI. Palestinian Arab Reaction, 1920.

In early 1920 Jerusalem Arabs, led by the Muslim-Christian Association, protested against Zionism to the British governor of Jerusalem. They warned him that Palestinian Arabs would fight for their rights. Rioting erupted on February 27 and again a few days later. The most serious rioting lasted four days, April 4-8, and was directed against the Jewish Quarter in Jerusalem's Old City. Arab police, who helped rioters, were withdrawn and disarmed by British troops. The latter, however, did not stop the rioting and did not allow Jews to organize their own defense. Of the nine people killed, five were Jews; of the 244 wounded, 211 were Jews. Most were old men, women and children.[49] Britain's military command in Palestine recommended that the area be put under the new King Feisal of Syria and that the Balfour Declaration be revoked.[50] Jews were furious with the British army, comparing it to czarist police during the pogroms. London did not share the views of its soldiers in Palestine. As soon as Britain's legal title to Palestine was secure, London replaced its military government there with a civilian administration. Sir Herbert Samuel became the first Lord High Commissioner of Palestine (1920-25). He was, author O'Brien writes, "a convinced (though gradualist) Zionist."[51] It was Samuel who had so effectively coached Weizmann during the Balfour negotiations. After he became high commissioner, Jewish immigration greatly increased, and with it Palestinian Arab objections, including unrest again in 1921.

Vladimir Jabotinsky (1880-1940), a Russian immigrant, became a hero to Jews because of his defense of Jerusalem Jews during the 1920 riots, for which Britain jailed him. He told the Zionist

Actions Committee in 1921 that it is impossible "to bridge this contradiction between us and the Arabs with words, gifts or bribery."[52] Instead he called for an "iron wall" of armed force to make Arabs understand that "here stands an iron wall; the Jews are coming and will keep on coming; we are unable to prevent this; we cannot kill them."[53]

Urofsky, reflecting on Zionists' attitudes in the late nineteenth and early twentieth centuries, wrote in 1974:

the Zionists failed to take into account the hope that arose among Arab groups with the breakup of the Turkish Empire, or that Palestinian Arabs would harbor as much love and devotion to the Holy Land as the Jews did. Most Zionists dismissed Arab claims to Palestine, since...many peoples had possessed the land; the Arabs were but the last in line. Centuries of Jewish rule in Biblical times, as well as God's promise of redemption, seemed to count for more than a few hundred years of recent occupation, especially one that had done nothing to reclaim the land.[54]

If Urofsky's reflection on Zionists' thinking is accurate, (a) they failed to distinguish between who *ruled* Palestine and who *lived* there; (b) they failed to realize that although the natives live according to Arab culture, their ancestral roots, at least in part, go back *within Palestine* for as many millennia as do Jewish roots; and (c) Zionists therefore mistakenly equated Palestinian Arabs' culture and language with being "but the last in line." When comparing a Chicago Zionist thinking of moving to the Holy Land and a Palestinian whose family has lived there for as long as it can remember, one can well ask who is really "but the last in line."

Regarding the implication which Urofsky relates, that Zionists had a greater claim to the land because Palestinian Arabs "had done nothing to reclaim" it: What neglect there may have been came partly from Ottoman neglect, over which Palestinians had little say. However, the Zionist charge itself is questionable. After a trip through Palestine in 1891 Ahad Ha'am wrote that it was difficult to find any *uncultivated* land there.[55] In 1883 a traveler found that "almost every acre of the plain of Esdraelon is at this moment in the highest state of cultivation."[56] This was again reported to be the case in 1914.[57] Arabs around Jaffa grew oranges "the exceptional size of which attracted attention as early as the eighteenth century."[58]

Moreover, to measure the right to statehood by the ability and desire to reclaim land (which involved draining scarce Mideast wetlands) is to say that political rights are based on economic and technological standards. Land development and use probably are factors which may help determine one's moral right to own land. But it is a major leap from arguing the moral right to own a particular piece of undeveloped land to establishing the moral right to statehood over the entire region. In the 1990s Israel decided that some of its previous wetland destruction was doing more harm than good; some farmland is being returned to wetland.

Wilson's eight-year presidency ended in March 1921. In Chapter Four we discussed the moral right to self-determination. The assumption there was that, within limits created by other people's rights, self-determination is a *moral* right, that is, it is inherent in a group of people and is not dependent on human legislation for its existence. To violate that *moral* right is thus *morally* wrong. It robs persons of the exercise of their right. To claim that *withholding* the exercise of the right would not violate the right would require that the conflicting rights of (a) the British to a mandate and (b) of Zionists to turn Palestine either wholly or partly into a Jewish state outweighed the rights of the indigenous people to self-determination. To respond to that in the light of the Golden Rule: How would - should - Americans react if their right to self-determination were withheld in order that America could become the mandated territory of some second nation so that it might become the national home of a third group of people? Would Americans consider that morally just?

Chapter Six

HARDING, COOLIDGE;
U.S. SUPPORT OF THE MANDATE

1921-33

Between the time Britain *de facto* gained its mandate over Palestine and Adolph Hitler became chancellor of the Third Reich, 12½ years passed. Woodrow Wilson's first two successors, with congressional concurrence, supported the Balfour Declaration and the mandate. Thus support for Zionism expanded from the policy of one president to that of three, buttressed by Congress. America became more involved morally in the Zionist-Palestinian conflict as the incidents of U.S. support increased and as the base of that support spread from the White House to Capitol Hill.

I. Developments During the Harding Presidency, 1921-23.

Republican Warren Harding (1865-1923) took office in March 1921. After his election, author Melvin Urofsky writes, anti-Zionists in the State Department "openly proclaimed that the country had made no commitments to a Jewish homeland in Palestine."[1] On June 21 Harding stated: "It is impossible for one who has studied at all the services of the Hebrew people to avoid the faith that they will...be restored to their historic national home and there enter a new and yet greater phase of their contribution to the advance of humanity."[2] This was vaguely supportive but no commitment.

Meanwhile, in March, Winston Churchill, head of Britain's Colonial Office, divided all mandate land east of the Jordan River (Trans-Jordan) from Mandate Palestine. He made one of Sherif Hussein's sons, Abdullah, Trans-Jordan's emir. (Abdullah was a brother of Feisal, who had briefly been king of Syria until ousted by the French. Abdullah was also the paternal grandfather of the future King Hussein of Jordan.) Abdullah was not fully independent but answered to a British "adviser." Churchill's action excluded any of Trans-Jordan from being considered by Britain as part of the Jewish National Home. Some Zionists objected, and still object. They consider areas of Jordan part of the historic Land of Israel because 2½ tribes lived there before the Babylonian Exile and because Jews lived there afterward as well.

In early June 1922 Britain published the first of eventually three white papers on Palestine. It stated that the Jewish community "should know that it is in Palestine as of right and not on sufferance. That is the reason why it is necessary that the existence of a Jewish National Home in Palestine should be internationally guaranteed, and that it should be formally recognised to rest upon ancient historic connection."[3]

By this "Home" did Britain now mean a Jewish state? On June 23, 1923, the Duke of Devonshire, Churchill's successor as head of the Colonial Office, stated: "The intention from the beginning has been to make a National Home for the Jews, but every provision has been made to prevent it from becoming in any sense a Jewish State, or a State under Jewish domination."[4] This statement displeased Zionists,[5] which indicates they desired a state, not just a semiautonomous enclave. Events would prove that Devonshire's position was not chipped in stone.

The 1922 white paper laid down a policy that limited immigration to what Britain judged Palestine's "economic absorptive capacity" to be. That policy stressed that immigrants should not become a burden on British taxpayers, nor should they deprive Arabs of their jobs. The latter objective was undercut, however, by the Histadrut, the federation of Jewish labor unions. It urged Jewish employers to hire Jewish laborers instead of the less expensive and frequently more efficient Arab workers. This Histadrut effort enabled more immigrant workers' families to become self-sufficient and thus meet Britain's first objective, that is, that immigrants not become a burden to British taxpayers. Meeting this objective made way for yet more Jewish families to immigrate.[6] However, the Histadrut action also helped to further institutionalize the discriminatory hiring practices that some Zionists had been advocating since the Second Aliyah.

On May 11, 1922, Harding wrote to a Zionist group:

I am very glad to express my approval and hearty sympathy for the effort of the Palestine Foundation Fund in behalf of the restoration of Palestine as a homeland for the Jewish people. I have always viewed with an interest...the proposal for the rehabilitation of Palestine, and I hope the effort now being carried on in this and other countries in this behalf may meet with the fullest measure of success.[7]

On June 30 the House passed Joint Resolution 322, already passed by the Senate,

That the United States of America favors the establishment in Palestine of a national home for the Jewish people, it being clearly understood that nothing shall be done which may prejudice the civil and religious rights of Christian and all other non-Jewish communities in Palestine, and that the holy places and religious buildings and sites in Palestine shall be adequately protected.[8]

Harding signed the resolution on September 22. Thus Congress added its moral support to that given by two presidents, one Democrat and one Republican.

In congresspersons' "extension of remarks" that accompanied the House discussion, they repeated several themes to support the resolution:

1. On several previous occasions Congress had passed resolutions supporting people struggling against oppression.

2. Jews had recently been persecuted in Russia, Ukraine, Poland, Romania and Hungary, and needed places to move to. They should be given a chance to do this.

3. Congress had recently (1921) limited immigration to America and so it was fitting that Congress support immigration to Palestine. (Congresspersons seemed oblivious of the irony which would place on Palestinian Arabs a situation they had recently rejected for America.)

4. Palestine was underpopulated and could absorb 6.3 million more people, at which point, they noted, it would have the same population as Belgium, (which was 13 percent larger and had

much more fresh water). (America had only half the population density of Palestine, yet Congress had already limited future immigration to America. Using their Belgium model, the congresspersons, if consistent, should have been willing to open America to a total population of more than two billion.)

5. The Balfour Declaration adequately protected the civil and religious rights of Palestine's non-Jews. Moreover, Jews, having themselves been treated unjustly, would not treat others unjustly.

Missing from these remarks was any desire by Congress to poll Palestinian Arabs to learn their wishes. Their objections were sometimes alluded to but dismissed. Walter Chandler, a congressperson from New York, in his "extended remarks," stated, "it does not become the American Congress or the American Government to prate too loudly at this time about the sacred rights of the Arabs in Palestine, in the light of our treatment of the Filipinos during the last quarter of a century."[9] He said that if Arabs "will not consent to Jewish government and domination, they shall be required to sell their lands at a just valuation" and move to another Arab territory. If they refuse to do this "they shall be driven from Palestine by force."[10] Chandler thus reflects a colonialist mentality. He also indicates that he envisions that a national home for Jews includes political domination over Arabs. He added that he had "feelings of intolerance" for "any attempted justification of Mahomet, his message, and his mission."[11] Chandler pointed out that he represented a congressional district in New York City that was at least 40 percent Jewish.[12]

Palestinian Arabs continued to press for a representative government; Zionists continued to oppose it because they would have been outvoted. During the 1920s Zionists developed an official formula which maintained that "Palestine belonged on the one hand to the Arabs living there but on the other it belonged to the whole Jewish people, not just to that part of it resident in Palestine."[13] Thus a Jew in Chicago had as much right to Palestine as an Arab resident whose family had lived there for centuries. But an Arab from nearby Amman did not have this right. According to historian Walter Zeev Laqueur, even socialist

Zionists such as Shlomo Kaplanski held that the Arabs did not have the sole right of possession of Palestine. From the socialist point of view, Kaplanski wrote, Jews also had a very good claim: the right of the only landless people of the earth, the right of the dispossessed masses.[14]

In 1923 Vladimir Jabotinsky, who two years earlier had urged his fellow *yishuv* to present an "iron wall" of force to the Arabs, pointed out: "The Arabs loved their country as much as the Jews did. Instinctively they understood Zionist aspirations very well, and their decision to resist them was only natural....*There was no misunderstanding between Jew and Arab, but a natural conflict.*"[15] Therefore, he argued, "No agreement was possible with the Palestinian Arab; they would accept Zionism only when they found themselves up against an 'iron wall,' when they realized they had no alternative but to accept Jewish settlement."[16] Jabotinsky's uncompromising stand against Palestinian Arabs and their rights was embraced first by many *yishuv* and then by many Israelis. An Israeli national park is named in his honor.

II. Developments During the Coolidge Presidency, 1923-28.

Calvin Coolidge (1872-1933) became president in 1923. Despite Palestinian Arabs' repeated protests against a Jewish national home, and despite State Department sympathy for Arab rights, the U.S. government in 1924 signed a covenant with Britain recognizing its mandate over Palestine. The Senate approved the treaty. America therefore also again recognized the Balfour Declaration, which was part of the mandate. (America entered into the treaty to protect American interests in Palestine, not to support Zionism, but it had that effect.) The 1924 covenant was a more formal government recognition than had been Wilson's approval of the Balfour Declaration in October 1917. It also probably had more international legal prestige than did the joint Senate-House resolution signed by Harding in 1922. Thus a second Republican president embraced and reinforced Democrat Wilson's undermining of Palestinians' moral right to (a) self-determination and (b) control of immigration into their territory.

In 1924 David Ben-Gurion (1886-1973), a leader in the Jewish labor movement in Palestine, pointed out that the disparity between Jewish and Arab wages could ruin both groups of workers. Jews received up to three times the wages paid to Palestinian Arabs,[17] who in turn received much higher wages than did Arabs in Syria and Iraq. "Together we shall rise or go under," Ben-Gurion asserted. In 1925 the Fourteenth Zionist Congress voted "that colonization must be based on Jewish labour."[18] This in effect rejected his plea.

The congress also established the Jewish Agency to represent the entire Jewish people. The congress stipulated "that all land acquired by the agency must be held as public property"[19] for the use of the Jewish people.

In 1925 a group of Palestinian Jews formed Berit Shalom (Covenant of Peace) to work for peace with Arabs. The group hoped to achieve this by convincing Zionists to make concessions to Arabs. It hoped this might lead to a binational state. Berit Shalom's goals were greeted with little enthusiasm among both Jews and Arabs. Jews did not want the national home put to a popular vote because the Arab majority would reject it. Many Arabs refused to negotiate with Jews because they viewed any concession to them as treason.[20] By now some Jews in Palestine openly discussed their goal of Jewish statehood. Sir John Russell, the director of an English experimental agriculture station, visited Jewish farm settlements in Palestine in 1927 and 1928. After his second visit he reported somewhat incidentally on what he called "this determination of the young people to make a Hebrew State": The "impression I formed last year was confirmed during my present visit....The purpose of the colonists is not to make money but to make a nation...they wish to found a state."[21]

III. Riots, Commissions and the Second White Paper, 1928-30.

Between 1920 and 1926 Jewish migration to Palestine was heavy. In December 1926 Palestine had 149,000 Jews and 770,500 Arabs. Jews, including postwar returnees, almost tripled from some 56,000 at war's end. By 1926 Jews were 15.8 percent of the people. The country's economy was quite strong. Between December 1926 and December 1931, however, Jewish immigration was very light. Immigration and births created an average annual increase of 5,500 Jews - from 149,000 in December 1926 to 176,500 in December 1931. During this same five years the Arab population increased from 770,500 to 852,000. If the two groups continued to grow at these respective rates, it would take perhaps a century for Jews to gain a majority.[22]

This forecast did not stop Arab fear and resentment. For almost a year during late 1928 and 1929 Jewish-Arab tension built. On August 22 and 23, 1929, large Arab crowds with knives and clubs entered Jerusalem. After a mass meeting in a Muslim sanctuary, some Arabs attacked Jews. The undermanned police and British army refused to use Jewish police or allow many Jews to arm. Rioting spread to other cities. In Hebron, a center of Jewish studies for four centuries, sixty-six Jews, mostly yeshiva (religious) scholars, were murdered. British reinforcements arrived from Egypt and ended the rioting within a few days. The toll throughout Palestine included 133 Jews and 110 Arabs killed, and 339 Jews and 232 Arabs wounded.[23] Some Arab leaders, especially Jerusalem's grand mufti, Haj Amin al-Husseini, were suspected of fomenting the violence.

In 1929 London appointed a royal commission, headed by Sir Walter Shaw, to investigate. It listened to Arab complaints that Zionists displaced Arab dock workers at Jaffa and Haifa and Arab farm workers from Jewish-owned orange groves. Arabs asserted that Jewish trade unions followed consistently a policy of Jewish labor only. Arabs pointed out that the constitution of the Jewish National Fund forbade it from ever selling land to Arabs, and from hiring Arabs to work on its land. The Arabs even contended that they had gained nothing from the introduction of Jewish capital into Palestine or from the expansion of Jewish social and education services.[24] Zionists interviewed by the commission brushed off these complaints as of no substance or consequence. They maintained that when the federation of Jewish trade unions, the Histadrut, tried to organize Arab workers it was accused of meddling in Arab politics. When it avoided doing so it was accused of willfully ignoring their interests.[25] In its Report, published in March 1930, Shaw's commission blamed the grand mufti for not having done more before the riots to encourage law and order.[26] However, the commission judged that the riots were "not premeditated" and not instigated by the mufti.[27] The report recommended that the British high commissioner for Palestine exercise more control over Jewish immigration to prevent large numbers from entering the country, as had happened in the mid-1920s.[28] On May 12 the Colonial Office halted issuing labor certificates, needed for immigration by poor Jews.[29]

Sir John Hope Simpson, a farmland expert, led a second royal commission. He estimated that 30 percent of the Arabs were already landless and that more than another 25 percent had farms too small to produce enough crops and livestock to provide even subsistence living. These farms were already too small to be productively subdivided further for their children. The Hope Simpson Commission applied the principle of "absorptive economic capacity" set forth in the 1922 white paper. On October 20, 1930, the commission concluded in its report that Palestine could not absorb more than fifty thousand more immigrants. The report urged: (a) close supervision of immigration, (b) severely limiting sale of Arab land to Jews, and (c) protection of tenant farmers from the sale of land on which they worked. In a confidential unpublished addition to the report, Hope Simpson accused the Zionists of consciously trying to buy all of Palestine in such a way that the Arabs would have no way to earn a living.[30]

In January 1930 the High Commissioner for Palestine, Sir John Chancellor, urged London to end all preferential treatment of Jews and to grant the Arabs self-government. He too warned that land sales to Jews were creating a class of landless Arabs.[31] Some Zionists assert, however, that the landlessness was being caused partly by Arab capitalists buying up land. Zionists maintain that Egypt, with no Jewish immigration, also experienced landlessness.[32]

The conclusions of the Shaw and Hope Simpson commissions were put into the Passfield White Paper, published October 21,

1930. Led by Weizmann, Zionists bitterly attacked it, and won when it was debated in parliament. The policies it urged were completely rejected. For the time being at least, there would be no further restrictions on immigration than those in effect before the two royal commissions issued their reports. According to author Conor Cruise O'Brien, "this was the last great victory which Zionism won by purely diplomatic means" and one of Weizmann's greatest diplomatic victories.[33] Ironically, it was not good enough for many Zionist leaders, who severely criticized him. At the Seventeenth Zionist Congress, held in June and July 1931, Jabotinsky, the "iron wall" proponent, outmaneuvered Weizmann. He lost the presidency of the World Zionist Organization until 1935.

By 1930 Jews were cultivating 273 square miles, some 175,000 acres, of land in 110 agricultural settlements - up from some fifty-one settlements in 1920.

IV. The Hardening of Zionist Positions, 1931.

When examining the Zionist-Arab relationship which began developing during the late 1890s, it was noted that Zionists tended to ignore or discount the presence of Arabs. This phenomenon continued during the 1920s. According to Laqueur, most Zionist leaders continued to misjudge the Arab national movement. They were firmly convinced that the vast majority of Arabs had no interest in politics and were concerned only with improving their living standards. Zionist leaders, Laqueur contends, considered most Arabs too backward and ignorant to form their own judgements and thus were easy pray for ambitious politicians.

The Zionist leaders were forever seeing a hidden hand behind the anti-Zionist movement. French and British agents were blamed in the early 1920s, Italian and German Fascism in the 1930s. The riots of 1921 and 1929 were explained in terms of religious fanaticism in the usual antisemitic (sic) tradition.[34]

Even politically sophisticated Zionists usually denied that Arabs had developed a national consciousness. Their riots were attributed to theft or murder perpetrated by criminals or by mobs incited by unscrupulous agitators.[35] An example of this was given by no less a leader than Nahum Sokolow (1859-1936), whom Laqueur says was more widely educated than Weizmann and "perhaps the most accomplished Zionist diplomat."[36] On June 30, 1931, in a speech at the Seventeenth Zionist Congress, Sokolow stated that there was no connection between the 1929 riots and the Balfour Declaration. Instead, he asserted, they were caused by Arab religious fanaticism.[37]

Thus after 1929 Jewish attitudes hardened. Militant "revisionists," led by Jabotinsky, became politically stronger. They deplored Jewish pleas for equality between Arabs and Jews. They rejected proposals for a binational state as incompatible with political Zionism as taught by Herzl. Revisionists wanted the Zionist congress to state clearly that the final aim of Zionism was the forming in Palestine of a specifically Jewish state. They did not get this but, as noted, they did oust Weizmann, whom they thought too "gradualist" and too pro-British. Jews who had hoped for some type of Jewish accommodation with the Arabs became much less hopeful as their peace movement became even more unpopular with the *yishuv*. In 1931 Jabotinsky formed the Irgun. Like the already-existing Hagana, it was an armed underground organization of militants. It would be dedicated not only to defending Jews, as was the Hagana, but to retaliation as well.[38]

The actions of the White House and Congress during the Harding and Coolidge administrations in support of Zionism were taken despite Wilson's pronouncements regarding peoples' right to self-determination, despite the findings of the King-Crane Commission, despite the 1920 and 1921 Arab riots, and despite the 1921 U.S. law to limit immigration to America. These factors seemingly should have been considered by the representatives of the American people as they weighed the moral aspects of their actions. Perhaps they did but found them of less import than pro-Zionist factors. Regardless of the motives behind the decisions reached then, we can still ask today whether, objectively speaking, America was then involved in an injustice against the Palestinian

Arabs. If so, what, if any, restitution should be made, even though few or no Americans alive today were involved in those early 1920s decisions?

The case is somewhat similar to that involving Americans of Japanese descent who were interned in U.S. concentration camps in 1942. More than forty years later Congress voted that an injustice had been perpetrated in the name of the American people and that they owed restitution to those who had been unjustly treated. Most of the taxpayers who incurred this onus were either children or not yet born in 1942, and were in no way personally guilty of the injustice. Yet as Americans they shared in the *corporate moral responsibility* incurred as a result of a decision by a few government officials in 1942. Corporate moral responsibility is therefore broader than individual moral guilt. Just as people inherit moral rights because of the actions of their forebears so they can also inherit moral responsibilities and burdens. Especially as citizens of a democracy they can inherit an obligation to correct a wrong that their ancestors committed even if they did not realize at the time that it was wrong. Thus, in the uncertainties following the Japanese attack on Pearl Harbor, the U.S. government officials who ordered the internment may not have *considered* their action unjust. But the next generation of Americans considered it unjust and felt an obligation to make at least a token compensation for it.

For how many generations does the corporate moral responsibility rest on citizens to correct a particular wrong committed by their ancestors? It would seem that with the passage of several generations the moral obligation would gradually decrease to the vanishing point. It seems difficult to pinpoint this time lapse; it would probably depend partly on circumstances.

Be that as it may, Palestinians today are still being denied the exercise of their basic moral rights because of the Balfour Declaration and the mandate, both of which were supported by three American presidents and by both houses of one congress and by the Senate of another.

Chapter Seven

ROOSEVELT;
AMERICANS' BALKING OVER ADDED REFUGEES

1933-45

During the twelve-year presidency of Franklin Roosevelt (1882-1945), European Jews suffered the Holocaust, Palestine's Arabs revolted in vain against Britain, British-*yishuv* relations deteriorated, and Zionists began looking more to America than to England for help. Roosevelt avoided involvement as much as he could, except for limited aid to Nazi victims. We saw in the last three chapters that between 1917 and 1924 three American presidents and two congresses at least in effect supported heavy Jewish immigration into Palestine. Roosevelt also supported it. However, Americans repeatedly balked at letting proportionately a much smaller Jewish immigration into their own country during the 1930s and 1940s, even when Jews faced severe persecution and genocide. Although Americans had reasons for balking, they were not as compelling as those of the Palestinian Arabs. Thus Americans were unwittingly working themselves into a double standard which would reach its climax during Harry Truman's presidency. Meanwhile, Americans were faced with the moral issues inherent in their response to the plight of European Jews. This chapter's purpose is to look not only at these events and issues but also at those which helped lay the groundwork for Israel's founding during Truman's first term.

I. Nazi Policies' Impact on Palestine, 1933-36.

Increasing anti-Semitism in Germany and several eastern European nations during the mid-1930s made many Zionists more determined to settle for nothing less than a Jewish state. This anti-Semitism also changed the thinking of many Jews who had been indifferent or hostile to Zionism. Jews poured into Palestine from these countries. Many immigrants were relatively wealthy because British-imposed quotas did not restrict those who brought enough capital. These non-quota immigrants mushroomed total legal immigration between 1933 and 1936 to 164,000. The large influx of well educated immigrants and of Jewish capital created a strong economy among some population segments in Palestine during those years. This during the worldwide depression![1] But poverty was still rampant among Palestinian Arabs, especially farmers.

According to one estimate, by December 1933 there were 236,300 Jews in Palestine; by December 1936 there were an estimated 385,400 - 27.8 percent of the people. Meanwhile, Arabs had increased to 983,200 in 1936, nearly a 50 percent increase since 1918.[2] The Peel commission *Report* stated in 1937 that unlike the Jewish growth, the Arab rise "has been due in only a slight degree to immigration."[3] The report estimated that "roughly nine-tenths of the growth has been due to natural increase."[4] According to Roberto Bachi, the Israeli demographer, Arab immigration was even less than the Peel commission thought. He maintains that between 1931 and 1945 an average of only nine hundred Arabs immigrated per year.[5] During 1931-36 this would account for only 3.4 percent of the Arab population increase. Thus 96.6 percent was due to natural increase, that is, to the degree that the birth rate was higher than the death rate.

In the months preceding the 1936 U.S. national elections, American Jewish leaders urged Roosevelt to take stronger action to help German Jews. In August he issued a statement criticizing British policy in Palestine. In September he urged London not to set tighter limits being considered for immigration there. He told Britain that America "would regard suspension of immigration as a breach of the Mandate."[6] Britain replied that it would delay further limits until a commission studying the matter had finished its report. In September Roosevelt gave to the Jewish *United Palestine Yearbook* an open letter supporting a Jewish homeland. "It is a source of renewed hope and courage," he wrote, "that by an international accord and by the moral support of the people of the world, men and women of Jewish faith have a right to resettle the land where their faith was born and from which much of our modern civilization has emanated."[7] Thus the wily president placated Jewish voters at the expense of Palestinian Arabs and perhaps of the British rather than at the expense of anti-immigration U.S. voters. London could weigh this election-year sop against FDR's hands-off policy regarding Palestine, and dismiss it as not serious. He won the election with 60 percent of the vote.

II. The Palestinian Arab Strike, 1936.

During the depression Palestinian grain prices fell, squeezing farmers' profits. To pay their debts small farmers had to sell their land. Often the buyers were Jews. Formerly most land sales to Jews had been by large owners whose life style was not hurt by the sale, although often their tenants were evicted. Now many small owners, who needed their land for their family's livelihood, found themselves landless, and often jobless, in an urban, overcrowded job market for which they lacked skills. Like ousted tenants in the Second Aliyah, many became manual workers in coastal cities. Stuck in urban slums, they had lost much of the social and cultural fabric which had helped sustain them in former tough times.[8] Moreover, prominent Arabs secretly added to this situation by their own very discreet and profitable land sales to Jews through secret agents. Their Arab tenants, evicted by the new Jewish owners who hired Jewish workers, joined the landless, formerly independent farmers in the slums. Leading Palestinian Arab families profited in the very land sales that these families' leaders publicly condemned. Thus, the Arab land base, already far too small in 1930 according to Hope Simpson, was shrinking even more, and the Jewish land base was greatly expanding.

Despite Arab involvement, willing or not, in land sales, many Arabs saw the incoming Jews and capital as a threat to their *numerical* superiority. In 1936 Arabs began attacking individual Jews. The Arab Higher Committee,[9] led by the grand mufti of Jerusalem, Haj Amin al-Husseini, called a six-month general strike. Armed Arab bands conducted guerrilla war. Palestinian Arabs widely supported the uprising. Arab countries, which formerly had shown little interest in the fate of Palestinian Arabs, also gave it aid. Despite this, Zionists again generally dismissed the strike as the work of a few demagogues who had incited unstable elements within Arab society. They also blamed Britain for not enforcing peace.[10] Britain brought in more troops from Egypt, and in October 1936 the Arab Higher Committee ended the strike.

III. The Peel Report, Jewish and Arab Reaction, 1936-39.

As it had done after previous Arab uprisings, Britain appointed a commission to investigate. Chaired by Earl Peel, it came to Palestine in November 1936. For two months it interviewed Jews, Arabs and British, and Trans-Jordan's Emir Abdullah. Although Jews were only 20 percent of the people and owned less than 5 percent of the land, Zionists testified that regardless of numerical size neither side should dominate the other. Instead, each side should have parity. Zionists said this principle should remain even when Jews increased enough to outnumber Arabs, as they intended to do.[11] In his testimony Ben-Gurion, head of the Jewish Agency's Palestine Executive, stressed that it was not Zionist policy to make Palestine a Jewish state. He said he recognized that Arabs lived there and that they did not want Jews to dominate them any more than Jews wanted to be dominated by Arabs. He added that a state may imply "domination of others, the domination by the Jewish majority of the minority, but that is not our aim. It was not our aim at that time[12] and it is not our aim now."[13]

Thus Ben-Gurion seemed, on the surface, to be willing to settle for a binational state. But his testimony was greatly influenced by Weizmann's insistence that Jews be diplomatic about their goals, and advance "step by step." This policy infuriated Ben-Gurion and other Zionists but rather than expose their acrimonious differences to the commission they presented a united front.[14] By 1942 Ben-Gurion definitely wanted all of Palestine to be a Jewish state. Weizmann's testimony to the commission stressed that there were six million Jews "pent up in places where they are not wanted, and for whom the world is divided into places where they cannot live, and places into which they may not enter."[15] Yet, twenty-six months later, on January 31, 1939, Weizmann himself discouraged trying to open up places into which refugee Jews could enter, because such efforts would "serve merely to distract attention from [opening up] the one country," Palestine.[16]

Meanwhile, Grand Mufti Haj Amin testified to the royal commission that immigration should stop, land sales to Jews should be outlawed, efforts to make a national home for Jews in Palestine should end, and Palestine should become an independent Arab state. When asked whether Palestine could absorb the 400,000 Jews already there, he replied, "No." When asked whether these Jews should be expelled or "somehow removed" he responded: "We must all leave this to the future."[17]

The Peel Commission considered cantonizing Palestine. This idea was based on the Swiss model of a single federal government with highly autonomous cantons - regions based on ethnic diversity. However, given the chasm between the two sides, the commission dropped the idea as needing more mutual good will than seemed possible. Instead, the Peel report recommended that the mandate be terminated and the country be partitioned in such a way that, (a) the partition would be practical, (b) it would conform to British obligations, and (c) it would respect the rights of both Arabs and Jews. The commission called for a Jewish state, an Arab state that would include Trans-Jordan, and a British enclave under permanent mandate, which would include Jerusalem, Bethlehem and a narrow corridor from them to the Mediterranean. The report urged that immigration be sharply cut while details of the plan were worked out. In July 1937 Peel released the report with a map of its planned division. The report was rejected by the Arabs, sharply criticized by most Zionists, and strongly questioned by several members of Britain's government. However, the Zionists and British, in principle, accepted partition.

In August, at the Twentieth Zionist Congress, most delegates rejected Peel's finding that national hopes of Jews and Arabs were irreconcilable. Delegates also thought that the size of the state that the plan assigned to Jews was far too small to be desirable for future immigration. However, they also knew that if they had their own independent state, even the one in the commission plan, they would be completely free to accept as many refugees as they could absorb, without British limits. The congress therefore voted to negotiate with Britain regarding its terms for a Jewish state. Meanwhile, Arabs were trying to put teeth into their rejection of the Peel plan. They organized a pan-Arab congress, held in September in Bludan, Syria. It passed a resolution that it was the sacred duty of every Arab to preserve Palestine as an Arab country. Rioting had already erupted throughout Palestine after Arabs learned that Britain had endorsed Peel's partition plan. Britain's acting district commissioner for Galilee was assassinated. The British arrested five members of the Arab Higher Committee; Haj Amin fled, and remained in exile until after World War II. The insurrection, against Britain rather than against Jews, continued. Britain vigorously hunted guerrillas, confiscated arms, jailed and deported guerrilla leaders, and killed several thousand Arabs. Even after the revolt was crushed in April 1939 Britain severely punished Arabs who possessed weapons. They were never allowed to rearm or reorganize politically. This left Palestinian Arabs unprepared when Zionist-Arab fighting erupted in 1947.

IV. The Evian Conference on Refugees, July 1938.

A poll in early 1938 showed that 82 percent of Americans surveyed opposed allowing many refugees into America. Concurrent polls had similar results. FDR decided that trying to pass more lenient immigration law was politically too risky.[18] It would be wiser to write more lenient guidelines within the Administration's authority, and to internationalize the problem, especially by trying to settle refugees in other countries. He therefore sponsored an international conference to coordinate refugee aid; thirty-two nations would attend it in July in Evian, France. That spring, to prepare for it, Bernard Baruch, a Jewish financier and sometime adviser to FDR, devised a refugee plan. By it, the U.S. government would help Jews to resettle in underpopulated host countries in Africa that would agree to more immigrants. Baruch said his plan (a) would leave U.S. immigration policy alone; (b) it would put no strain on the U.S. economy or job market; and (c) it would not discriminate in favor of any particular religious or racial group. Some Zionists, including Rabbi Stephen Wise, Supreme Court justice Brandeis and presidential adviser Felix Frankfurter, severely criticized the plan.[19] Some, echoing Russian Zionists thirty-four years earlier, opposed a national home for Jews in Africa because it would take pressure off Britain to expand immigration to Palestine.[20] This was not the first or last time that Zionists chose a national home for Jews in Palestine over a haven elsewhere.

Such ambivalence among Jews greatly weakened their ability at Evian to help refugees. According to historian Alan Kraut, the Jewish agencies preparing for the conference were quarreling among themselves and were poorly prepared for its diplomatic style. Instead of agreeing beforehand on their goals, the agencies came with differing proposals. Some wanted more immigration to Palestine, others wanted to settle refugees in unpopulated areas, while still others stressed protecting Jews in Europe itself. At the conference pro- and anti-Zionist Jews seriously clashed. Such feuding, notes Kraut, "only further muddled Jewish efforts to establish clear, achievable goals at Evian."[21]

Shortly before the conference met, the American Veterans of Foreign Wars voted for a resolution which urged suspending all immigration to America for ten years. London's conservative *Sunday Express* editorialized that "just now there is a big influx of foreign Jews into Britain. They are overrunning the country."[22] Britain stipulated that immigration to Palestine could not be discussed at the conference, and Weizmann's request to address it was refused. Virtually every delegate said that his nation had no land suitable for Jewish settlers. The Australian delegate claimed that his country had no racial problem and did not want to import one. The delegate from the Dominican Republic in the Caribbean offered to take large numbers of Jewish refugee farmers and provide land for them. But almost no Jewish refugees were farmers. Nothing came of the proposal.[23] (Yet many non-farmer refugees learned to farm in Palestine!) Other proposed areas,

British Guiana, Madagascar, the Philippines, Portuguese Angola, and Rhodesia, were investigated but nothing came of them. The Conference formed a permanent Inter-Governmental Committee on Refugees (IGCR). Roosevelt hoped IGCR would solve this international problem just as his New Deal agencies solved national problems. Investigating these other proposed areas received no encouragement from Weizmann. As noted, on January 31, 1939, he wrote: "They serve merely to detract attention from the one country [Palestine] which can offer both immediate help and the prospect of permanent settlement."[24] Zionists did not back IGCR and it was not effective. Thus, even after the intensification of Nazi persecution of the Jews, and with the likelihood of a major war breaking out, the Zionists forewent the possibility of other havens in favor of Palestine.

V. The British White Paper of 1939.

Between 1936 and 1939, Jews started or bought out fifty-five more settlements, bringing total Jewish farm settlements to 252.

In the months after the Peel Report's release, British talks with Zionists and Palestinian Arabs were fruitless. Britain therefore invited both sides to the London Round Table Conference, which began on February 7, 1939. Zionists feared that Britain would try to placate the Arabs, whom it would need for oil if war with Germany erupted. London told both sides that if the three parties reached no agreement it would impose its own solution. The talks ended March 17 with no agreement; on May 17 Britain issued its own solution, the watershed 1939 white paper. It stipulated that:

1. A single independent state should be formed within ten years.

2. Jewish settlements would be completely prohibited in some areas and restricted in others. Future land sales were to be severely restricted.

3. A maximum total of 75,000 immigrants could enter Palestine during the next five years. After March 1, 1944, immigrants could enter only with Arab consent.[25]

This last stipulation was designed to prevent Jews from becoming the majority within the ten year period before statehood. It would therefore prevent them from successfully voting that the single state would be Jewish. Instead, Zionists would have to form their national home within a predominantly Arab state and in a presumably hostile environment. Zionists thought this would be very difficult and "minimalist."[26] They were especially bitter in rejecting this third point, which limited immigration. It helped sour British-Zionist relations for the remainder of the mandate.

Actually, the white paper did not surprise Zionists; they and Britain had discussed it at the Round Table Conference. London could claim that it merely upheld that part of the Balfour Declaration (and therefore of the mandate document) which stated that "nothing shall be done which may prejudice the civil and religious rights of existing non-Jewish communities in Palestine." London assured Zionists it would always interpret the white paper in the light of Balfour and the mandate. Thus Britain would do nothing to undermine the Declaration's pledge to establish in Palestine "a national home for the Jewish people." Zionists were unconvinced. Weizmann, perhaps Britain's strongest supporter among Zionists, termed the paper a repudiation of the mandate, and lodged what he called the strongest possible protest. Ben-Gurion fumed: "the greatest betrayal perpetrated by the government of a civilized people in our generation had been formulated and explained with the artistry of experts at the game of trickery and pretended righteousness."[27] Several MPs agreed with the Zionists; one called the paper a cynical breach of pledges. Parliament approved it by a safe but slimmer than usual margin. On May 17 Britain began enforcing the white paper's provision which Zionists most opposed, the immigration lid.

Arab reaction to the paper was mixed, but mostly negative.

VI. The Deterioration of British-Zionist Relations, 1939-41.

World War II began September 1, 1939. During its first six months Britain issued no Palestinian immigration permits. Zionists increased illegal immigration by infiltrating Palestine's land borders and especially by running a British naval blockade along its coast. Violence between the Hagana and Britain escalated. The

British arrested forty-three Hagana officers in late 1939, and carried out many weapons searches in Jewish homes and businesses. In 1941 Lehi (the Stern Gang), the most radical of the Jewish underground military-terrorist groups, tried to contact German diplomats in Beirut to propose that they work together against Britain.[28] Most Jews found that abhorrent, but Zionists faced a dilemma: They considered Germany their worst enemy; most of them also considered Britain an enemy. Ben-Gurion's stated policy was to fight the war against Germany as if there were no 1939 white paper, and fight the white paper as if there were no war.[29] Representing the *yishuv*, the Jewish Agency offered to raise a division of Jewish soldiers to fight for the Allies. For several years Britain stalled accepting the offer, giving various reasons. Probably the main reason - unstated - was its fear that the division would reemerge in Palestine after the war to fight British forces there. This British rejection was another source of bitterness among the *yishuv* and led to a major split between the two at the end of 1941. Britain, however, accepted individual Palestinian Jews into its military and eventually allowed a small Jewish military unit, a 3,650-person brigade, to be formed.

Weizmann continued to favor reconciliation with Britain and attempted reconciliation with the Arabs. However, after the war started, he began to speak increasingly about what he considered the pressing need for a Jewish state in Palestine which would involve resettlement of at least some Arab Palestinians elsewhere.[30] Thus after 1939 the plight of Jews increased the danger of Palestinian Arabs becoming refugees. In 1940 Jabotinsky died and Menachem Begin (1913-1992) became head of the revisionist party and its underground military-terrorist unit, the Irgun. He would play a significant role in creating the Arab refugees.

VII. The Zionists' New York Biltmore Conference, May 1942.

After the war began, most Americans, including many Jews, were reluctant to endanger U.S. neutrality. "Mention of the Jewish tragedy was associated with war-mongering."[31] By early 1941, as America more openly supported the Allies, this attitude changed. In April Emanuel Neumann, an official of the American Zionist Emergency Council (AZEC), resurrected the moribund American Palestine Committee (APC), a pro-Zionist organization of Protestant leaders. Senator Robert Wagner of New York became its nominal head. He recruited twenty-six senators, including both the majority and minority leaders, Interior Secretary Harold Ickes and Attorney General Robert Jackson. The AZEC gave $50,000 of its own funds to the APC.[32] In April 1941 APC prevailed on seventy senators to sign an APC-sponsored declaration "to direct attention to the importance of Palestine in the solution of the problem of Jewish homelessness."[33] According to author Richard Stevens, the emphasis in the declaration on "'the tragic plight of refugees fleeing from persecution and finding no home,'" again tried to link the refugee problem with Palestine as the *only* solution.[34] Stevens contends:

For while many Americans might not support the creation of a Jewish state, traditional American humanitarianism could be exploited in favor of the Zionist cause through the refugee problem. Indeed, as later events were to show, *the refugee problem had to remain unsolved in order to insure the creation of a Jewish state in Palestine.*[35]

In December 1942 Neumann organized the Christian Council on Palestine for pro-Zionist Protestant clergy.[36] Many of them viewed Israel's restoration "in the light of Biblical prophecy."[37]

Meanwhile, because of the worsening British-Zionist relations, Zionists in early 1942 turned more to America for support. From May 6 to 11, Weizmann, Ben-Gurion and some 600 delegates of Zionist groups primarily in the New York area met at the Biltmore Hotel to set goals and policy. Their decisions reflected positions closer to those of Begin's militant revisionists than to those of Weizmann. The Biltmore delegates voted to: (a) reject the 1939 white paper, (b) demand that Palestinian Jews be able to form a military force that would fight against Germany under the *yishuv's* own flag, (c) declare that the new world order that would follow the war "cannot be established on foundations of peace, justice and equality, unless the problem of Jewish homelessness is finally solved,"[38] (d) urge that immigration to Palestine be opened and that the Jewish Agency be given control over it, (e) urge that the Jewish Agency be given "the necessary authority for upbuilding the country, including the development of its unoccupied and uncultivated lands,"[39] and (f) urge that "Palestine be established as a Jewish Commonwealth."[40] Thus what had previously been mainline Zionism's maximum demands became its minimum. Ben-Gurion's more hardline position gained favor over Weizmann's more gradualist approach. U.S. Zionists, if they considered the rights of Palestinian Arabs, apparently in effect decided that Zionists' rights superseded them. The Zionist Actions Committee, which was charged with implementing policy, overwhelmingly adopted the Biltmore Program.

Tragic news from Europe soon deeply impacted the Biltmore Program's premise. The Zionists who devised that program had assumed that after the war millions of Jewish refugees would want to move to Palestine. But within three months after the Biltmore conference, rumors of Hitler's "Final Solution" began to filter out. Zionists realized that if this took place, there would be virtually no Jewish refugees left for Palestine.[41] But the tragedy in Europe gave Biltmore a strong emotional appeal. Just "when the politico-diplomatic value of the Biltmore Program crumbled, the heart-touching summons, on which the program rested, grew stronger."[42] According to Stevens, within six years, culminating in U.S. recognition of the State of Israel, the Biltmore Program had become U.S. foreign policy.[43] Yet in 1942 the American Jewish Committee, which was then anti-Zionist, did not endorse Biltmore.

Six months after the Biltmore meeting, as reports of the Final Solution increased, the Balfour Declaration's twenty-fifth anniversary occurred. To observe it, sixty-eight senators, 194 congresspersons, hundreds of community leaders, and public figures signed a statement published on November 2, 1942, which called for a Jewish national home. Both the State Department and Britain's ambassador criticized such statements, contending that they could complicate U.S.-British relations and thus hurt the war effort.

According to Treasury Secretary Henry Morgenthau, Jr., FDR privately discussed with him on December 3 the possibility of deporting Palestinian Arabs to make way for Jewish refugees.

Whether Roosevelt really intended to create a new refugee group in order to settle an already-existing one is not clear. Was he again telling Jews what they wanted to hear? A few months later, on June 15, 1943, FDR assured Saudi Arabia's King Ibn-Saud that "no decision would be reached altering the basic situation in Palestine without full consultation of both Arabs and Jews."[44]

During 1943, with immigration to Palestine limited, Roosevelt made several efforts to open up many free-world nations, including America, to refugees. However, Zionists again opposed his plans because they did not include Palestine. According to Morris Ernst, FDR's international envoy for the project,

it did not work out....the failure of the leading Jewish groups to support with zeal this immigration program may have caused the President not to push forward with it at that time. I talked to many people active in Jewish organizations....I made clear that no Jews...would be compelled to go anywhere and certainly not to any assigned nation.

...active Jewish leaders decried, sneered and then attacked me as if I were a traitor. At one dinner party I was openly accused of furthering this plan of freer immigration in order to undermine political Zionism. Those Jewish groups which favored opening our doors gave little more than lip service to the Roosevelt program. Zionist friends of mine opposed it.[45]

FDR eventually told Ernst: "Nothing doing on the [Jewish refugee placement] program. We can't put it over because the dominant vocal Jewish leadership of America won't stand for it."[46]

By August 1943 Zionists had sufficiently increased their support among and control over American Jews that they were able more effectively to mobilize American public opinion. Under the militant leadership of Rabbi Abba Hillel Silver, American Zionists turned from "backstair diplomacy as the sole technique for achieving our goal"[47] and adopted a "program of public relations designed to create national agitation for a Jewish Palestine."[48] Silver urged Zionists to "build upon the broad base of public sentiment, the approval of public opinion which in the final analysis determines the attitude and action of governments in democratic society."[49] He warned Zionists not to put the future of their movement solely in the hands of individuals, however friendly, however great. Instead, they should "appeal to the masses...talk to the whole of America...carry on an active educational propaganda in your circle....That will sustain them [the masses] when they come to make important decisions which may involve America's participation in the ultimate solution of the Palestine problem."[50] Thus the strategy was to create such a substantial pro-Zionist opinion throughout the nation that Congress would be impelled to act.[51]

Throughout the war, Jewish leaders gave numerous plans to Allied leaders to alleviate the plight of European Jews. Some plans were enacted with varying success; others were rejected as impractical or too risky. Whatever the validity of the latter arguments, many Jews concluded that the world was indifferent to their tragedy. They lost trust in the likelihood of other people helping them in their hour of need. They felt that Gentile and even some Jewish humanity had failed them; henceforth they would rely on their own actions for their survival, whether the rest of the world approved or not. This hardening of attitude, which many Jews formed in the late '30s and '40s, was also formed by some Palestinian Arabs after 1947, for similar reasons.

VIII. Late Wartime American Zionist Developments, 1944-45.

In January 1944 U.S. Zionists successfully lobbied Senators Robert Taft of Ohio and Robert Wagner of New York to sponsor a Senate resolution opposing the 1939 white paper and calling for the constitution of Palestine as a Jewish commonwealth. On March 9 Roosevelt authorized American Zionist leaders to say that the U.S. government had never officially endorsed the white paper, which Britain enforced throughout the war. However, FDR also approved shelving the Taft-Wagner resolution. At the end of March Senator Harry Truman, following Roosevelt's lead, opposed raising the Palestine issue then, but he stated in letters that "when the right time comes I am willing to help make the fight for a Jewish homeland in Palestine."[52]

Zionists did not want Democrats in the 1944 national elections to assume that they automatically had the Jewish vote. They built a successful strategy to get both parties to compete for it by putting pro-Zionist planks into their party platforms. Significantly, both parties' planks, written to please Jewish voters and donors, called for opening Palestine to Jews but said nothing about opening the rest of the world to Jewish refugees.[53] The planks are another example of American Zionists stressing Palestine as the *only* solution rather than one of several possible solutions. If the planks accurately reflect American Jewish priorities in 1944, it would seem either that Palestine itself was a higher priority than the refugees or that Jews had given up on trying to place refugees elsewhere. However, this second option, the worldwide option, does not appear to have been pursued nearly as vigorously as was the Palestine option. Yet the worldwide option seemingly had greater potential for sheltering more refugees more quickly.

The planks had little noticeable influence on the presidential victor. A few months after winning his fourth term, FDR, while on his way back from the Yalta Conference, met for several hours on February 14, 1945, with Saudi Arabia's King Ibn-Saud. Saud apparently impressed him greatly, and was persuasive regarding America's need for Arab friendship. The king contended that Arabs should not be penalized for European anti-Semitism, and that if any part of the world should be turned into a Jewish state it should be a section of Germany, not of Palestine, since it was Germans, not Palestinians, who had killed so many Jews. Roosevelt told Saud that the U.S. government would make no change in its basic policy in Palestine without full and prior consultation with both Jews and Arabs. On April 5, just a week before he died, FDR repeated this promise in a letter to Saud.[54]

Meanwhile, in the fall of 1944 delegates of the Arab states signed a document supporting the 1939 white paper, which many Arabs had rejected in 1939. They now believed that it established the rights of the Palestinian Arabs as far as Britain and the League of Nations were concerned. In March 1945 Arab states formed the Arab League.[55]

In summary, Roosevelt repeatedly reassured both Zionists and Arabs. He told Rabbi Wise that he was for unrestricted immigration into Palestine. He told Arab leaders that America would not support any change in Palestine opposed by Arabs.[56] When a British diplomat was allowed to see State Department files he remarked that Britain was not the only country to promise the same thing to two different groups. David Niles, a Zionist who was an assistant first to Roosevelt and then to Truman, wrote that he seriously doubted whether Israel would have become a state if FDR had lived.[57]

IX. Morality in a Lifeboat Situation.

Although American response to European victims of the Nazis is outside this book's scope, it would seem, briefly, that those whose lives were in great danger had a moral right to immigrate to America and other free countries, including Arab countries. Each of these nations had a corresponding moral obligation to accept them insofar as "the common good rightly understood" would permit. After mid-1942 free-world leaders knew that this was a lifeboat situation and that the lifeboats of most free nations were not full. (If the threat of spies being planted among the refugees was sufficiently serious, the refugees could have been restricted to camps until the threat ended. This was done on a small scale in upstate New York, where the refugees at least were safe.) Against this lifeboat argument it can be pointed out that not only Jews and Gypsies were endangered. Half of the twelve million people who died in Nazi camps were Gentiles. Some fifty million people died in the war. Several hundred million people were in danger. Where draw the line? Between mid-1942 and early 1945 it was obvious that Jews were among the most endangered. During that time the line should have been drawn to include them among those most in need of rescue.

But did the Holocaust create for those trying to escape death a right to immigrate to Palestine (a) in large numbers and (b) with the intent of founding a Jewish state? The companion question is: Did Palestine's indigenous people, and Britain as the mandate authority, knowing of the Zionists' intent, have an obligation to accept Jewish refugees whose lives would be endangered if they did not enter Palestine? Were it not for that Zionist intent it would seem that within the limits imposed by the principle of "the common good rightly understood" the Palestinians and British theoretically would have had a moral obligation to admit at least some refugees. Presumably, however, the refugees immigrating to Palestine either (a) went there intending to establish a Jewish state which by its nature would seriously disrupt the Palestinians' common good, or (b) if they did not go there with that intent, they were recruited for that cause after they arrived. That this danger was serious was borne out by events within that very decade. It is therefore difficult to see how Palestine's indigenous people were morally obligated to accept people who so seriously endangered their own common good. To argue that they were so obligated requires that the indigenous people had a moral obligation to foster the deprivation of their own and their descendants' basic moral rights to their political self-determination, to their own culture, and to their own homes and land. It is difficult to see how people in a lifeboat are morally required to take in people whose friends who are already in the lifeboat have committed themselves to taking it over - especially if some of those friends have talked of expelling everyone but themselves. This very difficult situation has some of the appearances, at least, of a moral dilemma. For it is also difficult to place oneself in that lifeboat, decide not to accept the people trying to enter it, and then be morally comfortable with that decision. But with the Zionist leadership so clearly committed in the May 1942 Biltmore Program to having "Palestine be established as a Jewish Commonwealth," Palestinian Arabs could reasonably presume that each additional immigrant was a clear additional threat to their own common good.

Another factor in trying to evaluate the moral obligation of the indigenous people of Palestine and of the British with regard to the rights of the Jewish refugees was the effective opposition of the Zionists to the settling of Jewish refugees anywhere except in

Palestine. Partly because of this Zionist policy it has never been clear that Palestine was really the only place to which the Jewish refugees could flee. It was never clear that Palestine was the *only* lifeboat. Other havens might have been opened if Zionists had not opposed them. However, the rights of the Jews who needed to flee the Nazis nevertheless existed and should have been respected regardless of the policies of Zionists. For apparently it was not the refugees but Zionists who were safely in Britain, Palestine and America who were rejecting the other havens. If, even partly through Zionist policy, other havens as a matter of fact were not sufficiently open to accept all of the Jewish refugees, that apparently left only Palestine. Granted that the Jewish refugees were apparently the victims of Zionist manipulation, did that situation place a moral obligation on the indigenous people of Palestine to accept these refugees even though it would mean forfeiting their own rights outlined above? It would seem not, for the reasons already stated.

Chapter Eight

TRUMAN - PART 1;
SETTLING POSTWAR JEWISH REFUGEES

1945-46

With the Nazi defeat the lifeboat situation for European Jews eased. By the end of July 1945 most of some six million Gentiles displaced by the war had been repatriated. However, most surviving displaced Jews - a mere fraction compared to the surviving displaced Gentiles - did not want repatriation but emigration - preferably to America or Palestine. Their situation triggered a serious social and political problem for three years. Truman - and America - became deeply immersed in it. In the process they became more deeply entangled in the Zionist-Palestinian conflict itself, and thus more involved in the moral issues inherent in it.

I. Truman's Efforts to Increase Palestine Quotas, 1945.

In April 1945 the United Nations began; it took over the League of Nations' mandates. On April 12 Roosevelt died and Vice-President Harry Truman (1884-1972) succeeded him. On May 8 the war in Europe ended. On May 27 the Jewish Agency asked Britain to declare all of Palestine a Jewish state, even though 70 percent of its people were Arabs.

About one million Jews remained in non-Soviet Europe after the war. These included some fifty thousand or more in Germany and Austria who had eluded the Nazis or were camp survivors. Some 750,000 Jews were in Soviet-held eastern Europe. About 250,000 of these fled to western Europe, swelling the total postwar Jewish refugees there to 300,000.[1] Most reportedly did not want to remain in or return to their homelands. (Some 1,500 Jews would die in postwar strife in Poland between 1945 and mid-1947.[2])

115

Moreover, these nations' economies were shattered, a hardship Jews shared with these nations' Gentiles. What the Jewish DPs themselves really wanted may never be known. The *Yiddish Bulletin* complained editorially of the Zionists:

> By pressing for an exodus of Jews from Europe; by insisting that Jewish D.P.'s [displaced persons] do not wish to go to any country outside of Israel; by not participating in the negotiations on behalf of the D.P.'s; and by refraining from a campaign of their own - by all this they [Zionists] certainly do not help to open...America for Jews. In fact, they sacrificed the interests of living people - their brothers and sisters who went through a world of pain - to the politics of their own movement.[3]

Perhaps half of the Jews in DP camps wanted to come to America but U.S. immigration quotas, which also served Gentile DPs, did not allow such a large number. Palestine was popular, but fighting there between British and Jews made it less attractive. Britain still enforced the 1939 white paper in a modified way: Instead of allowing no immigration after March 1, 1944, without Arab approval, Britain in 1945 increased Jewish immigrants' permits from fifteen thousand to eighteen thousand annually. Refugees expecting quick transfers out of the camps often saw weeks turn into months before their papers came through. However, most of the fifty thousand Jews in Germany and Austria at war's end gradually found homes in Palestine or elsewhere. Jews still behind the Iron Curtain were not allowed to leave by the Communist regimes. In May 1945 Treasury Secretary Morgenthau, urged by fellow Jews, asked Truman to form a cabinet-level committee to address refugee problems. Truman, aware of voters' anti-refugee and anti-Semitic feelings, refused. But in late June he sent Earl Harrison to Europe to learn the refugee situation.

U.S. Jews, split between Zionists, non-Zionists and anti-Zionists, were sending Truman conflicting signals. On July 6, Joseph Proskauer, president of the then anti-Zionist American Jewish Committee (AJC), wrote to him:

> We distinguish...between the importance of Palestine as a place of homeland and refuge and the question of statehood

for Palestine. We have contended that it was ill-advised to agitate for Jewish statehood in Palestine under existing conditions....in a conference with Mr. Blaustein [chair, AJC Executive Committee] and me shortly before he left Washington for the last time, President Roosevelt stated to us that he had come to this belief and that he saw in the extreme Zionist agitation grave danger for the world and for Palestine itself. He added the belief that Great Britain could not presently consider Jewish statehood....we stress at this time as the main objective for Palestine the modification of the British white paper and the liberalization of Jewish immigration into Palestine, for that may become necessary for the relief of many thousand stricken European Jews.[4]

The AJC then told Truman: "while the population of Palestine remains two-thirds Arab, it is futile to raise this question of statehood, irrespective of its ultimate merits or demerits."[5]

In his *Memoirs* Truman wrote that early in his presidency "it was my feeling that it would be possible for us to watch out for the long-range interests of our country while at the same time helping those unfortunate victims of persecution to find a home."[6] He repeatedly indicated in his *Memoirs* that he thought of this home as Palestine. Thus he in effect embraced the Zionist position that Palestine was the only place to resettle Jewish DPs. Only when this seemed unlikely did he look elsewhere for a haven for them. In Truman's statement just quoted, he speaks of wanting to balance "helping those unfortunate victims of persecution to find a home" against "the long-range interests of our country." He mentions nothing about the long-range interests of the Palestinian Arabs. However, in a letter to Weizmann on November 29, 1948, he wrote that he would like to expand "financial and economic assistance on a large scale to the entire Middle East, contingent upon effective mutual cooperation."[7]

Meanwhile, at the Potsdam Conference of Allied leaders, July 17 - August 2, 1945, Truman urged Britain to lift its limit and permit large-scale immigration. Britain said this could ignite another Arab revolt. On August 16 Truman said he hoped Britain would be as liberal as possible with immigration but that any solution required Arab involvement. He added that he had no desire to send half a million American soldiers to keep the peace in Palestine - a policy he would stress on several occasions. Weizmann called his statement "phoney....He takes away with one hand what he gives with the other....He will never jeopardise his oil concessions for the sake of the Jews, although he may need them when the time of election arrives."[8]

In August Earl Harrison reported back to Truman that the camps had intolerable living conditions. He said the Jewish Agency had asked London to immediately issue 100,000 immigration certificates for Palestine. This figure was based not on the perhaps fifty thousand or more Jews remaining in what became DP camps at war's end but on Zionist immigration goals.[9] Harrison said the appropriate number of certificates was debatable but that meeting the Zionist request would clear the camps of many of their Jewish refugees. Truman sent the report to Prime Minister Clement Attlee (1883-1967) with his own request that he immediately grant 100,000 certificates. Thus Truman adopted the Jewish Agency request as his own. This request, which he repeated in vain over the next thirty months, caused friction between him and London. Foreign Secretary Ernest Bevin (1884-1951) publicly stated that Truman wanted the DPs in Palestine because he did not want them in America. This probably was inaccurate. If Bevin had said it was "because Americans did not want them" he would probably have been more correct. Bevin also implied that Truman requested the certificates and supported other Zionist priorities because he wanted the New York Jewish vote. This was probably only partly true. Truman seemingly had genuine compassion for DPs and wanted to help them; he also admitted that he had responded repeatedly to Zionist pressure.

Laqueur notes, "Bevin, like his chief Attlee, was neither pro- nor anti-Jewish. He simply believed that the Jews, unlike the Arabs, were not a nation and did not therefore need a state of their own."[10] If Laqueur is correct, Bevin would seem to have erred from the point of view of social justice. A group of people should have at least a theoretical right to form a state whether they are a nation or not - *if* such an action does not interfere with the weightier rights of other people.

Arab approval of Jewish immigration, required after March 1, 1944, by the 1939 white paper, was, of course, not forthcoming. Despite this, Britain allowed eighteen thousand immigrants per year, a 20 percent increase over the permitted 1939-44 annual average of fifteen thousand. Zionists thought this totally inadequate. After World War II they greatly expanded illegal immigration. Most illegals were caught in the blockade; after mid-1946 Britain detained them in camps on Cyprus.

On September 29, 1945, Truman met with AJC leaders. Three days later he met with two U.S. Zionist leaders, Rabbis Wise and Silver. He told them he was very occupied with Cold War problems and would not be rushed, or bound by previous commitments. He complained to them of excessive "ethnic pressure"[11] on him from Poles, Italians and Jews. He said he objected to a religious state, "be it Jewish or Catholic."[12] But when, according to Israeli historian Michael Cohen, the Zionists refuted these objections, "Truman then stated somewhat disingenuously that he had no objection to the Zionist conception of a Jewish state."[13] However he again stressed that he would never send U.S. troops to Palestine. A few minutes after the Zionists left, he met for the second time within a week with the AJC's Proskauer and Blaustein, who repeated their opposition to Jewish statehood. According to Blaustein, Truman told them he was annoyed with Wise and Silver, who had been "insisting as they do constantly for a Jewish State. Truman said that [a Jewish state] positively is not in the cards now (or at any time in the foreseeable future) and would cause a third World War."[14]

On the day he met with these leaders, senators in both parties called for a quick, productive response to Jewish DPs' needs. They strongly criticized Britain for enforcing the white paper's limit, even with its expansion to eighteen thousand per year. London needed a $3.5 billion loan from America. Senator Taft proposed that British easing of the immigration limit into Palestine be made a condition for the loan. Rabbi Silver, against State's wishes, began to organize U.S. Zionists to kill the loan completely. The White House, siding with State, countered Silver's efforts with pro-loan statements from moderate Zionists.[15] Dean Virginia Gildersleeve, then a prominent American educator, wrote of the atmosphere at that time:

> Of the few who had any real knowledge of the circumstances, almost no one was willing to speak out publicly against a project of the Zionists. The politicians feared the Jewish vote; others feared the charge of anti-Semitism; and nearly all had a kind of "guilt complex" in their emotions towards the Jews because of the terrible tragedies inflicted upon them by Hitler. It seemed to me, however, that someone ought to speak out against the cowardly and immoral course to which our nation was being urged.[16]

The October 9, 1945, issue of the *New York Times* printed a letter from Virginia Gildersleeve which urged America to admit 200,000 Jews rather than force them on Arabs. That letter, she said, "brought a storm on my head. Many Zionists denounced me vehemently; some threatened violence."[17] This was yet another example of Zionists putting their own political agenda ahead of the settlement of Jewish refugees.

In October Zionists' anti-British warfare in Palestine vastly expanded. Hagana's leader urged Zionists to make London know it would pay a high price to continue the white paper's limit, even though expanded. More Zionists talked of going underground to fight the British. That same month Palmach, Hagana's full-time core group, sank three patrol boats used to stop ships with illegal immigrants. On the night of October 31 Palmach destroyed or damaged some fifty parts of Palestine's railroad. The Voice of Israel, an underground radio station, began broadcasting that month.[18]

II. The Anglo-American Committee, October 1945.

On October 4 Bevin, to get America to act in a way he considered more "responsible" - without losing the U.S. loan - proposed forming a joint Anglo-American Committee of Inquiry to study the Jewish refugee issue and make both short- and long-term proposals. Despite the offer of cooperative effort there was mutual mistrust. Bevin told Lord Halifax, the British ambassador to America, that he thought Truman was "dishonest" about Palestine. Bevin referred to the tight New York City mayoral election race then being hotly contested, in which both parties courted the large Jewish vote. He added: "My only fear of bringing the United States into the picture at this stage is this: the propaganda in New York has destroyed what looked to me a few weeks ago as a reasonable atmosphere in which we could get Jews and Arabs together."[19] Zionists suspected that Britain wanted to take the focus off Palestine; they therefore assured Truman "that any attempt to secure Jewish immigration into other countries would come to naught."[20] Thus Zionists continued to insist that Palestine was the *only* solution to the Jewish refugee problem and discouraged the search for any other solution. Truman, reflecting Zionist distrust of London, feared that the proposed Anglo-American Committee might provide a pretext to stall on the immigration issue. He accepted Bevin's offer with the proviso that the committee report within four months and limit its inquiry to the suitability of Palestine as a home for refugees. Britain reluctantly agreed.[21] Thus other possible havens were excluded or at least ignored.

Truman continued to be annoyed with what he considered constant badgering by U.S. Zionists. He pointed out that Palestine did not belong to America and that the U.S. government had no right to dispose of it. Moreover, he added with a foresight he would later abandon, to impose a political structure on the Mideast would certainly create even more conflict there. He also said that he no longer believed in the advisability of resolutions calling for a Jewish state. But he continued to vacillate: At the end of October his staff told Taft and Wagner that he would not object to their introducing a revised Senate resolution backing Zionist goals; but on November 29 he told Secretary of State James Byrnes that he opposed it. He thought it would undercut the Anglo-American Committee and threaten U.S. diplomatic relations with Arab states. On December 4 Truman again told an AJC leader and Weizmann that he feared that Zionists would create a racial or theocratic state at odds with America's concept of a pluralistic state. Zionists themselves were thus frustrated with Truman. They had more success in the Senate, which passed an amended Taft-Wagner on December 17. The House passed a concurring resolution two days later. Some resolutions lack the value of law; Cohen notes that these two resolutions "had no practical impact whatever on America's Palestine policy."[22]

Britain, meanwhile, was not yet fully intimidated by the Palestine war. On November 13, 1945, Bevin reaffirmed London's commitment to the white paper. Weizmann, in a speech in Atlantic City, again pleaded for the immediate issuance of 100,000 certificates.

When the members of the Anglo-American Committee interviewed Weizmann he argued in effect that because the Arabs in Palestine were part of the larger Arab community they had less right to Palestine than they would have had if they had not been Arabs. He said the Arabs already had several independent countries whereas the Jews had none. Weizmann argued in effect that because some Arabs elsewhere had been able to achieve independence, the Arabs in Palestine no longer had that right, at least not to the degree that Jews had it. Weizmann also argued that because Jews had suffered more casualties during the war than Arabs had, Jews had a greater right to Palestine than did Palestinian Arabs. Weizmann told committee members that there is no absolute justice but only rough human justice. He contended that there was bound to be injustice.[23] He argued that in this situation injustice to the Palestinian Arabs was appropriate: "I say there may be some slight injustice politically if Palestine is made a Jewish State....the line of least injustice demands that we [Jews] should be given our chance."[24]

On December 22 Truman issued a presidential order that DPs, especially orphans, receive preference within existing U.S. immigration quotas. At that time the annual U.S. quota was still 26,000 for Germans, and thirteen thousand for all eastern Europeans, so the order would have little impact on U.S. society. However, reflecting national sentiment, there was opposition in

Congress to his order lowering barriers against DPs even to this extent.[25]

On May 1, 1946, the Anglo-American Committee of Inquiry publicly issued its report. It said that trying to form any kind of state, either a single state or two states, one for Arabs and one for Jews, would ignite civil strife which could threaten world peace. Therefore Britain should temporarily continue to administer the mandate and then turn it over to the UN. The report proposed that the 100,000 certificates be granted and that the 1939 white paper and its limit on land sales to Jews be revoked.[26] The Arabs and British fully rejected the report's proposals. Bevin said it would take another division of British troops and 200 million pounds to enforce them. Zionists liked some proposals, rejected others and were divided on still others, including the state issue. Supreme Court Justice Felix Frankfurter, perhaps the leading U.S. Zionist, reportedly told Truman aide David Niles that the more militant Zionists "prefer a Jewish State on paper rather than doing something real for human beings."[27] Weizmann said that perhaps Zionists should not have asked for a Jewish state. "We are always trying to push too hard," he stated.[28] For Ben-Gurion, however, Zionist pressure on the committee had been too weak, or at least not successful enough. He complained that the committee had proposed a "British colonial-military state, which was no longer to be a homeland for the Jewish people, and which would never become a Jewish State."[29]

On April 30 Truman publicly backed the Anglo-American Committee's call for 100,000 certificates and an end to the white paper. His statement, which endorsed only *part* of the committee report, was drafted by Emanuel Neumann, a Zionist who worked with Rabbi Silver. The State Department had urged Truman in vain not to make the statement as it would seriously hurt Anglo-American consensus on Palestine. Predictably he pleased U.S. Jews but displeased Bevin and Attlee. To reconcile their differences Truman and Attlee set up yet another bilateral committee, which became known as the Morrison-Grady committee or team. That summer it tried to devise a mutually agreeable adaptation of the Anglo-American Committee proposals.

III. Zionist Warfare, the Morrison-Grady Plan, Mid-1946.

Zionists in Palestine, doubting that their goals would be won by British and U.S. diplomats, tried to force the issue by open warfare and terrorism. In mid June Hagana sappers blew up nine bridges - destroying all but one bridge linking Palestine and its neighbors. They also damaged Haifa railroad shops. On June 29 the British sealed off Jewish Agency offices, searched public buildings and Jewish settlements, and ordered the arrest of the Zionist executive and other Jewish leaders. Begin's Irgun terrorists, cooperating with Hagana officials, blew up part of Jerusalem's King David Hotel on July 22, killing almost one hundred British, Jews and Arabs. Part of the hotel housed British government offices. Irgun leaders later said their plan to warn people to leave before the explosion was not properly followed, causing more deaths than Irgun expected. The British arrested 787 people but did not catch the bombers. Most detainees were soon released.[30] The Hagana attacked British naval vessels and radar stations, the Irgun attacked army equipment and installations, and Lehi (the Stern Gang) attacked British personnel.[31]

By late July the Morrison-Grady team devised a compromise that both London and Secretary of State Byrnes accepted. It allowed entry of 100,000 refugees. It proposed federalization of Palestine, which was interpreted by some to mean a type of partition. Zionists opposed this latter feature because it would not allot as much land to Jews as Zionists wanted. Truman was for backing the Morrison-Grady Plan, which he thought fair. At a July 30 cabinet meeting held to discuss endorsement, Undersecretary of State Dean Acheson and Navy Secretary James Forrestal were for approving it. However, Zionists had launched an intense campaign against it. Byrnes (in Paris) realized the issue could hurt Truman in that congressional election year and wired that he took a neutral position. Commerce Secretary Henry Wallace warned Truman that Morrison-Grady was "loaded with political dynamite" and asked him to examine it more fully before endorsing it. According to Wallace, Truman brought to the meeting "a sheaf of telegrams about four inches thick from various Jewish people." He stated that he was "put out" with the Jews, that he had no use for them and did not care what happened to them. Despite his exasperation, he decided not to endorse the plan. Acheson later told British ambassador Lord Inverchapel that Truman could not endorse it because "intense Jewish hostility" made it a political liability.[32]

Ironically, on August 5, within a week of Truman's cabinet meeting, the Jewish Agency Executive Committee voted to give up some of the demands of the 1942 Biltmore Program. The Agency said it would negotiate for space in *part* of Palestine. Thus it quit demanding all of Palestine. This narrowed the gap between Zionist demands and the Morrison-Grady Plan. Nahum Goldmann, representing the Jewish Agency, went to Washington to negotiate, but little came of it and Morrison-Grady died.[33] Truman, increasingly frustrated with the battle over Palestine, threatened to wash his hands of it. He later told the head of the Jewish War Veterans of America that he and Bevin "had agreed on the best possible solution for Palestine [Morrison-Grady] and it was the Zionists who killed that plan by their opposition."[34] With its death, the chance of 100,000 DPs being admitted to Palestine, a goal requested of Truman by Zionists themselves the year before, was scuttled. Thus Zionists again sacrificed the future of European Jews because of the statehood issue.

IV. Truman's Efforts to Open America to More DPs, 1946.

By August 1946 almost 250,000 Jews had fled eastern Europe, especially Poland, to DP camps in Austria, Germany and Italy. Here they awaited transfer to Palestine or elsewhere. Meanwhile, some 600,000 Gentiles, mostly from eastern Europe, had also become DPs seeking permanent homes. Stymied in trying to open Palestine to more DPs, Truman on August 16 announced that he would ask Congress to allow more of them to enter America. Without saying how many, he hoped that perhaps 300,000 would be admitted. That month a national poll showed that 72 percent of those asked opposed such a law. Congresspersons publicly opposed any change in quotas; one congressperson threatened to halve present quotas.[35] Zionists opposed easing quotas for DPs because this would ease Jewish refugee entry into America; this would lower pressure on London to allow the 100,000 into Palestine. Truman kept running up against the same obstacle that Roosevelt had faced in 1938 and 1943.[36] Zionists, who had pleaded for emptying the DP camps, again sacrificed these people rather than endanger immigration to Palestine.

Non-Zionist Jews, including the AJC, strongly objected to making Jewish refugees hostages to Zionist political goals. They formed a high-powered lobby fronted by prominent American Gentiles to work for passage of the pro-DP law. The AJC hoped for a bill that over a four-year period would allow the entry of 400,000 of the estimated 850,000 Jewish and Gentile DPs then in Europe. Because some 29 percent of these were Jewish, it was hoped that the goal of 100,000 Jews would be nearly reached within the four years. However, the AJC did not want the legislation to appear to favor Jews. Instead of setting large quotas for doctors, lawyers and other professions with many European Jewish practitioners, advocates of the bill urged large quotas for farm and construction workers, which included few Jewish practitioners but met U.S. job openings. The strategy therefore somewhat backfired. The lobby's efforts resulted in an April 1947 bill introduced by Representative William Stratton.[37]

V. The Zionist Lobby and Zionist Government Advisers.

Because 1946 was a congressional election year, Congress and the White House faced great pressure from the Zionist lobby, which had become much stronger since war's end. The Zionist Organization of America (ZOA) formed several proxy groups to give the lobby a seemingly broader base. These groups also worked through individual Zionists in sensitive positions on White House, State Department and congressional staffs. Such Zionists were in excellent spots to influence their government superiors regarding decisions affecting Zionism. They could also inform Zionist groups of developments and nuanced thinking within the government. Historian Cohen notes that the lobby worked "among advisers and aides, mostly without officially specified positions, who played a key role in shaping President Truman's Palestine policy. This group enabled Truman to believe in what he was doing and not simply to feel that he was bowing to electoral blackmail."[38]

Two such individuals were David Niles and Max Lowenthal. Niles, the former FDR aide, was Truman's liaison with Jewish, liberal and labor groups, especially those on the northeastern seaboard. He advised Truman on which Jewish leaders it was important to meet. Lowenthal held various government jobs; in 1947-48 he was Clark Clifford's legal adviser on Palestine affairs when Clifford was an adviser to Truman. According to Cohen, Lowenthal "visited and obtained material from the Zionist office in Washington regularly. On the basis of the briefings he received there, Lowenthal drafted the memoranda on Palestine that Clark Clifford would present to the president and to the State Department."[39]

Lowenthal had direct access to Truman and advocated his pro-Zionist views informally during numerous talks with him. Thus Zionists had a direct and very short line to Truman; Palestinian Arabs lacked even smoke signals. Truman later told Lowenthal that he was the one most responsible for Truman's recognition of the state of Israel.

Several "brain trusts" - informal groups of government and non-government individuals - included Zionists. These groups developed advice on Zionist affairs for the White House and other government entities. Niles sat in on some meetings of one brain trust. It included at various times: Israel Sieff, a very wealthy Anglo-Jewish businessman; presidential adviser Ben Cohen; Robert Nathan, an economist working for U.S. intelligence; David Ginsburg, a lawyer and New Deal government official; and David Lilienthal, head of the Tennessee Valley Authority. Michael Cohen notes: "This little group was strategically placed to carry the... Zionist lines to the highest quarters in the administration, either directly or through well-calculated remarks 'among well-placed colleagues in the corridors of power and the salons of social Washington.'"[40]

Such pro-Zionist brain trusts took on increased importance as debate over forming a Jewish state multiplied during 1947 and early 1948. Truman had no comparable mechanism, aside from some personnel at State perhaps, to present Palestinian Arabs' interests. This imbalance resulted in a truly extraordinary arrangement for guarding the chicken coop.

By 1946 one of Emanuel Neumann's Zionist front groups, the Christian Council on Palestine, had a membership of almost three thousand Protestant clergymen. According to Cohen:

> Their prestige and authority were used by the Zionists in many appeals to the American public and to the administration....Christian Zionist support for the Zionist cause, both spontaneous and organized, would prove a valuable...asset in the Zionist diplomatic struggle. At the very least, it provided a crucial counter to the aspersions cast both by anti-Zionist Jewish elements and by the State Department that the Zionists were a narrow, parochial lobby, not representative of even the Jewish community let alone the larger non-Jewish one.[41]

Before 1946 ended, the American Zionist Emergency Council (AZEC) expanded its subsidy to Senator Wagner's American Palestine Committee (APC), a pro-Zionist Protestant group, from $50,000 in 1941 to $150,000. The Committee's membership of fifteen thousand American leaders included sixty-eight senators, two hundred congresspersons and several governors. The APC had seventy-five chapters and was "the preeminent symbol of pro-Zionist sentiment among the non-Jewish American public."[42] Virtually all of its business was actually conducted by the AZEC. This included opening and answering letters from the White House and State Department; Wagner merely received a copy of the letters.

VI. Anti-Zionist Influences in Washington.

Pro-Zionist influences were not alone in Washington. State

Department officials saw the postwar Mideast as ripe for U.S. diplomatic and business interests. Britain and France, dominant in the area between the world wars, were battered economically. They were losing their colonies and much of their influence to rising African and Asian nationalism. America, in Arab eyes, was not tainted with British and French imperialism. Arabs saw that America had become the world's strongest economic and military power, the one that could best thwart whatever ambitions the Soviets might have for either military aggression or Communist infiltration in the Mideast. Although America bought little Arab oil then, it paid for Arab oil sold to western Europe. During the war, Aramco had become by far the largest U.S. economic investment in the area, much larger than any investment by Americans in Palestine. Aramco helped King Saud see Saudi Arabia's future as being with America.

Officials at State viewed their jobs as promoting both U.S. diplomatic *and* commercial interests. They saw much Arab good will that would be undercut by U.S. support of a Jewish state in Palestine. According to historian Phillip Baram, State judged that the nationalisms of the Sunni Arabs, who comprised most of the Mideast people, were benevolent, progressive, and overdue from World War I, "while the political Zionism represented chiefly by the Jewish minority in Palestine and in the United States was retrograde, a chimera in the 'Arab world' and, in the context of pro-Zionist American politics, an albatross around the Department's neck."[43]

State Department officials therefore argued, sometimes vehemently, that U.S. support of Zionism ran against U.S. national interests and should be opposed despite domestic pro-Zionist pressure. State strongly criticized the type of lobbying done by what it termed "hyphenated Americans." It asserted that the ethnic vote should not be a factor in shaping U.S. foreign policy.[44]

As the Cold War intensified, the western allies strengthened a tier of countries, Greece, Turkey and Iran, as military and political bulwarks against possible Soviet penetration southward toward the Mideast. State repeatedly warned Truman that it was pointless to fortify the three nations forming the top of this arch while undermining the loyalty of the pillars, the Arab states below it. Perhaps through hindsight one may question whether the danger was as great as some officials at State portrayed it. Russia was not about to buy Arab oil; atheistic communism was abhorrent to politically conservative and religiously devout Muslim Arab monarchs. Yet several Arab countries, including Egypt, Syria, and Iraq, eventually turned to Moscow for economic and military aid, although some of these moves were not entirely related to U.S. policy regarding Palestine. Dean Acheson, undersecretary of state from September 1945 to January 1947, and responsible for Palestinian affairs, later wrote of that period:

> The number [of DPs] that could be absorbed by Arab Palestine without creating a grave political problem would be inadequate, and to transform the country into a Jewish State capable of receiving a million or more immigrants would vastly exacerbate the political problem and imperil not only American but all Western interests in the Near East.[45]

VII. Truman's Yom Kippur Speech, October 4, 1946.

On September 30, six weeks before the 1946 congressional and gubernatorial elections, the newly formed Greater New York Zionist Actions Committee ran a large ad in the *New York Herald Tribune*. It listed Democrats' past support for opening up Palestine and then stated: "We do not seek new promises or new planks. The old ones are good enough. What we ask is that our Administration fulfill old promises now."[46] Zionists also urged Democratic politicians to have Truman speak out. Abraham Feinberg, business magnate and Truman friend, told him that if he made a pro-Zionist statement on October 4, the eve of Yom Kippur, the Day of Atonement, "every single Rabbi in every single synagogue will broadcast what you say. Forget the newspapers, forget any other of the media. You will have word directly to the Jewish people."[47] On October 4 Truman gave a speech urging a change in U.S. quotas so that more refugees could enter America. He again asked for the 100,000 Palestine certificates, and said the U.S. government could support a "viable Jewish state...in an adequate area of Palestine."[48] He did not specify what he meant by a "viable" state or how much area he had in mind. Thus Zionists, who were themselves divided, were not sure how close Truman's speech was to their own position. But this was the first time that a U.S. president had so publicly and explicitly backed the idea of a Jewish state.

Truman's speech angered the Arabs and British. It was thought political because it came shortly before the elections. Acheson, who helped revise an early draft of the speech written by Eliahu Epstein and Judge Sam Rosenman, later wrote that Truman "never took or refused to take a step in our foreign relations to benefit his or his party's fortunes."[49] Yet on the day before the speech was given, Acheson told the British ambassador that domestic political pressures had increased on Truman during the past ten days. Truman later said his talk was not politically motivated and just "happened" to be made on the eve of synagogues' best attended holy day. But on December 8 he told Bevin that *with elections over* he could give Britain greater latitude regarding Palestine.[50]

In November, four heads of U.S. diplomatic missions in Arab states met with Truman and warned him that his pro-Zionist statements threatened U.S. interests. He reportedly replied, "I'm sorry, gentlemen, but I have to answer to hundreds of thousands who are anxious for the success of Zionism; I do not have hundreds of thousands of Arabs among my constituents."[51]

Truman was not alone in seeking pro-Zionist votes. Before his Yom Kippur speech Niles warned him that New York Republican governor Thomas Dewey planned to strongly endorse immigration to Palestine. Loy Henderson, head of State's division for Near Eastern Affairs, strongly opposed Truman's pro-Zionist statements. But he later conceded that Truman was merely reflecting aspects of the U.S. political system. Henderson noted that many Republican Party leaders, including Dewey, frequently criticized Truman for not giving Zionists his full support. If the Jewish state had failed to be established because of his lack of action, "he would almost certainly have been defeated in the November [1948] elections since the Zionists had almost the full support of the Congress, the United States media, and most of the American people.

The new Republican Administration would then have gone along with the Zionists."[52]

Despite Truman's speech on the eve of Yom Kippur, Republicans trounced Democrats in the November 1946 vote, particularly in New York, including heavily Jewish New York City. But the speech had a great effect in Britain. According to Cohen it marked a watershed in the political and diplomatic struggle for the Jewish state. "The British saw in the statement a demonstration of Jewish political power and gave up their quest for an Anglo-American consensus on Palestine."[53] In February 1947, four months after Truman's speech, Britain asked the UN to take over the Palestine problem. Meanwhile, in late October 1946, following Truman's speech, the ZOA, at Rabbi Silver's urging, passed a resolution that Jews should have a state that included all of Palestine.[54] This struck a harder line than did the Jewish Agency in Palestine. But Truman, stung by the severe criticism he received for bowing to Zionist pressure, stopped urging London to admit 100,000 DPs. He did not address the Palestine issue for many months.[55]

VIII. Zionist Developments, Late 1946.

On December 9 the Twenty-Second Zionist Congress opened in Basel. The first congress since 1939, its international makeup differed radically from all previous congresses. In pre-meeting votes, U.S. Jews cast 40 percent of the ballots; at the meeting their group was the largest. Weizmann criticized what he considered its excessive militancy. He was himself accused of being too pro-British and too gradualist by those wanting more illegal immigration and armed resistance. He was not reelected Jewish Agency president. Later he wrote bitterly that, as had happened before, he was scapegoated for British policies opposed by Zionists.[56] U.S. delegates were split as well. Veteran leader Wise, also bitter, quit his office in the ZOA.[57]

As noted, during Truman's first two years in office there was opposition in Congress to his December 22, 1945, order giving DPs, especially children, preference within existing U.S. immigration quotas, even though his order did not expand the quotas. Yet during these same two years Congress and Truman pressured Britain to vastly expand Palestine's quotas in order to admit these very same DPs. U.S. absorptive capacity was many times that of Palestine. The DPs were no threat to Americans' common good, as they were to the common good of Palestine's indigenous people. Thus Americans, especially through their representative leaders, seemingly were entering farther into the trap of a moral double standard.

Chapter Nine

TRUMAN - PART 2;
PALESTINE'S PARTITION, ISRAEL'S STATEHOOD

1947-48

I. The Stratton Bill's Troubled Introduction, April 1947.

On April 1 Representative William Stratton of Illinois introduced a bill to admit 400,000 DPs into America over the next four
years. The mail response to Congress and the White House was 88
percent against his bill. The postwar housing shortage, lack of
jobs, anti-Semitism, fear of Communist infiltration among DPs,
and the threat to the "American way of life" were frequently cited
motives.[1] Truman urged Congress to pass some type of bill to
help DPs, but he did not endorse the Stratton bill, which he
thought unrealistic in asking for 400,000 DPs. He estimated
Congress at most would approve only 100,000.

II. The *Yishuv's* Pre-war Expulsion of Arabs, Spring 1947.

Father Elias Chacour is a Melkite Rite[2] Catholic priest born in
1939 in Biram, an Arab farming village in northern Galilee. He
relates that in the spring of 1947, when Palestine was still a British
mandate, the Hagana told Biram's elders that Jewish soldiers
would soon be coming for a few days and would want to live in
the villagers' homes. Though apprehensive, villagers provided
them with hospitality - free board and room. After a few days the
Hagana commander told the elders that Biram was in serious danger; it would be safer for the villagers to leave for a few days.
The soldiers would protect their homes and property while they
were gone; the villagers should give the keys to their homes to the
soldiers living in them, and leave immediately. The villagers knew
of fighting between the Hagana and British forces, so the danger

134

sounded believable. All the families - several hundred people - hurriedly left with little more than the clothes on their backs. They slept in an olive grove just below town. They could hear trucks coming and going from the village. After almost two weeks of sleeping on the cold, wet ground, with no word about returning, a few elders went back to talk to the Hagana commander. They found their homes smashed into and ransacked. Their belongings had been trucked off. Furniture that had not been stolen had been smashed. The soldiers told the elders - at gunpoint - that the village was no longer theirs but now belonged to the Jews. The elders must get out. Thus was their hospitality repaid.

The elders returned to their families in the olive grove; they decided they should all walk to Gish, the next village, and request hospitality until the matter could be resolved. When they arrived in Gish it was deserted except for ten elderly Arabs, who said soldiers had come and immediately, at gunpoint, driven out the rest of the villagers. They did not know where they went but presumed they fled to Lebanon, just a few miles north. The old people said they had heard shooting when this happened. They invited the refugees from Biram to use the deserted houses, whose belongings had been smashed or carried off in the soldiers' trucks. A few days later a refugee discovered a blackened hand sticking out of recently shoveled sand. The refugees dug down and exhumed the bodies of two dozen victims of the gunfire.

In the following days, stragglers arrived from other Arab villages in Galilee that had suffered similar fates. The refugees were left alone in Gish until the spring of 1949. Then Israeli troops came at night and trucked off all of the men in the village. They took them, without any belongings, to the armistice line between Israel and West Bank, and fired over their heads as the men ran for their lives into West Bank. Elias Chacour's father and three oldest brothers were among the deportees. The family heard nothing of their fate for three months. The four Chacours, nearly starving, walked almost to Damascus, then southwest into Lebanon, then sneaked across the border into Galilee and back to Gish. Several other men made it back. Others died or were reported to be in refugee camps, or simply were never heard from again.

Israeli authorities sold the Chacour fig orchard to a wealthy Jewish immigrant, with no compensation to the Chacours. Because immigrants from Europe and America lacked farming skills the new owner turned to Arab labor, which was both skilled and, under the circumstances, very cheap. Elias's father, needing work and loving the orchard, arranged that he and his older sons be hired to work the very land that had been stolen from them.[3]

III. Britain's Request that the UN Solve the Conflict, 1947.

In early 1947 Bevin held separate, futile meetings with Jews and Arabs. Stymied, Britain announced on February 18 that by mandate terms it lacked authority either to give Palestine to Arab or Jew, or to divide it between them. Britain said it thus had no choice but to submit the issue to the UN, which it did. The UN General Assembly (UNGA) opened a special session in late April. America wanted to avoid committing U.S. troops to keeping peace in Palestine. Therefore it did not want whatever policy the UN decided on to appear to be a result of U.S. politicking at UNGA. Thus U.S. strategy was to be quiet in the UN debates and await the emergence of a consensus. On May 13 UNGA formed the UN Special Committee on Palestine (UNSCOP) to study the issue and report by September. No major states were on the eleven-nation committee, which took evidence for more than three months.

IV. The Stratton Bill's Gaining of Support, Summer 1947.

By mid-1947 Stratton's immigration bill was gaining support among prominent Americans, including religious leaders. With Palestine before the UN, State promoted easing U.S. quotas in order to weaken Zionist arguments for the need for a Jewish state. Assistant Secretary of State John Hildring developed two proposals for Truman to submit to Congress. One provided that 150,000 DPs be admitted to the U.S. as its "fair share." The other would have given DPs all of the 571,000 unused wartime U.S. immigration certificates. Truman did not use either proposal.[4]

Many DPs had resettled by mid-1947. Of the Jews in camps on

December 22, 1945, the date of Truman's DP immigration directive, ten thousand remained unresettled. The rest had gone to Palestine, America or elsewhere. Of the Jews in camps in mid-1947, more than 100,000 had fled either from Russia in early 1946 or from Poland. The camps' population by mid-1947 was composed more of postwar, east European refugees than of war refugees. The new total was some 850,000: 250,000 Jews and 600,000 Gentiles, mostly from eastern Europe, with nearly 1,660,000 refugees - many outside camps - eligible for DP status.[5] In the fall of 1947 the Stratton bill was still far from becoming law. Few Jewish groups testified in its favor - and only briefly.[6] If the bill had passed at that time it would have weakened Zionists' argument that opening Palestine was necessary to solve the refugee problem. Yet the AJC, which then had not yet fully embraced Zionism, seems to have sincerely tried to open America to more Jewish refugees. Meanwhile, the Fulton Committee, a subcommittee of the House Foreign Relations Committee, agreeing with the Zionist position, stated: "If the Jewish facet of the problem could be cleared up, the solution of the remainder of the problem would be greatly facilitated. The opening up of Palestine to the resettlement of Jewish displaced persons would break the log jam."[7]

V. The UNCSOP Report and Subsequent Maneuvering, Fall 1947.

On August 31 UNSCOP finished its report, which offered both minority and majority plans. (Australia rejected both plans.) The three-nation minority, India, Iran and Yugoslavia, proposed a federation, with a common citizenship. A federal authority would manage foreign policy, defense, immigration and most economic matters. During a three-year transition, a UN-appointed authority would govern Palestine. This minority plan was similar to one submitted to the joint Anglo-American Committee in early 1946 but rejected. It also resembled the ill-fated Morrison-Grady Plan set forth in July 1946.

The UNSCOP seven-nation majority consisted of committee members from Canada, Czechoslovakia, Guatemala, The Netherlands, Peru, Sweden and Uruguay. It advocated political partition rather than the minority's proposed federation. However, the majority also favored an economic union because it thought that otherwise the Arab state would not be economically viable. The Holy Places were to be accessible to all; Jerusalem was to remain under international trusteeship. The transition period was to be as short as feasible, with both states to be independent by September 1, 1949. The Jewish state was to comprise three geographic areas: upper Galilee and the Jordan and Beisan valleys; the coastal plain from just south of Acre to just north of Isdud, including most of the Valley of Esdraelon and the city of Jaffa; and most of the Negev, that is, the southern desert next to the Sinai. The Arab state was also to comprise three areas, western Galilee, most of the West Bank down to and including Lydda, and the Gaza Strip from the Egyptian border north to a point about twenty miles south of Tel Aviv.[8]

At this time those against U.S. support for a Jewish state included Defense Secretary James Forrestal, Secretary of State George Marshall, Assistant Secretary of State Dean Acheson, Undersecretary of State Robert Lovett, State's Near Eastern Affairs Director Loy Henderson, as well as other State Department personnel. According to Henderson, these included all U.S. legations and consular officials in the Mideast and all State Department officials who had responsibility in the area.[9] They still thought such support would so anger the Arabs that they might (a) cut their crucial oil supply to western Europe, and (b) become Soviet allies. Washington's oil lobby played on these fears. As noted above, western nations were Arab oil's major market and so there was probably little danger that the oil-producing states would cut off their major income to help Palestinian Arabs. The political danger was probably greater; some Arab states became quite anti-American and moved closer to the Soviets.[10]

During the UNGA *Ad Hoc* Committee's debate over partition, a resolution was introduced which recommended that the UN member states absorb the Jewish DPs who were unable to be repatriated. The vote was sixteen to sixteen with twenty-six abstentions. America voted against it and thus supported the Zionist position that Palestine was the *only* solution. According to Rabbi Silver, one of those who urged this position, the Jewish problem was not just homelessness in the way that DPs experienced homelessness. Rather the Jewish problem was homelessness in the way that all Diaspora Jews experience it: not having a national home. Therefore the solution was not to place Jewish DPs in better living conditions in various host nations, because this would just continue their Diaspora "homelessness." The solution was to establish a national home to which all Jews could come if they so desired; that home could be only Palestine.[11]

After his October 1946 Yom Kippur eve speech, Truman remained quiet about Palestine until the UNSCOP report and its UN debate reheated the issue. He reportedly felt that Congress, the Democratic Party, the press and the public wanted him to support Zionism. U.S. Zionists strongly pressured him to endorse the UNSCOP majority's partition plan. Three cabinet members encouraged by aides Clark Clifford and David Niles also urged him to endorse it. He did, publicly, on October 9; two days later the U.S. delegation announced this at the UN. Leo Sack, a Zionist public relations professional, told an American Zionist Emergency Council meeting: "We had won a great victory, but" none of us should "believe or think we had won because of the devotion of the American Government to our cause. We had won because of the sheer pressure of political logistics that was applied by the Jewish leadership in the United States."[12]

The USSR also supported the majority plan. It thus seemed unlikely that the UN would endorse the minority or any other plan. The State Department, through its UN delegation, therefore tried to change the UNSCOP majority plan map of the partition to make it less loathsome to Arabs. State especially tried to shift highly Arab Jaffa and the Bedouin-occupied Negev from the proposed Jewish state to the Arab. Virtually no Jews lived in the Negev but some 66,000 Bedouin did. Even the Zionist *Encyclopedia of Zionism and Israel* states: "This area [the Negev]...had been occupied only by Bedouins...."[13] Israeli demographer Bachi states that in 1944 the Negev "was inhabited almost exclusively" by Bedouin, and that less than .1 percent of the Jews in Palestine, that is, less than 536 Jews, lived in the Negev, including the town of Beersheba. This changed little by 1948.[14]

A UN subcommittee was to decide on the Negev during the afternoon of November 19, 1947. Undersecretary of State Lovett told the U.S. delegates working with the group not to submit to Zionist demands for the area. However, Weizmann learned of the situation. Niles got him a secret lunch with Truman on November 19, and Weizmann may have changed Truman's mind - a feat he repeatedly accomplished at especially critical moments during the next year. Weizmann told Truman that the Negev would be strategically important to the Jewish state, and thus the border proposed by UNSCOP should not be changed. Shortly after 3:00 that afternoon Truman himself, bypassing State's chain of command, phoned directly to the U.S. delegates, telling them to vote for allotting the Negev to the Jewish state. That evening Truman told Lovett that he had not wished to countermand his directives but only wanted to keep America from being a noticeable minority opposing Zionist demands.[15]

VI. The UN Vote on Partition, November 1947.

The UNSCOP majority plan was to be voted on in late November. Initially the U.S. delegation was told not to lobby other members to vote for partition. On Tuesday, November 25, UNGA members, *sitting as an ad hoc committee on Palestine*, voted; twenty-five were for partition and thirteen against; seventeen abstained. With this simple majority, partition passed the committee. In the next step UNGA, *sitting as a plenary group*, would take the final vote on partition. Now it would need a two-thirds majority to pass. The 25/13 vote it had just received would be one vote short. Even more "yes" votes would be needed if any of the abstainers switched to "no" or if some "yes" nations changed their minds. The Zionists desperately needed time to influence "no" states at least to abstain, and abstaining states to vote "yes." Pro-Zionist members therefore conducted a successful filibuster to avoid a vote on Wednesday. Because the next day was Thanksgiving, the vote was set for Friday. It would be a busy holiday weekend. Silver said later:

> we marshalled our forces. Jewish and non-Jewish opinion, leaders and masses alike, converged on the Government and induced the President to assert the authority of his Administration to overcome the negative attitude of the State Department....The result was that our Government made its intense desire for the adoption of the partition plan known to the wavering governments.[16]

Michael Comay, head of the Jewish Agency's New York office, later wrote that over Thanksgiving Day "an avalanche descended upon the White House while some newspapers openly accused officials in the State Department of sabotage. The President...threw his personal weight behind the effort to get a decision....we really got the full backing of the United States."[17]

According to Cohen, during the last forty-eight hours before the final vote, "the crucial influence of Truman himself, and of his White House, was finally brought into play. Presidential aides, ex-secretaries of state, members of Congress, and even Supreme Court justices joined together in an intensive lobby to secure more positive votes."[18]

These are only three of numerous Jewish sources which attest to the very active role of Truman and his administration in influencing UN members to vote for partition. Actions which were reportedly taken include these:

Supreme Court justices Felix Frankfurter and Frank Murphy cabled the Philippine president, threatening him with negative consequences to Philippine interests in America if his country did not change its vote from "no" to "yes." Ten U.S. senators sent him a similar threat. Seven bills which would impact the Philippines were then pending in Congress.[19] On Friday Truman aide Clifford conferred with its ambassador in Washington. Later that day the Philippine UN delegate said he would vote "yes."[20]

Truman aide Niles orchestrated similar pressure on Liberia, which had abstained Tuesday. Its delegate was told that if he did not vote "yes" former Secretary of State Edward Stettinius had business contacts who could harm Liberia. Stettinius contacted Harvey Firestone, a major buyer of Liberian rubber, who feared that Jews might boycott his products unless he intervened. Firestone reached Liberia's president, warning him to change the vote or he would perhaps revoke his planned expansion there. Liberia voted "yes."[21]

Niles had Bernard Baruch warn France's government, which feared alienating its Arab colonies in North Africa, that America would terminate its economic aid if France voted "no." Weizmann contacted the French premier. It voted "yes."

Haiti was promised U.S. economic aid if it changed its vote to "yes," which it did. According to Stevens, Adolph Berle, a former assistant secretary of state, "reportedly" made the promise.[22]

At UNGA Zionists were given U.S. delegates' passes so that they could talk to delegates on the Assembly floor.[23]

Later, Truman said he himself had gotten several nations to vote "yes." However, in his *Memoirs* he states that he did not approve of pressure tactics; he thus implies that he did not use them.[24] According to staunchly pro-Zionist Sumner Welles, who had been undersecretary of state under Roosevelt:

By direct order of the White House every form of pressure, direct and indirect, was brought to bear by American officials upon those countries outside of the Moslem world that were known to be either uncertain or opposed to partition. Representatives or intermediaries were employed by the White House to make sure that the necessary majority would at length be secured.[25]

Dean Rusk, head of the State Department's UN desk in Washington, later wrote, "when President Truman decided to support partition, I worked hard to implement it....The pressure and arm-twisting applied by American and Jewish representatives in capital after capital to get that affirmative vote [on November 29] are hard to describe."[26] Rusk added: "There likely would never have been a state of Israel had it not been for American support."[27]

Additional pressure on nations came from non-governmental sources. Cuba's UN delegate maintained that one Latin American nation accepted a bribe of $75,000 to vote "yes." A Central American state reportedly refused a $40,000 bribe, but then voted for partition. Robert Nathan, who had previously worked for the government, told several Latin American delegates that their "yes" votes would make a Pan-American highway construction project more likely. He used the name of the State Department and of President Truman in making these promises - as he later admitted in writing to Dean Acheson. Wives of Latin American delegates reportedly received mink coats. A former president of Costa Rica, Jose Figueres, reportedly received a blank check book.[28] Paraguay, which had not voted on Tuesday, voted "yes" on Saturday. To increase the number of "no" votes, the Arab nations also lobbied but were not as effective.

UNGA reconvened on Friday but the Arabs, fearing they would lose and hoping that with time they would gain more votes, got the Assembly to adjourn for a day. It did not work. When UNGA voted on Saturday, November 29, thirty-three states voted for partition, thirteen opposed it, and ten abstained. (Cf. Table One, p. 146.) The necessary two-thirds majority was achieved.[29] Nine states that on Tuesday had either abstained or not participated in the vote, on Saturday voted for partition. One former "yes" nation, Chile, abstained. Greece, perhaps because of Arab pressure, switched from abstaining to opposing.

If Greece had not done this, and if Haiti and the Philippines had voted against partition, as they had so indicated before being pressured into voting "yes" by the United States, there would have been fourteen "no" votes. This would have required twenty-eight "yes" votes for partition to pass. If France and Liberia had abstained instead of bowing to U.S. pressure and voting "yes," partition would have carried by twenty-nine to fourteen. But if Liberia had voted against partition, as there is reason to think it might have done had it not been for U.S. pressure, the vote would have been twenty-nine to fifteen and thus partition would have been defeated. Moreover, the alleged threats and bribes may have influenced other nations to vote "yes" when otherwise they would have abstained or voted against partition.

Whether or not the Zionists would have gotten the two-thirds vote they needed without the alleged strong U.S. threats is speculative. The facts are that the vote change resulted partly from America imposing its will on several states beholden to it. The American action resulted not from U.S. national interests but from extreme domestic pressure by a small but influential part of the population on Congresspersons, on the Democratic Party especially, and above all on Truman. However, this pressure group apparently was not acting against most Americans' sympathies. A November poll showed that 65 percent of those questioned supported partition.[30] Whether they would have supported the tactics, had they known of them, is another question.

In trying to reconstruct what took place during those four days one is caught between unproved allegations and a large amount of evidence indicating that the allegations should not be just dismissed. One can say with certainty that before United States officials and former officials began to apply threats and other types of pressure, partition did not have enough votes to pass. After the actions of these people, it did. American threats certainly contributed to its passage; perhaps they were essential to it. Either way, it would seem that America was a party to a grave injustice against the Palestinian Arabs. The reasons for maintaining this are:

1. The people of Palestine had a clear moral right to self-determination. The fact that Britain had denied them the exercise of this right since the beginning of the mandate did not decrease the moral right itself.

a. The UN partition plan denied to the 500,000 or so Arabs living in the area *allotted to the Jewish state* the ability to exercise the right of self-determination.

b. The plan gravely diminished the exercise of this right to the Palestinian Arabs living in the area *allotted to the Arabs* because it dismembered their country and took away from them the control of more than half of it.

2. The plan forcefully split the Palestinian Arabs from each other, against their wishes, into two different political countries (assuming the Palestinian part will become a country).

3. It forced the Arabs who would be living in the Jewish state to be a minority among a hostile majority. (It would also force the

Jews living in the area allotted to the Arabs to be a minority among a hostile majority, but partition was not an Arab idea.)

4. The partition plan was a form of diplomatic aggression. America was a major collaborator in that diplomatic aggression.

5. The partition vote does not seem to pass the tests of:

a. "Was it fair?"

b. "Do to others as you would have them do to you." Would Americans complain if the UN dismembered the United States and let other nations be formed from parts of it? (Cf. Maps Two and Three.) Yet it would seem that historically the Palestinians have a stronger moral claim to their land than non-Native Americans have to theirs.

At the time of the partition vote the *yishuv* owned about 5-6 percent of Palestine. If the partition plan had concerned itself with allotting the Jewish state only this territory or an equivalent amount, it would seem that the morality of the partition would have been greatly different. However, that did not happen. The UN, "the moral conscience of mankind," as it was then sometimes referred to, had spoken. This time it seemingly spoke through a grave miscarriage of justice. The Arab states immediately served notice that they would not be bound by the vote. It would seem that they had a moral right to do this.

The Zionists now had a UN resolution which not only favored a Jewish state but also called for allotting 5,579 square miles, 53.46 percent of Palestine, to the Jews even though they then occupied only 5-6 percent of its territory. The areas allotted to the Jewish state encompassed 499,000-to-538,000 of the more than 600,000 Jews in Palestine. Most of the remainder lived in Jerusalem, which, according to the resolution, was to be internationalized. Some ten thousand Jews lived in about thirty-five settlements outside the areas allotted to the Jewish state. Some 510,000 Arabs lived in areas assigned to the Jewish state. Thus the Arab population assigned to the Jewish state was about as large as its Jewish population.[31]

Table One:[32] UNGA Partition Votes

Votes in *Ad Hoc* Committee Nov. 25:			Votes in plenary meeting Nov. 29:		
For	Against	Abstain	For	Against	Abstain
Australia	Afghanistan	Argentina	Australia	Afghanistan	Argentina
Bolivia	Egypt	China	Bolivia	Egypt	China
Brazil	India	Columbia	Brazil	India	Columbia
Byelorussia	Iran	El Salvador	Byelorussia	Iran	El Salvador
Canada	Iraq	Ethiopia	Canada	Iraq	Ethiopia
Costa Rica	Lebanon	Honduras	Costa Rica	Lebanon	Honduras
Czechoslovak	Pakistan	Mexico	Czechoslovak	Pakistan	Mexico
Denmark	Saudi Arabia	UK (Gr.Br.)	Denmark	Saudi Arabia	UK (Gr.Br.)
Dominican R.	Syria	Yugoslavia	Dominican R.	Syria	Yugoslavia
Ecuador	Turkey	*Changed:*	Ecuador	Turkey	*Added:*
Guatemala	Yemen	Greece	Guatemala	Yemen	Chile
Iceland	Cuba	Belgium	Iceland	Cuba	*Absent:*
Nicaragua	*Changed:*	France	Nicaragua	*Added:*	Siam
Norway	Siam	Haiti	Norway	Greece	Total: 11
Panama	Total: 13	Liberia	Panama	Total: 13	
Peru		Luxembourg	Peru		
Poland		Netherlands	Poland		
Sweden		New Zealand	Sweden		
Ukraine		*Absent:*	Ukraine		
U. So.Africa		Paraguay	U. So.Africa		
USSR		Philippines	USSR		
USA		Total: 19	USA		
Uruguay			Uruguay		
Venezuela			Venezuela		
Changed:			*Added:*		
Chile			Belgium		
Total: 25			France		
			Haiti		
			Liberia		
			Luxembourg		
			Netherlands		
			New Zealand		
			Paraguay		
			Philippines		
			Total: 33		

VII. Response to the Partition Vote.

Because of the intense U.S. lobbying, most nations viewed the partition plan as an American project. This was the very situation that State - and Truman until overwhelmed by political pressure - hoped to avoid. As Britain began to see an end to its tunnel, America blissfully entered it. America's role in Palestine would often be a most time-consuming problem for both the State Department and the White House, and a constant drain on U.S. resources - with no end in sight for either the State Department or the taxpayer.[33]

The American Jewish Committee opposed partition before the UN vote. Afterward, after extensive debate, the AJC supported partition, and continues to do so. Zionists were profuse in their gratitude to Truman - at least for a few months. On hearing of the vote, Zionists danced in Palestine's streets. On November 30, Palestinian Arabs called a three-day strike and physically attacked Jews. Neighboring Arab states announced that they would invade Palestine as soon as Britain left. Many wealthier Arabs who lived in areas allotted by the UN plan to the Jewish state began to flee to Beirut and other parts of Lebanon, and to other Arab states. The Jews in the thirty-five or so settlements in the areas allotted to the Arab state were ordered by the Jewish Agency not to flee.[34] They were to keep the settlements as outposts that could be used for both defensive and offensive military operations in establishing the Jewish state.[35]

On December 11, Britain, as it had said it would, announced that it would end its mandate. Eventually it specified that it would withdraw all its personnel by the end of May 14, 1948. London indicated it would not offend Arabs by cooperating with the UN in implementing the partition. Thus the UN Committee of Five, five nations chosen to oversee the transition to partition, received almost no recognition or help from Britain while British forces remained in Palestine. Britain did nothing, in fact probably could have done nothing, to set up cooperative procedures between Arabs and Jews to make the transition peaceful and smooth. Britain's primary goal between November 29 and May 14 was to ship out its materiel, gradually evacuate its personnel and their families, and avoid loss of British life in the growing warfare and chaos. Usually, if combatants did not shoot the British, the latter did not stop them from shooting each other. However, Britain warned the Arab Legion not to advance into areas allotted by the UN to the Jewish state. The Legion served under Trans-Jordan's Abdullah but was trained by British officers. Britain continued its coastal blockade to intercept immigrants and Zionist arms.

On November 14, 1947, two weeks before the final UN partition vote, State had imposed an embargo against the sale or shipment of U.S. arms to either the *yishuv* or the Arab states around it. Because Britain had contracts to sell arms to Arab states, the U.S. embargo worked to the disadvantage of the *yishuv*. Weizmann in April 1948 begged Truman to lift the embargo. This time his charm did not move Truman, who faced the threat of the Cold War turning into armed conflict with the Soviets. The *yishuv* therefore bought and smuggled in arms from eastern Europe. Palestinian Arabs outnumbered the *yishuv* but the latter had 50 percent more males in the 20-44 age bracket and thus 50 percent more potential soldiers. Each side increased its forces either with non-Palestinian Arab soldiers or with Jewish men from Europe or America infiltrating Palestine.

In December 1947 Arabs attacked Jewish workers at the Haifa oil refinery, killing thirty-nine of them. In reprisal, two companies of the Hagana attacked the nearby village of Balad el-Sheikh, killing more than sixty villagers, many of them women and children.[36] On January 5 the Hagana blew up part of the Hotel Semiramis in an Arab part of Jerusalem, killing twenty-six people, fourteen of them civilians. Part of the hotel was used by Arab military.[37] By the end of January some 15,000 Arabs had fled Jerusalem and Haifa. This was before Begin's Irgun began most of its terrorist attacks in Jerusalem, Tel Aviv and Haifa. Arabs responded with terrorism but on a much smaller scale.[38]

VIII. The Revised Stratton Immigration Bill of March 1948.

In March Stratton introduced a revised immigration bill in the

House. Because of the November 29 UN approval of partition, it was widely assumed that most Jewish DPs still in the camps would go to the new Jewish state as soon as it began. The AJC had supported increased Jewish immigration to America both on humanitarian grounds and as a way to deflate Zionist pressure to found a Jewish state. Now that the AJC had ceased its opposition to the state it was forced to reassess its position. The new Stratton bill called for admitting 100,000 DPs into America over two years. However, it would admit only those who had been in the camps prior to December 22, 1945. This was the date Truman had used in his former presidential order. The bill would therefore admit any Jewish DPs who had been in the camps since war's end. However, few of these remained. The bill, reflecting the AJC strategy noted in Chapter Eight, gave priority to farm workers, who were in greater demand in America than people in some other professions. Jewish DPs were apt to be in these other professions but were not apt to be farm workers. Moreover, the bill excluded more than 100,000 Polish and Russian Jews who had entered the camps since December 22, 1945. Many of those helped by the new bill would be Polish and Baltic Gentiles, including many presumed to be anti-Semitic. Despite these drawbacks from a Jewish viewpoint, the AJC supported the Stratton bill because it would admit some Jews and many Gentiles stuck in the camps.

Truman castigated the bill as discriminating "in callous fashion against displaced persons of the Jewish faith."[39] His statement, made near the start of the presidential and congressional election campaign of 1948, jabbed at the Republican-controlled House and Senate immigration committees. He ignored the fact that many Democratic lawmakers opposed admitting many Jews.

The State Department, hoping the UN would reverse its vote calling for a Jewish state, opposed Stratton's bill because it would admit few Jews and thus not deflate pressure for a Jewish state. State's Marshall told Bevin that Congress was "strongly anti-Jewish" and was acting "entirely on anti-Jewish prejudice."[40] The bill was revised to double the total quota to 200,000, of whom forty thousand - 20 percent - were expected to be Jewish. It passed both houses; Truman, despite his criticisms, signed it into law on

July 1, 1948, by which time Israel was a state. Thus the law did not affect the statehood issue.

The American people's representatives in 1945 had called for the admission of 100,000 Jews into Palestine's 10,435 square miles. Three years later the American Congress could find room for only forty thousand Jews in America's 3.62 million square miles. Not only was America 347 times the size of Palestine, geographically, in 1948 it was also seventy-seven times the size of Palestine in population. Many of the representatives of the American people did not hesitate to impose 100,000 DPs on the then 1,288,000 Palestinian Arabs, yet adamantly refused to let more than 200,000 DPs be absorbed by a U.S. population that was then seventy-seven times as large.

IX. The Reconsideration of Partition, Spring 1948.

Continued Palestine warfare throughout early 1948 and the chaos expected after Britain's pullout undercut UN and White House hopes for the feasibility of partition without committing a large UN peace-keeping military force. U.S. opinion polls backed Truman's policy of not sending American troops to Palestine. Sentiment was growing within the government to abandon or at least delay partition and settle for at least a temporary UN trusteeship instead. Leaders at State and Defense reminded Truman of the possibility of war with the USSR. They told him he should accept losing the fall presidential election rather than endanger U.S. security by jeopardizing Western bases and oil sources in the Mideast. American Zionists opposed this assessment of national interests. They did not ask for U.S. troops in Palestine but worked to ensure that Truman would not abandon his support for partition. However, some non-Zionist U.S. Jews and prominent Protestant clergy publicly supported a retreat from partition. For instance, the American Council for Judaism supported trusteeship, the only Jewish organization to do so.[41]

For the moment Truman again let State handle Palestine matters. He approved beforehand a speech which Warren Austin, U.S. ambassador to the UN, made in the UNSC on February 24:

The Security Council is authorized to take forceful measures with respect to Palestine to remove a threat to international peace. The Charter of the United Nations does not empower the Security Council to enforce a political settlement....The Security Council's action, in other words, is directed to keeping the peace and not to enforcing partition.[42]

Austin's speech warned that America was not committed to a military imposition of partition, or even to a political enforcement if this would endanger world peace. Zionists tried to counteract the thinking behind the speech.

On March 19 Austin, acting on prearranged instructions from Truman and Marshall, proposed that the UN set up a trusteeship for Palestine. This would reverse or at least delay the partition which Truman had forced through UNGA on November 29, 1947. Zionists, except Weizmann, were furious; some of them called Truman a traitor. What they did not know, and what Marshall and Austin did not know, was that on the previous day, March 18, Truman had again met secretly with Weizmann and assured him that he would support partition. However, Truman did not know that Austin would be making the prearranged speech favoring trusteeship, on March 19. On learning he had made it, Truman sent Weizmann a message that, regardless of the speech, the policy they had secretly discussed would be carried out.[43]

On March 24 a meeting was held at the White House to draft a press release to backpeddle from Austin's March 19 speech. That showdown session pitted State's staff, including Marshall, against White House staffers involved in Palestine affairs. State lost. Max Lowenthal, with Clifford and others, drafted a release stressing the temporary nature of the trusteeship the U.S. proposed, with the intent to enact partition as soon as feasible.[44] The release did little to stop U.S. Zionists' anger with Truman.

Many at the UN thought trusteeship would be as unenforceable without a major military commitment as partition would be: Both Arabs and Zionists rejected trusteeship. Moreover, U.S. policy regarding Palestine had flipflopped so often during the past few months that other nations doubted America's ability to stick to a policy. Nations did not want to be left holding America's bag.

X. The Massacre at Deir Yassin, April 9, 1948.

From December 1947 to April Arabs achieved more military successes than did the *yishuv*. In particular, Arabs cut communications and blockaded roads so that Jews found it difficult and dangerous to travel between settlements. However, the *yishuv*, having resolved to stay in its settlements, kept all but one of them. Golda Meir went on a very lucrative fundraising trip to U.S. Jews to finance buying arms. By April the *yishuv* smuggled in enough arms to take the offensive. It especially tried to reopen the blockaded Tel Aviv-Jerusalem road to supply 100,000 Jews isolated in Jerusalem. The small Arab village of Deir Yassin, on Jerusalem's southwest outskirts, was near the canyon through which the road passes. Whenever a *yishuv* convoy tried to run the blockade, word quickly spread to nearby Arab villages. Their men would run to the road with whatever arms they had to stop it. However, according to Jerusalem's Hagana commander, Deir Yassin did not join in these battles; in fact "the village had made a non-aggression pact with the Hagana and had abided by it strictly."[45] On April 9, men and women members of the Irgun and of the Stern Gang attacked the village at 4:30 am. Author Rosemary Sayigh claims that the Hagana's Palmach troops joined in the attack and massacre,[46] but the British high commissioner questioned this.[47] The *yishuv* attackers lined up families - men and women, grandparents and children, even infants - and shot them. They ripped off earrings, sometimes taking part of the ear with them. They loaded villagers onto open trucks, paraded them around the Jewish area of Jerusalem, returned them to Deir Yassin and shot them.

Jacques de Reynier, the Swiss representative of the International Red Cross, entered Deir Yassin after the fighting stopped but while the massacre continued. That night he wrote in his diary that Jews were still entering houses with guns and knives. He said they seemed half insane. He saw a beautiful young Jewish woman carrying a blood-covered dagger. Explaining screams, a German Jewish Irgun member told Reynier that they were still finishing off the massacre. He saw a young woman stab an old couple at the doorway of their home. The Red Cross agent wrote that the scene reminded him of S.S. troops he had seen in Athens.[48] He entered some homes and found Arabs still alive. He got some of them to the hospital before the Irgun ordered him to leave. Reynier estimated he had seen two hundred corpses. One was that of a woman who was about eight months pregnant. She had been shot in the abdomen. Powder burns on her dress indicated, according to Reynier, that she had been shot point blank.[49]

Eliyahu Arieli, commander of the Gadna, the *yishuv* youth organization, was one of the first people to enter Deir Yassin after the massacre. He found the scene "absolutely barbaric." "All of the killed, with very few exceptions, were old men, women or children....the dead we found were all unjust victims and none of them had died with a weapon in their (sic) hands."[50]

Richard Catling, the assistant inspector general of the Criminal Investigation Division of the (British) Palestine government, on April 13, 15, and 16, sent three reports of his investigation of the massacre to that government's chief secretary:

> I interviewed many of the womenfolk in order to glean some information on any atrocities committed in Deir Yasseen but the majority of these women are very shy and reluctant to relate their experiences especially in matters concerning sexual assault....The recording of statements is hampered also by the hysterical state of the women who often break down many times whilst the statement is being recorded. There is, however, no doubt that many sexual atrocities were committed by the attacking Jews. Many young school girls were raped and later slaughtered. Old women were also molested. One story is current concerning a case in which a young girl was literally torn in two. Many infants were also butchered and killed.[51]

One woman testified that a man shot her nine-month-pregnant sister in the neck. "Then he cut her stomach open with a butcher's knife." She said another woman who saw this happen was killed when she tried to extricate the unborn infant from the dead mother's womb.[52] According to Sayigh, this atrocity of cutting open the pregnant woman was "particularly calculated to horrify

Arab peasants....This was the clearest of messages warning them
that the Arab code of war, according to which women, children
and old people were protected, no longer held good in Palestine.
Men now had to choose: their country or their family."[53]

Thus the atrocities were not the result of soldiers running amok
but were coolly calculated to force peasant militia members who
were fighting in the blockaded area at Kastel to return to their
villages to protect their families. Kastel fell to the Palmach on
April 11, two days after the massacre.[54]

Sayigh maintains that at least three hundred villagers were killed
at Deir Yassin;[55] author Nafez Nazzal writes that more than 250
died.[56] According to a member of the Hagana who witnessed part
of the massacre, 245 Arabs were killed in the fighting and
massacre. It is not clear if this includes some twenty-five young
Arabs who were paraded around Jerusalem and then shot in the
quarry outside the village.[57]

Zionist leaders denied responsibility for the massacre. Ben-
Gurion, the leader in Palestine of the *yishuv*, apologized to Emir
Abdullah of Trans-Jordan. He blamed "unofficial" terrorist
groups. The Irgun and the Stern Gang were such groups. The
Hagana was not an "unofficial" terrorist group but part of the
official underground military, answerable to the Jewish Agency.
Three days after the massacre the Irgun and the Hagana entered
into an open alliance.[58]

The Zionists tried to prevent reports of the massacre from
reaching the outside world. Irgun leaders in vain threatened
Jacques de Reynier's life to get him to falsify his report to the Red
Cross. However, the *yishuv* eagerly publicized the massacre
among Palestinian Arabs. *Yishuv* radio stations broadcast in Arabic
about Deir Yassin. *Yishuv* forces about to attack Arab villagers
reminded them by loudspeakers about Deir Yassin in order to
panic them into fleeing rather than staying and fighting.[59] Arabs
also publicized the massacre but later realized this was a mistake
because it frightened Arabs into fleeing when *yishuv* forces
approached. Irgun leader Menachem Begin stated that after the
massacre Arabs throughout Palestine "started to flee for their
lives....Of the about 800,000 Arabs who lived on the present

territory of the State of Israel, only some 165,000 are still living there. The political and economic significance of this development can hardly be overestimated."[60] According to Mideast scholar Seth Tillman, Begin claimed that in effect "the terror associated with Deir Yassin precipitated events that enabled the new state of Israel to rid itself of the bulk of its Arab population and thus to acquire its demographic character as a Jewish state."[61]

Even if the Palmach did not join the Irgun and the Stern Gang in the Deir Yassin massacre, regular units of the Hagana and its successor after statehood, the Israeli Defense Forces, massacred many civilians. For example, on April 10, 1948, the Hagana attacked the village of Nasr al-Din near Tiberias. It dynamited all of the houses in the village, killing ten civilians trapped inside them.[62] As will be noted in the next chapter, civilians were also massacred in 'Ain al Zeitouneh, al-Bi'na and Safsaf (all in Palestine), Hula (Lebanon), and elsewhere. Deir Yassin was anything but an isolated aberration or the result of *yishuv* panic.

Dr. Benny Morris, an Israeli, studied Palestinians' exodus. He concluded that of the 400,000 who left between November 29, 1947, and June 1, 1948, 70 percent (280,000) left because of Jewish military action: 15 percent from actions of the Irgun and the Stern Gang and 55 percent from actions of the Hagana/IDF. Dr. Morris obtained his figures from a report prepared by the IDF Intelligence Branch in 1948. Thus the Israeli government itself at least partly admitted the roll of the Hagana/IDF in expelling Palestinians.[63] Before the Arab exodus ended, between 614,000-626,000 (an Israeli's figures) and 840,000 (an Arab's figures) left. (Cf. Table Two, p. 176.)

XI. Ambush on the Mt. Scopus Run, April 13, 1948.

Arabs also massacred civilians. On three occasions between February and March 1948, bombs were placed in vehicles which entered Jerusalem's Jewish section and blew up. One of them killed fifty-seven people and wounded eighty-eight. Jews set off a bomb in an Arab crowd waiting for a bus, killing seventeen.[64]

Mt. Scopus is part of a long, high, north-south ridge that forms the east side of the Kedron Valley and the Mount of Olives. Hebrew University was founded on it in 1925. Nearby Hadassa Hospital, the best in Palestine, was started in 1939 by a U.S. women's Zionist group. The Hagana had a military outpost on Mt. Scopus, from which it had attacked Arabs. To supply these three facilities with personnel and materiel, Jews had to drive 2.5 miles from the western, Jewish section of Jerusalem. Much of the route traversed Arab land, including an area called Sheikh Jarrah, north of the Old City of Jerusalem. After the November 29 UN vote, Arabs had attacked vehicles making the run. This limited Jews to weekly convoys under military escort. However, since March Arabs had usually let the convoys through. On April 13, four days after Deir Yassin, a ten-vehicle convoy was making the weekly run to Mt. Scopus. It comprised an armored car in the front and rear; in between were an armored ambulance, two civilian passenger busses, another armored ambulance and four supply trucks, in that order. The second ambulance carried two Irgun members wounded during the battle for Deir Yassin. Many convoy passengers were members of the Hebrew University Faculty of Medicine or medical personnel for Hadassa Hospital. This included its director, one of the world's best known ophthalmologists, Chaim Yassky.

At about 9:30 am, near the east end of the Arab area, a large bomb buried in the road blew up just in front of the lead armored car, which fell into the crater. A score of armed, hidden Arabs attacked the convoy. Soon hundreds of other armed Arabs arrived. The last six vehicles - the rear ambulance, the four trucks, and the armored car - turned around and escaped to western Jerusalem. A British armored car, a truck and a half-track arrived from Mt. Scopus and urged the people in the two trapped busses to run the few feet to the half-track, which would take them to safety. The passengers thought it too risky and decided to wait for help from the Hagana. The British, with their wounded half-track gunner dying, left in frustration to get medical aid. Further British help was not immediately forthcoming. Three Hagana armored cars came from Jerusalem but so many soldiers in two of them were killed or wounded before reaching the convoy that they had to rush to hospitals with their own wounded. The third car helped the trapped convoy hold off some Arabs but many of its own soldiers were killed or wounded. The Arabs, who had been shouting "Deir Yassin," set the two busses on fire. Some people in the ambulance and two busses ran for safety in a nearby mansion that was a British military post. Some were killed before reaching the house. The British came again at about 3:30 pm and rescued the few people still alive in the vehicles. At least seventy-five people, mostly nurses, medical researchers and doctors, had been killed. Humanity had lost one of its best known ophthalmologists.[65]

XII. The Massacre at Kfar Etzion, May 12-13, 1948.

Zionists picked the site for the farm settlement of Kfar Etzion, south of Bethlehem, for its militarily strategic value. In an otherwise Arab area, it overlooked the Hebron-Jerusalem road. On April 12, three days after Deir Yassin, the Hagana ordered Kfar Etzion's settlers to harass Arab traffic on the road. On April 30 they were told to cut the road to prevent Arabs from moving military reinforcements from Hebron to Jerusalem. The settlers made barricades, cut telephone lines, and ambushed passing vehicles. At dawn on May 4 the British-trained Arab Legion, together with irregular militia from nearby villages, attacked the settlement, reopened the road and then withdrew.[66] At 4:00 am on May 12 the Arab forces returned to destroy Kfar Etzion and its military usefulness before Israel was to become a state three days later. After almost two days of hard fighting, some fifty surviving *yishuv* soldiers and civilians, men and women, including wounded, surrendered. They were assembled in a little square surrounded by Arab irregulars shouting "Deir Yassin!" One of the irregulars began machine-gunning prisoners. Some were bayonetted. About six were able to flee.[67] Four of these hid in a vineyard, where an old Arab discovered two of them. He told them, "Don't be afraid." However, a group of irregulars found them and threw the two Jews against a wall. The old Arab stood in front of them, protecting them with his own body. "You have killed enough," he told the irregulars. They threatened to kill him too. "No," he replied; "they are under my protection." Two Arab Legionaries came and took the two Jews into the safety of Legionary custody as war prisoners.[68]

Eliza Feuchtwanger, a young Polish Jew, was the radio operator for the Palmach unit helping to defend Kfar Etzion. When it fell she and several others hid in a ditch but were found by the Arab irregulars. While she and her companions were being shot at she screamed. The Arabs pulled her out and began arguing about who would get to rape her. Two of them dragged her away from the others and resumed the argument between themselves. An Arab Legion officer rescued her, told her she was under his protection, gave her bread and took her to the safety of his armored car.

Of the 152 *yishuv* soldiers and settlers in Kfar Etzion when the battle began, about ninety-six died in the battle, some fifty-two were massacred after it, and four survived - the female soldier and three settlers.[69] It was one of the worst military defeats and one of the worst massacres the *yishuv* suffered in the war. The next day, May 14, Britain finished its pullout from Palestine.

XIII. Arab Expulsion Before Israeli Statehood, Early 1948.

Meanwhile, Arabs were being either driven from their homes or frightened into leaving. The three major, largely Arab, coastal cities, Acre, Haifa and Jaffa, had been "de-Arabized" well before the British left on May 14. The two principal Arab cities of eastern Galilee, Safed and Tiberias, fell to *yishuv* troops in late April and early May. In these two areas, that is, along the coast and in eastern Galilee, that left only the villages which had not already fallen. Most of them had enough ammunition for their ancient guns for only a few hours of resistance. They could not turn to the cities for help. Many of these villages fell either at the approach of *yishuv* troops or after a brief battle. Thus, by the time Britain withdrew on May 14 large areas of the coastal plain, eastern Galilee, some of western Galilee, and all of the cities except Gaza, Old Jerusalem, and those of the West Bank "had already been 'cleaned' of most of their Arab inhabitants."[70] Unlike Kfar Etzion, the militarily strategic Jewish settlement on the Hebron-Jerusalem highway that the Arabs destroyed, most, but not all, of the de-Arabized villages had little strategic military value - aside from being inhabited by a virtually unarmed populace that was unhappy to be included within the Jewish state.

While the British were making their final withdrawal, the *yishuv* were still "encouraging" Arab villagers to flee. Survivors described what happened in al-Bassa, about eleven miles north of Acre, after it was occupied by the Hagana on May 14:

The day the village fell, Jewish soldiers ordered all those who remained in the village to gather in the church. They took a few young people - including Salim Darawes and his sister Ellen - outside the church and shot them dead. Soon after, they ordered us to bury them. During the following day, we were transferred to al-Mazra'a....There we met other elderly people gathered from the surrounding villages.[71]

This is one of many eyewitness accounts of *yishuv* atrocities committed *before* statehood and therefore before Truman recognized Israel as a state.

By May 14, when Truman recognized Israel as the *de facto* government of the areas allotted to it by the UN, most Arabs within those areas had either been driven from their homes or fled. In either case, according to the Fourth Hague Convention of 1907, they had a right to return home in this sense: "It is especially forbidden to destroy or seize the enemy's property, unless such destruction or seizure be imperatively demanded by the necessities of war" (Article 23g; cf. Appendix Two).[72] Moreover, the Fourth Hague Convention stipulates that "private property...must be respected" (Article 46),[73] "pillage is formally forbidden" (Article 47),[74] and the property of municipalities, that of institutions dedicated to religion, charity and education, the arts and sciences, even when State property, shall be treated as private property (Article 56).[75] Many who fled fully expected to return within a few days or weeks. Most of them have never been allowed by Israel to return. Truman urged the Jews to allow them to but he did not fully use his influence first over the *yishuv* and then over Israel to gain the refugees' return. Israel did offer that as part of a peace treaty it would allow 100,000 Arabs to return, a fraction of those who had a right to. The Israeli-Egyptian peace treaty of 1979 was not a comprehensive treaty which included the other Arab states with which Israel was technically still at war. The 100,000 refugees were not allowed to return.

XIV. American Zigzagging at the UN, May 1948.

On April 23 Truman secretly informed Weizmann that if UNGA did not change the partition plan, and if the *yishuv* declared a Jewish state, he would recognize it. On May 11 Niles told Truman that a poll showed that 80 percent of the U.S. press favored recognition if statehood were declared. Moreover, added Niles, most Democrats and Republicans in Congress and most governors supported recognition. Did this support stem from politicians' personal conviction or from election year realities? According to Cohen, Truman "was deluged by appeals for recognition from prominent Jewish figures."[76] Lowenthal, with Clifford, had prepared a brief given to Truman on May 9. It asserted that as soon as the *yishuv* declared a state there would be great domestic pressure, including Republican pressure, for quick recognition. Lowenthal argued that recognition was in the best national interest. Eleanor Roosevelt, a member of America's UN delegation, wrote to Truman that she personally believed in a Jewish state. Zionists had told her that the Soviets planned to recognize Israel as soon as it was declared. She urged Truman to beat them to the punch. State, still trying to isolate policy making from domestic politics, hotly opposed recognition.[77] This clash between White House aides and Truman on one side and State on the other sharpened during the final two days before Israel was due to be declared. Zionist pressure also greatly increased.

On Friday, May 14, at 4:00 pm in Tel Aviv (10:00 am, EDT), Ben-Gurion proclaimed that the State of Israel would begin at midnight (6:00 pm, EDT). He did not say what its geographic boundaries would be. However, the Israeli Proclamation of Independence promised that its leaders would be "ready to cooperate with the organs and representatives of the United Nations in the implementation of the Resolution of the Assembly of November 29, 1947."[78] That resolution called for establishing an Arab state in part of Palestine. Thus Israel promised to be ready to cooperate with the UN in establishing an Arab state in part of Palestine.

After a day of wrangling between Clifford and State's Lovett over when Truman would announce recognition, Clifford, at 5:45 pm, EDT, phoned Dean Rusk, head of State's UN desk in Washington, that Truman would make his announcement shortly after 6:00 pm - in just a few minutes. Rusk objected that this would conflict with the U.S. delegation's efforts going on at that very moment at the UN to arrange a truce in Palestine, and that these efforts had most nations' support. Clifford responded that Truman would go ahead anyway. Rusk phoned Ambassador Austin at the UN to warn him. Austin did not go to the UNGA meeting room to inform the U.S. delegation. Instead he let its members manifest their surprise before the rest of the UN delegates so that they would know that the American delegates were not privy to Truman's decision.[79] At 6:11 pm Truman publicly announced U.S. recognition of the State of Israel as the *de facto* government of the area allotted to it by the UN declaration of November 29, 1947. Within a few minutes the U.S. delegation learned that the announcement was on the UN teletype. Reportedly a copy was retrieved from a waste basket in the office of UN Secretary General Trygve Lie. It was given to Phillip Jessup, a U.S. delegation member, who called Washington for confirmation and then publicly read Truman's statement from the retrieved piece of scrap paper.[80]

Cuba's delegate (pre-Castro Cuba, then friendly with America) tried to go to the rostrum to announce his country's withdrawal from the UN in protest against U.S. duplicity. However, a U.S. delegation staff member physically kept him from leaving his seat. Marshall sent Rusk to New York to keep his delegation from resigning *en masse*. Marshall reportedly stated privately that America "had hit its all-time low before the UN."[81] Four days later Austin wired Marshall that Truman's action "has deeply undermined the confidence of other delegations in our integrity." Austin pointed out that in the view of many delegations:

although the Jews had not accepted the truce they disregarded the admonitions of the SC, violated spirit of truce effort, and prevented conclusion of formal truce. US immediately not only condoned but endorsed these violations, thus striking heavy blow at prospect of concluding any truce and equally heavy blow at prestige and effectiveness of SC and UN generally.[82]

Austin said that delegations believe that the "US...violated the terms of the SC truce resolution." He added that "other delegations, such as those of Canada, [pre-communist] China, and a number of Latin American states," frankly feel "double-crossed."[83] Several delegations told Eleanor Roosevelt, a member of the U.S. delegation, that they would certainly be reluctant to back American projects again "because the United States changed so often without any consultation."[84]

As author Richard Stevens notes, citing Arthur Koestler, thus there was "brought into existence a state which, by Zionist admission, constitutes an 'historic injustice' from the viewpoint of national sovereignty and self-determination."[85]

Chapter Ten

TRUMAN - PART 3;
THE FIRST ISRAELI-ARAB WAR AND ITS REFUGEES

1948-53

I. Internationalization of the Palestine War, May 1948.

Five Arab states, Lebanon, Syria, Trans-Jordan, Egypt and Iraq, warned the *yishuv* that if it declared a Jewish state they would attack. It seems clear that from the viewpoint of morality the UN partition vote of November 29, 1947, was an act of diplomatic aggression primarily because it gave to the Jewish state so much Arab land and Arab people. The declaration of Israel's statehood on May 14, 1948, did not specify its borders, but it did not repudiate the areas allotted to it by the UN. Clearly Israel intended to incorporate all of these areas, including those that were almost entirely Arab. The statehood declaration thus ratified the diplomatic aggression committed by the *yishuv*, and by America on its behalf, in the days leading up to the partition vote on November 29. It would thus seem that the Arab states' declaration of war on May 15 was a declaration of a defensive war to the extent that it was intended as a protection against Israeli aggression. As noted above, by that time the *yishuv* had already expelled many Arabs from their homes while the British still theoretically controlled Palestine. This situation strengthens the argument that the Arab states entered an already existing war to defend other Arabs. However, *if* the Arab states also intended to repossess land that Jews had legally purchased in a moral manner, the moral issues become more difficult to unravel. It seems quite clear that the *yishuv* at that time did not have a moral right to a state that included so many Arabs and their land. It also seems clear that the *yishuv* had a right to their own property. However, they did not have a right to use it as a base for launching aggression against

163

Arab Palestinians. Moreover, the *yishuv* may have had a moral right to form a state on the 5-6 percent of Palestine that they owned. However, this would have been such a checkerboard that it would have been impractical and perhaps would also have interfered with the rights of their Arab neighbors.

Ben-Gurion had strong reasons for declaring statehood despite the Arab states' warning that such a move would precipitate a war with them. Moreover, he apparently thought war had advantages for the new state and was winnable. In early August 1948 he told *Time*, "I can quite imagine a Jewish state of ten million." Asked if that many Jews could live within the area the UN had allotted to the Jewish state, he replied, "I doubt it." Then he added the significant statement, "We would not have *taken on* this war merely for the purpose of enjoying this tiny state."[1] Ben-Gurion thus seemingly indicated (a) that Israel could have avoided the 1948 war had it so chosen and (b) that it actually "took on" the war to expand its territory. This would seem to make it a war of aggression.

Although the five Arab states declared war on Israel they did not recognize it as a state. They immediately sent troops, including small contingents from Saudi Arabia and Yemen, into Palestine. It was hardly an all-out effort. The total Arab military sent against Israel was about 25,000-32,000 men, plus some poorly armed Palestinians.[2] With the exception of Trans-Jordan's British-trained Arab Legion, most of the Arab troops were poorly armed, poorly trained, and poorly led. Most had no experience in modern warfare. An Iraqi general was in nominal command of the whole operation but had almost no authority. The five states' leaders distrusted each other and therefore reserved to their own generals the effective command of their own troops. Four of the states allegedly entered the war not only to fight Israel but to keep the fifth state, Trans-Jordan, from dividing Palestine with Israel - an idea Emir Abdullah and *yishuv* officials discussed on several occasions, though nothing came of it.

Verbally the leaders of the five states entered the war whole-heartedly. However, their uncoordinated military probes certainly did not equal their rhetoric. Leaders of most of the states had severe economic and social problems at home. Saving Palestine was definitely not their top priority. However, their rhetoric was so bellicose that rescuing Palestine became a high priority and expectation among their own citizens. The Arab leaders were caught in their own propaganda. Moreover, Britain had warned Abdullah not to allow his Arab Legion to move beyond the line drawn by the UN partition resolution, that is, into the area allotted to Israel. This prohibition hurt the Legion militarily because it gave the IDF a safe base from which to operate, whereas the Legion's own area was subject to IDF attack. If the IDF was losing a battle it needed merely to retreat to the sanctuary behind the line, rearm, regroup, and attack again. Initially the Arabs were better armed than the Israelis, and Egypt had an air force. However, Britain prevented the Arabs from resupplying their armies, so that they lacked ammunition and replacement parts.

On May 15, 1948, Israel had 35,000-80,000 soldiers. They were soon joined by Jewish volunteers from other countries, including U.S. citizens. American law forbids fighting for a foreign country without U.S. permission. Israeli troops, except perhaps for new recruits, were usually more highly motivated, much better trained, and better led than Arab troops. Some 20,000-25,000 had military experience during World War II.[3] Despite jealousies and disputes in the Israeli general staff, it was reasonably well coordinated. Initially many Israeli troops were poorly armed but shortly after statehood Israel purchased and smuggled large quantities of arms and substantially improved its equipment. It soon acquired its first warplanes. Thus from the beginning of the phase of the war that started May 15, the Arabs were outpersoned, outled, outtrained and outmotivated. Soon after that date they were out armed. Essentially they were beaten before they began, which may help explain why some of their leaders entered the war so reluctantly. Israel soon retook areas it had initially lost to Arab soldiers and captured much land that the UN had allotted to the Arab state.

II. The Dispute Over Why Refugees Left Their Homes.

Meanwhile, as noted in the preceding chapter, Arab civilians were driven out of or were fleeing cities and towns in the area allotted by the UN to Israel. This exodus started well before May 15; most refugees originated from this earlier period rather than from post-May 14 fighting. The *yishuv*, and later Israel, refused to let most refugees return home. This refusal was not in accord with the Hague Conventions. (Cf. Appendix Two.) Although Israel was not a signatory of the Hague Conventions, they reflect some basic human moral rights in the conduct of warfare and are looked to as international law. Israel tried to justify its refusal to let the refugees return, by arguing that they had left voluntarily. Israel maintained that because they left their homes they forfeited any moral or legal right to them. At the same time, as noted in Chapter Two, Israel argued that Jews, whose ancestors had left their homes centuries earlier, had a right to come in and take the property.

Israel maintains that the Arabs left because they had been instructed by Arab leaders, on Arab radio stations, to leave the area allotted to Israel so that they would be out of harm's way when Arab armies invaded the area.[4] Arabs deny that such broadcasts ever took place. They make four points to support this:

1. The British Broadcasting Corporation (BBC) monitored the Mideast stations; its records indicate no such broadcasts.

2. According to Sayigh, the first known source of the "Arab orders" charge was a pamphlet distributed by Israel's Information Office in New York City many months after the war's end. The allegation was later put into a statement "presented by 19 prominent Americans to the U.N."[5] British writer Erskine Childers also investigated the charge that Arab leaders had broadcast instructions to Arabs to leave: "The charge, Israel claimed, was 'documented;' but where were the documents?....no dates, names of stations, or texts of messages were ever cited."[6] Childers added that Israel's Foreign Office assured him in 1958 that the proofs existed and repeatedly agreed to provide them to him but as of April 1961 had not.

3. Sayigh maintains that there is evidence that the Arab Higher Committee in Damascus broadcast pleas to Arabs to remain in their homes and *not* to flee.[7] According to Childers, in 1961 the British government still possessed "repeated monitored record of Arab [radio] appeals, even flat orders, to the civilians of Palestine *to stay put.*" He then gave two examples from April 4 and 24, 1948.[8] However, the impact of these leaders' directives was weakened because the leaders themselves were safely out of the war zone.[9]

4. Only when Arab soldiers were about to *retreat* from an area did they warn Arab villagers that they were about to leave, in case the villagers wanted to flee while they still had military protection. "Only in the case of one or two cities, for instance, Haifa, could local Arab authorities be said to have 'ordered' flight by organizing evacuation. But in most of the country there was not even this slight degree of organization."[10]

Many Arabs, aware of massacres at Deir Yassin and elsewhere, were extremely afraid of the Israeli military. The IDF produced a booklet in which Lt. Col. Rabbi Abraham Avidan (Zemel), Chief Rabbi of the Central Command, wrote an article, "An Army Rabbi Calls for the Killing of Civilians." In that article he stated that when Israeli forces encounter Arab civilians during the war the soldiers "may, and by Halachic [religious] standards even must... [kill them if] it cannot be ascertained that they are incapable of hitting us back."[11] Rabbi Avidan added that an Arab should never be trusted "even if he gives the impression of being civilized." The rabbi justified this policy by citing a highly authoritative interpretation of the Babylonian Talmud, which is second only to the Bible as a source of Jewish moral law. He said that in the opinion of the Tosafot, when Israeli troops attack the enemy during war "they may, and by Halachic [religious] standards even must, kill conforming civilians," that is, "civilians whose conduct is proper." Rabbi Avidan cited the religious opinion that in such a case it is proper to "'Kill the best of the Gentiles.'" He contended that "no trust should be accorded a Gentile who will not bring harm to our troops" because in some phase of the fighting the Gentile may cause harm either by supplying resources or information to the enemy.[12]

Israeli historian Arieh Yitzhaqi, for many years a researcher in the history section of the IDF, lists several Arab villages where the Israeli military seemingly followed this policy, at least to some extent. He claimed that the Palmach itself engaged in operations similar to those used by the Irgun and the Stern Gang at Deir Yassin: He cites the night attack by the Carmel Brigade on the village of Balad el-Sheikh, mentioned in the preceding chapter, in which more than sixty Arabs, mostly non-combatants, were killed in their homes.[13] On the night of February 14-15, 1948, a force of the Third Palmach Battalion raided the village of Sa'sa' and blew up twenty houses while people were in them, killing some sixty Arabs, mostly women and children.[14] On May 21, 1948, Israeli troops attacked al-Ghabisiya. They shelled the villagers as they fled, killing and injuring many of them.[15] On July 12, 1948, in Lydda, where the IDF said the Arabs revolted, any Arab seen in the streets was fired on; Israeli troops entered homes and fired at every moving target; 250 Arabs were killed. One Palmach commander admitted firing into rooms containing women and children.[16] In October 1948 some fifty to seventy men were herded into the mosque in the Lebanese border town of Hula and machine-gunned. The mosque was then blown up to entomb them.[17] In Ed-Dawayimeh, near Hebron, some two hundred Arabs, mostly elderly who could not flee, took refuge in the village mosque, where the Israelis massacred all of them.[18] Rosemary Sayigh notes that "mass killings" were also carried out by ordinary units of the Haganah in 'Ain al-Zeitouneh and al-Bina.[19]

As noted above, the Israeli military played on Arabs' fear resulting from reports of these atrocities. Yigal Allon, a Palmach leader in 1948 and later a member of the Israeli cabinet and a deputy prime minister, is quoted as having written:

> We saw a need to clean the inner Galilee and to create a Jewish territorial succession in the entire area of the Upper Galilee....We therefore looked for means which did not force us into employing force, in order to cause the tens of thousands of sulky (sic) Arabs who remained in Galilee to

flee....We tried to use a tactic which took advantage of the impression created by the fall of Safed and the (Arab) defeat in the area which was cleaned by Operation Metateh - a tactic which worked miraculously well!

I gathered all the Jewish mukhtars, who have contacts with Arabs in different villages, and asked them to whisper in the ears of some Arabs, that a great Jewish reinforcement has arrived in Galilee and that it is going to burn all the villages of Huleh. They should suggest to these Arabs, as their friends, to escape while there is still time.[20]

After May 14 the IDF continued to expel Arabs from the area allotted to Israel. In many cases it would start shelling a village late at night, without warning. Lt. Col. Yosef Tabenkin, the commander of Harel, one of three Palmach brigades, wrote a description of a typical plan for a night attack on a village by a Palmach unit during the 1948-49 war. According to the plan a detachment of sappers - explosives experts - joins the Israeli force attacking the village. As soon as the village is captured the sappers begin to destroy positions and buildings. "A unit specially chosen by the command, and no one else, begins to collect the booty."[21] When the attack is finished the force completely withdraws. As examples of how the plan had worked in action, Col. Tabenkin cited the capture of the villages of Biddu and Beit Surik.

Thus, testimony regarding *yishuv* actions is given not only by Palestinians but also by *yishuv*. These villages were near Abu Gosh on the Jerusalem-Lydda road, an area of several strategic villages. Israelis sometimes destroyed strategic villages they could not hold because they did not want them reoccupied by Arab military. (But cf. pp. 158-59.)

Nafez Nazzal interviewed many eyewitnesses of *yishuv* and Israeli military actions. Although he perhaps did not always obtain corroborating witnesses of the same incidents, the experiences told by the refugees reveal a pattern of actions by members of the *yishuv* military and the Israeli military. For example:

On March 28, 1948, villagers from Kabri in western Galilee destroyed a *yishuv* armored convoy. On May 21, in the ensuing battle for Kabri itself, *yishuv* soldiers took Amina Musa and her husband, with other captured villagers, to an officer. The men were then led away and at least her husband was shot dead. The prisoners' wives were abandoned on the Kabri-Tarshiha road. The next morning Amina Musa found her husband's body; she and another woman buried him. She stayed in the village six days without eating and then left.[22]

On the night of July 9/10 the IDF surrounded three sides of the village of Kuweikat, a few kilometers east of Acre, and attacked it with artillery. A villager recalled: "'We were awakened...shells exploding and artillery fire...the whole village was in panic. ...Most of the villagers began to flee with their pajamas on. The wife of Qassim Ahmed Sa'id fled carrying a pillow in her arms instead of her child.'"[23] In the panic and confusion of fleeing, especially in the middle of the night, it was common for families to become separated and children to get lost.[24] Interviewees told Nazzal that although old people were sometimes allowed to stay on in their villages or in nearby caves, this was not always true. In December 1948 Israelis ordered villagers, including the elderly, into an open truck and drove them in the rain to Zububa, near Jenin. "When they reached the border the Israelis ordered them to cross to the Arab side. Many of the villagers were too sick to walk and were left behind in the rain. No one knows what happened to Nimr's parents."[25]

These are a few of many eyewitness accounts of atrocities. In what sense can one claim that these people left their homes and lands voluntarily?

Wealthier Arabs who fled to Lebanon during the early months of the war, before they would have been driven out, found lodging. But many people driven from their villages and forced to flee the new state of Israel found themselves shelterless just beyond the Israeli-West Bank frontier. An article in the *Economist* recorded that in the hills at Bir Zeit, north of Jerusalem, about 14,000 destitute refugees were ranged on terrace upon terrace under olive trees - a tree to a family. They were forced to eat the bark and burn the wood of trees that had provided livelihood for generations but were now being destroyed. Both at Bir Zeit and at

Nablus, the *Economist* reported, there was little milk for babies.[26]

Count Folke Bernadotte, the UN mediator for Palestine, wrote:
I have made the acquaintance of a great many refugee camps; but I have never seen a more ghastly sight than that which met my eyes here, at Ramallah [a West Bank city north of Jerusalem and still the site of a refugee camp in 1995]. The car was literally stormed by excited masses shouting...that they wanted food and wanted to return to their homes. There were plenty of frightening faces in that sea of suffering humanity. I remember not least a group of scabby and helpless old men with tangled beards who thrust their emaciated faces into the car and held out scraps of bread that would certainly have been considered quite uneatable by ordinary people, but was their only food.[27]

The fact that 7 percent of the Arabs remained in Israel was due in some cases to Jews urging them not to flee. For instance, Tuvia Arazi, a Jewish Agency official, urged Arabs not to flee Haifa.[28] Was the expulsion and encouraged flight of 93 percent of the (non-Bedouin) Palestinian Arabs only a war measure to eliminate what a pro-Zionist referred to as a potential fifth column, or was it also intended to clear Israel of non-Jews permanently? In their dealings with Arab leaders, Zionist leaders stressed that their goals were peaceful and no threat to Palestinian Arabs. However, for many years they had discussed with British individuals and among themselves the possibility of deporting Arabs from Palestine. In 1940 Joseph Weitz, an official of the *yishuv* responsible for Jewish colonization, noted in his diary:
Between ourselves it must be clear that there is no room for both peoples together in this country....We shall not achieve our goal of being an independent people with the Arabs in this small country. The only solution is a Palestine, at least Western Palestine (west of the Jordan river (sic)) without Arabs....And there is no other way than to transfer the Arabs from here to the neighbouring countries, to transfer all of them; not one village, not one tribe, should be left.[29]

Writing again in 1950, while head of the Jewish National

Fund's department of land and afforestation, Weitz wrote more publicly:

> The struggle for the redemption of the land means...*the liberation of the land from the hand of the stranger*, from the chains of wilderness; the struggle for its conquest by settlement, and...the redemption of the settler, both as a human being and as a Jew, through his deep attachment to the soil he tills.[30]

Thus this high official wanted the land to be somehow transferred from Arab to Jewish ownership and use. Weitz sees the redemption of Jewish settlers through deep attachment to soil they have just acquired. Yet he seems oblivious to the deep attachment Arab farmers may have had to that same soil, which their families had tilled for generations. Weitz did not just show great concern for the redemption of Jews and seemingly none for the redemption of Arabs. He also envisioned the redemption of Jews at the expense of the Arabs. This double standard continually manifests itself in both Israeli literature and action. America, by its actions, loyally supported and continues to support this double standard.

In June 1948 Prime Minister David Ben-Gurion ordered that the government should "see to the settling of the abandoned villages."[31] Thus, immediately after statehood, he moved to have Arab homes become occupied by Jews.

British Army Major Edgar O'Ballance, in his book, *The Arab-Israeli War 1948*, states that "Arab leaders...early in the war had ordered Arabs *living on the edges of the 'mixed' areas* to evacuate their villages so as to leave the field clear for the Arab Liberation Army to conduct military operations."[32] But he also indicates that Zionist forces applied pressure to promote what he terms "an unusual feature" of the war, "the complete and voluntary evacuation of the Arabs from their towns and villages as the Jews advanced."[33] He notes in passing that "as the Jews advanced and took Arab villages, they expelled the inhabitants, and blew up the place if they did not want to occupy it themselves...."[34] This was hardly "voluntary evacuation" by the Arabs. O'Ballance emphasizes Zionist use of 'psychological' methods: "It was the Jewish policy to encourage the Arabs to quit their homes, and they used psychological warfare extensively in urging them to do so. Later, as the war wore on, *they ejected those Arabs who clung to their villages.*"[35] Concerning the suffering this created, O'Ballance blandly concludes:

This policy, which had such amazing success, had two distinct advantages. First, it gave the Arab countries a vast refugee problem to cope with, which their elementary economy and administrative machinery were in no way capable of attacking, and secondly, it ensured that the Jews had no fifth column in their midst.[36]

One of the bitter ironies of this situation was that the Arabs, much against their will, had been allotted by the UN to the Jewish state. Then they were considered a threat to that state and forced to move out of it. The reverse side of this was that the Zionists demanded that the UN allot to the Jewish state territory that was heavily populated by Arabs. Once it was allotted, the Zionists expelled them as a threat to that state. This situation again raises the question: Had at least some highly placed Zionists long intended that somehow the Arabs would leave the Jewish state?

This much is clear: Some of the very people who wanted America to solve Jewish refugee problems, at least knowingly created the Palestinian refugee problem. One is reminded of what Weizmann said at a March 1, 1943, rally at Madison Square Garden concerning the Holocaust:

When the historian of the future assembles the bleak record of our days, he will find two things unbelievable; first the crime itself, second the reaction of the world to that crime ....He will be puzzled by the apathy of the civilized world in the face of this immense, systematic carnage of human beings ....He will not be able to understand why the conscience of the world had to be stirred. Above all, he will not be able to understand why the free nations...required appeals to give sanctuary to the first and chief victim of that barbarism ....The world can no longer plead that the ghastly facts are unknown or unconfirmed.[37]

The Truman Administration and Congress would not have known of all of the atrocities but they certainly were in a position to know of some of them from their own intelligence apparatus and the reports of the UN peacekeepers in the Holy Land. They were well aware of the refugees.

Arab villages which resisted IDF attacks soon depleted their meager ammunition - usually within a few hours. In some villages, for instance, al-Ghabsiyeh, the IDF directly fired on fleeing villagers. Palestinian casualties were high and medical resources in such circumstances were virtually non-existent. After occupying a village, IDF sappers would often blow up its houses.[38] In al-Zib, for example, the remaining villagers "said that the Jewish soldiers had destroyed most of the al-Ramel area south of the village, and the eastern section."[39] Thus the IDF continued Palmach policies.

Sometimes, after a village fell, some people tried to remain. Consequences varied. The villagers of Mi'ilya were permitted to return after they had fled; this was a rare case. Sometimes the elderly were allowed to remain or were removed to other villages. However, arrest, imprisonment, deportation or being killed were the lot of most individuals who attempted to stay or were caught trying to return to their homes. For example, in al-Bi'na, al-Bassa, Kabri, Mejd al-Kroon and Safsaf, mass killings were used to frighten everyone into fleeing. Mass deportation was common.[40] After the war ended, only one of fifteen non-Bedouin Arabs (60,000) remained in Israeli-controlled territory.

As to whether Arabs left voluntarily or not, Nathan Chofshi, a Russian Jew who moved to Palestine in 1908, and who witnessed the Arabs' departure, wrote:

we Jews forced the Arabs to leave....Here was a people who lived on its own land for 1,300 years. We came and turned the native Arabs into tragic refugees. And still we dare to slander and malign them, to besmirch their name. Instead of being deeply ashamed of what we did and of trying to undo some of the evil we committed by helping these unfortunate refugees, we justify our terrible acts and even attempt to glorify them.[41]

Erich Fromm, a Jewish author, wrote:

It is often said that the Arabs fled, that they left the country voluntarily, and that they therefore bear the responsibility for losing their property and their land. It is true that in history there are some instances - in Rome and in France during the Revolutions - when enemies of the state were proscribed and their property confiscated. But in general international law, the principle holds true that no citizen loses his property or his rights of citizenship; and the citizenship right is *de facto* a right to which the Arabs in Israel have much more legitimacy than the Jews. Just because the Arabs fled? Since when is that punishable by confiscation of property and by being barred from returning to the land on which a people's forefathers have lived for generations? Thus, the claim of the Jews to the land of Israel cannot be a realistic political claim. If all nations would suddenly claim territories in which their forefathers had lived two thousand years ago, this world would be a madhouse.[42]

Erich Fromm added: "there is only one solution for Israel, namely, the unilateral acknowledgement of the obligation of the state toward the Arabs - not to use it as a bargaining point, but to acknowledge the complete moral obligation of the Israeli state to its former inhabitants of Palestine."[43]

In its October 2, 1948, issue, the *Economist* urged sending humanitarian aid to the refugees. It did not ask for an inquiry into the causes of their exodus. Sayigh maintains that this became the principal Western response to the problem: give material aid to the refugees but ignore the political causes.[44]

In that same article the *Economist* estimated that there were 360,000 refugees, but Sayigh contends that there were at least twice that many. She estimates that this was the approximate redistribution of Palestinian Arabs during 1948 and early 1949:[45]

Table Two: Redistribution of Palestinian Arabs:

Arab population of Palestine early 1948:	1,400,000
Arabs in 77% of Pal. that became Israel:	900,000
Arabs in first Israeli census*: about	60,000
Total displaced from Israel: about	840,000
Prewar population of West Bank:	425,000
Refugees from Israel to West Bank:	360,000
Postwar population of West Bank:	785,000
Prewar population of Gaza: about	80,000
Refugees from Israel to Gaza:	200,000
Postwar population of Gaza:	280,000
Refugees to Lebanon:	104,000
Refugees to Syria:	82,000
Refugees to Trans-Jordan:	100,000
Refugees to other countries:	14,000
All Palestinians displaced from Pal.:some	300,000
Total Palestinian refugees:	860,000
Discrep. with all displaced from Israel:	20,000
Palestinians killed in 1948 war:	15,000
*Excludes Bedouin	

Some of these figures are disputed, especially by Israelis. Bachi estimates that 614,000-626,000 Arabs left Israel.[46] In addition to these, of the approximately 60,000 non-nomadic Arabs[47] who stayed within the state of Israel, some were forcibly moved by Israeli authorities out of their own homes and into houses of Arabs who had left. For example, in 1972 Haj 'Ali Fayyad went to visit al-Birwa, which had been his home village before it fell. He discovered that, like many other Arab places taken over by the Israelis, it had disappeared. "When I arrived there, there was no al-Birwa. The village was levelled and the few Arabs who remained had been transferred to other villages. The Jews had built a new village in place of ours."[48]

America, especially through the UN, has helped provide food, clothing, housing and medical aid for the Palestinian refugees outside of Israel. But in his *Memoirs*, Truman expresses no feelings of compassion for them. He repeatedly expressed great concern for Jewish DPs, whose deplorable situation he had done nothing, or virtually nothing, to initiate. He expressed no concern, at least in his *Memoirs*, for the Palestinian refugees, whose deplorable situation he knew was developing but which arguably he allowed to transpire.[49]

III. The Expulsion of Jews From Old Jerusalem, May 1948.

Jews had lived in Jerusalem's walled city during most of the time since Arabs conquered it in 638. On May 28, 1948, the Arab Legion captured its Jewish Quarter and safely escorted all its surviving residents through angry Arabs to the Jewish New City, a few blocks away. Ancestors of some of these residents had lived in the Jewish Quarter for generations. Probably most of the survivors were anti-Zionists. They too were not allowed to return to their homes at the end of hostilities - a violation of the Fourth Hague Convention of October 18, 1907, because their homes were seized. (Cf. Appendix Two.) They returned only after Israel conquered the Old City in 1967. Thus Arabs were as unjust to these Jews as the Israelis were to the Arabs whom they either drove or frightened out of their homes.

IV. UN Truce, July; Bernadotte's Murder, Sept. 1948.

The UN arranged two truces, the second of which went into effect on July 19 (Palestine time), 1948. It left Israel with five hundred square miles of land that had been allotted by the UN partition plan to the Arab state. This included 112 Arab villages. Arab forces retained 129 square miles and fourteen sites that had been allotted to the Jewish state.[50] Thus Israel gained a net 371 additional square miles. However, both sides in the truce agreed that the new truce line was not a permanent border but only a cease-fire line. Some fifteen thousand Arab and six thousand Israeli military personnel and civilians died in the war, one human life for about every three hundred acres of Palestine's soil. Many more would die in the decades to come.

Despite the truces, both sides committed frequent small, localized violations, such as sniper fire and looting. Many displaced Palestinians tried to return to their homes and shops - if they were still standing - to retrieve belongings. Cease fire lines cut through many Arabs' farms, so that their homes were on the Arab side but their fields on the Israeli side. These farmers tried to return to their fields to work them. Israel called these acts "hostile infiltration" and killed many "infiltrators." However, some Israelis, because of UN mediators, allowed Arab farmers to cross the cease-fire line to work their fields.[51] But when harvest time came, Israelis often did not allow them to cross but harvested the fields for themselves.[52] It is difficult to see how this was anything but outright robbery of civilian property, an action prohibited to signatories by Article 47 of the Annex of Hague Convention IV. (Cf. Appendix Two.) Between December 1, 1951, and November 30, 1952, four years after the Arabs fled, Israelis killed 394 Arabs who tried to return, injured 227 and captured 2,595. During that same period sixty-nine Israelis were killed, seventy-nine wounded and thirty-six kidnapped.[53]

The UN mediator, Folke Bernadotte, reported on August 12 that in the Jerusalem area "the Jews have generally speaking though not on all occasions been the more aggressive party since the renewal of the truce."[54] However, on September 16 he reported that Arabs had cut off Jerusalem's water supply, including water to its Jewish civilians; Arab irregular troops were suspected of blowing up a plant pumping water to the city.[55] On August 19 the UNSC passed Resolution 981 sponsored by America, Britain and France. It forbade both sides (a) to break the truce on the ground of reprisals or (b) to gain military or political advantage through truce violations.

Bernadotte's lengthy September 16 progress report contained his recommendations to UNGA. He told it that the refugees' "unconditional right to make a free choice [between return and compensation for lost property] should be fully respected."[56] He stated:

no settlement can be just and complete if recognition is not accorded to the right of the Arab refugee to return to the home from which he has been dislodged....It would be an offence against the principles of elemental justice if these innocent victims of the conflict were denied the right of return to their homes while Jewish immigrants flow into Palestine, and indeed, at least offer the threat of permanent replacement of the Arab refugees who have been rooted in the land for centuries.[57]

Bernadotte added:

There have been numerous reports from reliable sources of large-scale looting, pillaging and plundering, and of instances of destruction of villages without apparent military necessity. The liability of the Provisional Government of Israel to restore private property to its Arab owners and to indemnify those owners for property wantonly destroyed, is clear.[58]

Bernadotte favored redrawing Palestine's map to change boundaries drawn by the UN partition plan so that it would be less of a patchwork. This would make areas allotted to the Jewish state more contiguous, and thus reduce the need to travel through areas allotted to Arabs. The same would be true for the Arab areas. Israel objected that there should be no change from the boundaries set forth in Resolution 181 of November 29, 1947. Israel stated that 181 "was a valid instrument of international law, while the conclusions in the Mediator's report were merely the views of a distinguished individual which were not embodied in any decision of a United Nations organ."[59] As noted below, within a few months Israel reversed its position when a part of Resolution 181's allocation provision no longer suited its purpose.

Bernadotte urged UNGA to take prompt, firm action to execute his report's recommendations. On September 17, the day after he released them, he was gunned down - by Israelis, according to eyewitnesses - in the Israeli-held part of Jerusalem. Israel never apprehended his murderers. Both Israel and the Arabs opposed Bernadotte's plan; nothing came of it. Both sides reinforced their armies, so that by October 1948 Arab forces were about 50,000-55,000 and Israeli forces were some 75,000-120,000.[60]

V. America's Support of Israeli Truce Violations, 1948-49.

A few days before Bernadotte's murder, Israel had planned a major truce violation - an attack on the Arab Legion in West Bank. But his murder created so much world opinion against Israel that it delayed the offensive. A month later, politically protected by the U.S. presidential campaign, Israel opened the first of three offensives. (Cf. Map Four.) On October 14 it launched "Operation Ten Plagues" against Egyptian forces in the Negev. It overran their lightly held positions and surrounded a large Egyptian and Sudanese unit at Faluja.[61] Ralph Bunche, an American who had become acting UN mediator after Bernadotte's murder, blamed both sides for the truce's breach. But, he asserted, the Israeli "military action of the last few days has been on a scale which could only be undertaken after considerable preparation, and could scarcely be explained as simple retaliatory action for an attack on a [Israeli] convoy."[62] Bunche ordered Israel to stop its offensive and return to its pre-October 14 lines. Israel refused, saying that it "stands by its claim to the whole of the Negev."[63] Thus Israel scrapped the truce pact it had signed less than three months before the offensive.

Bunche and other UN leaders saw the issue as a test of UN authority. He asked the UNSC to order a cease-fire and the return of Israeli troops to their pre-October 14 positions. Britain and China sponsored a resolution demanding this under pain of possible sanctions. Marshall supported it. Truman, facing in a few days an election that many Americans thought he would lose, ordered the U.S. delegation at the UN not to support the resolution. Canada then entered a milder resolution which the UNSC passed on November 4. Although it threatened sanctions, both America and the Soviets indicated they would not support strong sanctions. Thus Truman undercut Bunche's authority and again reminded Israel, if it needed reminding, that while he was president it had little to fear from the UN.[64] Truman's actions also undercut the UNSC's Resolution 981 of August 19, which America had cosponsored. That is the resolution which forbade both sides (a) to break the truce on the ground of reprisals or (b) to gain military or political advantage through truce violations. Truman thus used the power of his office and America's power in the UN in such a way that Palestinian rights would be continually violated in the future.

Meanwhile, on October 28, a few days before the elections, even as the UN debated how to react to Israel's Negev offensive, Israel launched its second offensive, to conquer western Galilee. Israel could not claim this area as its own because it had been allotted by the UN plan to the Arabs. Again Bunche ordered Israel to withdraw to the truce lines, but it refused. He also reported that Israeli troops were looting Arab villages. Israel continued its offensive until it conquered all of western Galilee and about 15 villages in southern Lebanon. The campaign spawned a new movement of refugees into Lebanon - and a new, ineffectual resolution passed by the UNSC on November 16.[65]

Thus in its Negev offensive, Israel claimed it had a right to land assigned to it by the UN but which was in Arab hands at the time of the July 19 armistice. In its western Galilee offensive, Israel refused to recognize Arabs' rights to land assigned to Arabs by the UN. By this offensive Israel violated both its signed truce agreement of July 19 and its promise to honor the terms of the partition plan of UNGA Resolution 181 of November 29, 1947. In his *Memoirs*, Truman asserted that "all promises made by responsible, civilized governments should be kept."[66] But when Israel repeatedly broke its truce agreements Truman was strangely less insistent. On the contrary, on November 29, in the wake of several truce violations by Israel, Truman wrote to Weizmann, who was by then Israel's first president: "how happy and impressed I have been at the remarkable progress made by the new State of Israel....you have more than made the most of what you have received, and I admire you for it."[67] In that letter Truman talks approvingly of "a substantial long-term loan to Israel" then being arranged by the U.S. Export-Import Bank. He utters no criticism of the truce violations in which Israel had just been engaged.

Three weeks after Truman sent his letter, on December 22, Israel launched its third offensive. It was a second major offensive against Egyptian forces in the Negev. Israel said it was in response to a series of "provocations." Bunche rejected this, stating, "I have no knowledge of any incidents which could be claimed as a provocation for the fighting in the Negeb."[68] He cited several ways in which Israel had not complied with UN resolutions or his directives. Israel also justified its offensive by claiming that Egypt had not entered into armistice negotiations, as required by the November 16 UNSC resolution. Bunche replied that he believed that Egypt was prepared to negotiate an armistice if Israel would resolve the condition of the Egyptian troops trapped at Faluja. Israel was refusing to allow Egypt to send them food and other non-military supplies even under close UN supervision. UN officials claimed that as Egypt moved closer to negotiation, Israel kept increasing its demands. This delayed the start of negotiations and gave Israel more time to conquer land militarily.[69] On December 29 America abstained as the UNSC passed Resolution S/1163, which was similar to its predecessors in content and lack of effect.

On December 1, 1948, Abdullah announced that Trans-Jordan was annexing the area it occupied, that is, West Bank, including East Jerusalem. This illegal action was strongly objected to by the other Arab states.

On December 10, 1948, UNGA approved the Universal Declaration of Human Rights. Its thirty articles include these:
2: "Everyone is entitled to all the rights and freedoms set forth in the Declaration, without distinction of any kind.... Furthermore, no distinction shall be made on the basis of the political, jurisdictional or international status of the country or territory to which a person belongs, whether it be independent, trust, non-self-governing or under any other limitation of sovereignty."
6: "Everyone has the right to recognition everywhere as a person before the law."
7: "All are equal before the law and are entitled without any discrimination to equal protection of the law. All are entitled to equal protection against any discrimination in violation of this Declaration and against any incitement to such discrimination."

8: "Everyone has the right to an effective remedy by the competent national tribunals for acts violating the fundamental rights granted him by the constitution or by the law."

9: "No one shall be subjected to arbitrary arrest, detention or exile."

10: "Everyone is entitled in full equality to a fair and public hearing by an independent and impartial tribunal, in the determination of his rights and obligations and of any criminal charge against him."

13: "1. Everyone has the right to freedom of movement and residence within the borders of each State. 2. *Everyone has the right to leave any country, including his own, and to return to his country.*"

17: "1. Everyone has the right to own property alone as well as in association with others. 2. No one shall be arbitrarily deprived of his property."

28: "Everyone is entitled to a social and international order in which the rights and freedoms set forth in this Declaration can be fully realized."

30: "Nothing in this Declaration may be interpreted as implying for any State, group or person any right to engage in any activity or to perform any act aimed at the destruction of any of the rights and freedoms set forth herein."[70]

As a UN member, America pledged beginning December 10, 1948, to uphold the Universal Declaration of Human Rights (UDHR). But Truman's Administration, in its actions which impacted Palestinian Arabs, continued to support the violation of its articles. It did this knowing that they were being violated. The UDHR is not a moral code as such but embodies moral principles. It would seem that America repeatedly violated these moral principles by supporting the ongoing violation of the UDHR.

On December 11 UNGA passed Resolution 194, which in Paragraph 11 stated:

that the refugees wishing to return to their homes and live at peace with their neighbours should be permitted to do so at the earliest practicable date, and that compensation should be paid for the property of those choosing not to return and for loss of or damage to property which, under principles of international law or in equity, should be made good by the Governments or authorities responsible.[71]

Resolution 194 also established a Conciliation Commission and in Paragraph 11 instructed it "to facilitate the repatriation, resettlement and economic and social rehabilitation of the refugees and the payment of compensation."[72] Because it was a GA rather than an SC resolution, 194 did not require compliance. Israel, both before and after becoming a UN member, refused to comply. In 1965 Israel unilaterally claimed that this Paragraph 11 of 194 "had long since been made obsolete by the course of events."[73]

As part of Israel's Negev offensive, particularly its advance toward the Gulf of Aqaba, it fought Trans-Jordan's troops south of the Dead Sea. On February 8 Trans-Jordan agreed to enter armistice talks. Israel, however, delayed signing even a preliminary cease-fire agreement until after its troops reached the Gulf on March 10. Even after the two sides signed an agreement on March 11, Israel continued to conquer more of the area - in violation of the agreement it had just signed.[74]

Israel's repeated violations of the July 19, 1948, truce agreement, especially its two major offensives in the Negev, its Galilee offensive, and its Negev warfare with Trans-Jordan, belie the image of a nation under siege. The war was advertized as one in which 600,000 Israelis were being attacked by 40 million Arabs. This was hardly the reality. The U.S. government knew the reality. Despite strong State Department objections, Truman chose to act according to the newly created myths. In doing so he sacrificed the basic rights of some 1.4 million Palestinians and their descendants. On January 20, 1949, Truman began his only full term as president.

VI. UN Armistices, 1949.

Early in 1949 the UN negotiated a series of separate armistices between Israel and: Egypt February 24, Lebanon March 23,

Trans-Jordan April 3, and Syria July 20. These left Israel in control of about 8,000 square miles, 77.4 percent of Palestine's total of 10,435. Thus, through its violations of the July 19, 1948, truce, Israel gained some 2,000 square miles, some 20 percent of Palestine's total. America first bullied through the UN partition plan of November 29, 1947, which gave Jews 53.46 percent of Palestine even though Jews then owned only some 5-6 percent of it. Then through its role in the UN, America encouraged and helped Israel to take even more land through truce violations. This left only 22.6 percent of Palestine under Arab control; this was ruled by either Trans-Jordan or Egypt, not by Palestinians, which was not directly due to U.S. action.

In theory the armistices formally ended the fighting but did not formally end the war. Each armistice agreement included this or a similar statement: "No provision of this agreement shall in any way prejudice the rights, claims and positions of either party hereto in the ultimate settlement of the Palestine question."[75]

On March 10, Israel, thirteen days after it signed the armistice with Egypt, invaded Egyptian-held land in the Negev between the armistice line and the Gulf of Aqaba. It drove out the Arab villagers of Umm Rasrash, confiscated their property and started the port city of Eliat. Thus Israel achieved its goal of an outlet on the Gulf. The UN did not even demand that Israel return to the armistice lines. Thus the UN again signaled Israel that it could scrap its agreements with impunity.[76]

VII. America's Influence in the UN.

Conor Cruise O'Brien, author of *The Siege: The Saga of Israel and Zionism*, was a member of Ireland's UN delegation from 1956 to 1961. He maintains that during the first Israeli-Arab war and for a long time after, the UN Secretariat, as a whole, was far more influenced by America than by any other country. This happened partly because of U.S. economic dominance after World War II, partly because America was paying for much of the UN's operation, and partly because the UN was headquartered in America, where it received extensive U.S. media coverage.

Americans then had high hopes for the UN and tended to consider it humanity's moral conscience. This situation, contends O'Brien, made the UN far more important to the U.S. government than to any other government. America could use the UN to make its own policies look good. The UN also gave Washington opportunities to bring about a certain policy or situation without seeming to be directly responsible for it. O'Brien adds that Americans who were senior officials in the Secretariat were in a much better position than non-Americans to talk confidently with State and White House officials. They had a better idea of what Washington would accept or reject.[77] If his assessment is correct, UN actions and inactions, at least during Israel's founding and early years, greatly reflected U.S. policy.

Eventually America became more isolated in the UN over its support of Israeli actions. Yet, because of U.S. veto power in the SC, America usually thwarted the will of the majority of SC members when this collective will was unfavorable to Israel. Meanwhile, the GA, which has no veto, repeatedly passed resolutions demanding that Israel change its actions. GA resolutions, unlike those of the SC, do not bind member nations, nor even the SC. Israel could therefore scorn GA resolutions with impunity. Thus the UN could exert little influence over the state it had helped bring into existence.

VIII. Israeli Reneging on International Zone, 1949.

UNGA Resolution 181 of November 29, 1947, which called for Palestine's partition, stipulated that Jerusalem should not be part of either the Jewish or the Arab state but under international control. In March 1949 Israel began moving its government agencies into the part of the city that it had occupied. By this time Israel had also reapplied for UN membership. Its first request had been rejected in December 1948. Several nations hesitated to admit Israel because it kept land conquered outside the area allotted to it by the UN, because it refused to allow refugees to return home, and especially because many UN members feared that Israel would prevent the internationalization of Jerusalem. Israel maintained that

it "held no views and pursued no policies on any question which
were inconsistent with...the resolutions of the Assembly and the
Security Council." Israel indicated it would be somewhat cooperative on these issues.[78] Moreover, the Israeli representative, in
December 1948, gave the Columbian delegate to the UN "formal
assurance in writing that Israel would not oppose the internationalization of Jerusalem."[79] The GA then voted on May 11, 1949,
to admit Israel as a member. However, the resolution of admission, 273 (III), contained this preamble:

> Recalling its resolutions of 29 November 1947 [#181 on
> partition] and 11 December 1948 [#194 on refugees] and
> taking note of the declarations and explanations made by the
> representative of the Government of Israel before the *ad hoc*
> Political Committee in respect of the implementation of the
> said resolutions, the General Assembly...decides to admit
> Israel to membership in the United Nations.[80]

Within seven months Israel repudiated its promise regarding
Jerusalem. Ben-Gurion stated that "Jews will sacrifice themselves
for Jerusalem no less than Englishmen for London."[81] On December 9, 1949, the GA voted for Resolution 303(IV), which
requested the UN Trusteeship Council (a) to draw up a statute to
internationalize the city and (b) to implement it. Despite Israel's
promise not to oppose internationalization, it voted against the
resolution. Israel also increased the movement of its government
offices from Tel Aviv to Jerusalem. On December 26 the Knesset
began to meet there. Four weeks later the Knesset proclaimed that
Jerusalem had been the capital of Israel since it declared independence. In December 1950 the GA again considered proposals to
internationalize the city but nothing came of the discussion.
Jordan, which then controlled East Jerusalem, also opposed
internationalizing the city.[82] As of August 1995 the issue was still
unresolved. The entire city was still controlled by Israel, which
has made numerous statements that it will never give it up.
Moreover, Jerusalem has annexed several square miles of the
surrounding area of West Bank and thus has expanded the area
that Israel has stressed is a "non-negotiable" part of Israel.

IX. The Lausanne Protocol Regarding Refugees, May 12, 1949.

Meanwhile, again regarding Israel's admission into the UN, the UN Conciliation Commission for Palestine, trying to carry out UNGA Resolution 194 of December 11, 1948, regarding refugees, wrote the Lausanne Protocol. It was based on the partition plan of Resolution 181. Israel and the Arab states signed the protocol on May 12, 1949, a few hours after Israel had been voted into the UN.[83] By signing, Israel left the impression (a) that it was willing to give up the areas, including Jerusalem, which it had seized militarily but which were outside the area allotted to it by the partition plan, and (b) that it would allow the return of the refugees. As noted above, believing that Israel would soon agree to these two protocol points, several nations that had not approved Israel's membership now voted for it. They were soon disappointed. Israel later obliquely admitted that it had cooperated during the talks leading up to the protocol signing because it wanted to be accepted. Israel's own *Government Yearbook 1950* stated:

Some members of the United Nations wished at this opportunity to test Israel's intentions with regard to the refugee, boundaries and Jerusalem issues, before approving its application for admission. In a way, Israel's attitude at the Lausanne talks aided its Delegation at Lake Success in its endeavour to obtain the majority required for admission.[84]

However, within six weeks of signing the Lausanne Protocol regarding refugees and being admitted into the UN, Israel's delegation to the Conciliation Commission for Palestine indicated to it that the delegation "could not accept a certain proportionate distribution of territory agreed upon in 1947 as a criterion for a territorial settlement in present circumstances."[85] Thus Israel repudiated the allocation provision of the partition plan of Resolution 181. This was the very plan that Israel, in arguing against the Bernadotte plan some seven months previously, had insisted "is a valid instrument of international law."[86] Israel again used a UN resolution that it had agreed to, as long as it worked to Israel's advantage, but discarded part of it when it became disadvantageous.

Within six weeks of signing the Lausanne Protocol and being admitted into the UN, Israel also renewed its refusal to let the refugees return to their homes. The Conciliation Commission reported:

> The Arab delegations continue to hold the view that the first step must be acceptance by the Government of Israel of the principle set forth in the resolution of 11 December 1948 concerning the repatriation of refugees who wish to return to their homes and live at peace with their neighbours. The Commission has not succeeded in achieving the acceptance of this principle by the Government of Israel.[87]

On August 12, 1949, delegates of seventeen nations signed four Geneva Conventions, including the Fourth Convention relative to protecting civilians in time of war. (Cf. Appendix Two.) Within six months sixty-one nations had signed the conventions. On October 21, 1950, they became a part of positive international law. By early 1956, fifty-two nations, including America and Israel, had either ratified or acceded to them.[88]

On April 24, 1950, Abdullah's parliament followed his instructions that it formally ratify his December 1, 1948, proclamation annexing West Bank, including East Jerusalem, to Jordan.

Shortly after its declaration of statehood, the government of Israel passed a development authority law. According to the *Israel Yearbook, 1950/51*, it specifically authorized the Jewish National Fund (JNF) "to acquire abandoned Arab land on a large scale."[89] This land was not truly abandoned; the Arab owners had either fled or been driven off and then kept at gunpoint from returning. The *Yearbook* article indicated that largely because of that law, the JNF had acquired well over 405 square miles of land just since statehood, and was in the process of acquiring another 386 square miles of "abandoned land," a total of more than 791 square miles. The *Yearbook* added the significant phrase, "With the path to land acquisition cleared ...,"[90] that is, the owners had been frightened or driven off and the government had set up the legal machinery to confiscate the land. With the land, Israel also acquired thousands of Arab homes which the IDF had not blown up or bulldozed. Israel was thus able to provide this ready housing to many of the 400,000 or so Jews who entered Israel during the first two years after statehood,[91] without the great expense of building homes.

The U.S. government knew Israel was confiscating properties but continued to support it against the properties' owners, Arab Palestinians. It is hard to see how the Israeli acts were anything but outright thefts, at least in the meaning of objective, not subjective, morality, despite Israeli claims that the properties were "abandoned" and that the takeovers were the lands' "redemption." It is hard to see how America's actions were not cooperation in such thefts. For America aided and abetted them by protecting Israel in the UN and by its financial support, which were also signs of approval and practical aid in maintaining such thefts.

Israel, at least until August 1995, refused to either return the lands or otherwise make restitution. The moral obligation therefore seems to fall on America, as Israel's principal accomplice, either to persuade Israel to make full restitution or, failing that, to make restitution itself. The probability that America has gained nothing from its participation in such thefts does not change this. To argue against this position seems to require either (a) that Israel's takeover of Arab land without payment was not theft, at least in a moral sense, or (b) that America's actions did not make it an accomplice even in a moral sense, or (c) that nations do not have the same moral obligation to restitution that individuals have.

During the U.S. government's Fiscal Year 1951, which began July 1,1950, it sent $100,000 in economic grant aid to Israel.[92] Thus began annual U.S. grants and/or loans, plus other aid, totaling some $60 billion, some of which has been repaid.

X. The Israeli Occupation of DMZs, 1950-51.

The 1949 armistices provided for four demilitarized zones - three between Israeli and Syrian forces, and one between Israeli and Egyptian forces. The two main purposes of the DMZs were to physically separate opposing troops to minimize friction and incidents, and to restore normal civilian life within the DMZs. Troops from neither side were to enter the zones. By March 1950, however, Israeli troops occupied the Arab village of Bir Qattar in the DMZ along the Egyptian frontier.

The UN chief of staff reported that on August 20 Israeli troops began forcing Bedouin out of Israeli-held land in the Negev and onto Egyptian-held land. Israelis then burned crops, tents and other possessions the Bedouin left behind. Israelis also killed thirteen Bedouin in the operation. On September 2, the UN chief of staff reported, Israeli soldiers rounded up some four thousand Bedouin living in and around the DMZ and drove them out of Israeli-controlled land into Egyptian-held land. Some of these Bedouin had been displaced two years earlier from the Beersheba area by Israeli pressure. Thus they were uprooted twice.[93]

On December 14, 1950, two years after UNGA passed Resolution 194 regarding refugees, it passed Resolution 394, which stated in part,

> *noting with concern* that...repatriation, resettlement, economic and social rehabilitation of the refugees and the payment of compensation have not been effected, *recognizing* that...the refugee question should be dealt with as a matter of urgency...*directs* the United Nations Conciliation Commission for Palestine to...continue consultations with the parties concerned regarding measures for the protection of the rights, property and interests of the refugees....[94]

In other words, "keep talking." The resolution's mildness confirmed that the UN, dominated by America, either could not or would not do anything effective to ensure justice for the refugees.[95] Israel was thus allowed by both the UN and America to continue its policy of refusing to grant either repatriation or compensation to the refugees. That policy was still operative and, in effect, sanctioned or at least tolerated by the U.S. government in August 1995.

Israeli efforts to take over DMZs surfaced again in March 1951.

General Vagn Bennike, chief of staff of the UN Truce Supervision Organization in Palestine, reported to the SC that 785 Arabs had been removed (by Israel) from the DMZs between Israel and Syria.[96] Israel, in violation of the armistice agreement, also prevented Arabs who had fled during the war from returning to their homes in the DMZ. Syria complained. The SC ruled that "Arab civilians who have been removed from the demilitarized zone by the Government of Israel should be permitted to return forthwith to their homes and that the Mixed Armistice Commission should supervise their return."[97] The SC warned that "no action involving the transfer of persons across international frontiers, armistice lines or within the demilitarized zone should be undertaken without prior decision of the Chairman of the Mixed Armistice Commission."[98] Despite this ruling, Israel continued to try to gradually take over the DMZs.

In 1951 the U.S. government increased its economic grants to Israel from $100,000 for FY 1951 to $86.4 million for FY 1952, an 86,300 percent increase.[99] These were not military grants. However, they enabled Israel to allocate to the purchase of arms funds that it would otherwise have had to spend for non-military items.

On July 20, 1951, a Palestinian refugee killed Jordan's King Abdullah in Jerusalem. In 1953 his grandson succeeded him as King Hussein. In July 1952 young Egyptian army officers, led by Gamal Abdel Nasser, deposed the ineffectual King Farouk. Nasser became the unofficial leader of the new government and, in 1956, Egypt's president.

In 1952 the U.S. government allotted $73.6 million in economic grants to Israel for FY 1953, a 15 percent decrease.[100] By the time Truman left office on January 20, 1953, Israel occupied everything in Palestine except Gaza Strip, West Bank, and the Arab section of Jerusalem. That situation continued until the June 1967 war.

XI. Truman on Truman.

Truman devotes forty pages of his *Memoirs* to the issues of DPs and Palestine. In several places he reveals a great compassion for Jews. However, he expresses no *feelings*, either positive or negative, toward Palestinian Arabs. Except as a factor to be dealt with, they seem not to exist. For example, he writes:

The question of Palestine as a Jewish homeland goes back to the solemn promise that had been made to them [the Jews] by the British in the Balfour Declaration of 1917 - a promise which had stirred the hopes and the dreams of these oppressed people. This promise, I felt, should be kept, just as all promises made by responsible, civilized governments should be kept.[101]

Truman, says nothing, however, about that part of Balfour in which the British also state that "nothing shall be done which may prejudice the civil and religious rights of existing non-Jewish communities in Palestine." Should not that part of Balfour also have been kept?

When Secretary of Defense Forrestal pointed out to Truman the need for Saudi oil in case of war, Truman responded that he would handle the situation in the light of justice not oil.[102] But justice for whom - the Palestinian Arabs, Jewish DPs, Jews already in Palestine, or all of them? The political history of the late 1940s leaves the impression that in the tension between Truman and those in his administration who questioned his Mideast policy, the focus of his critics was on safeguarding American interests in the region. These interests particularly concerned oil and the exclusion of Soviet influence. Justice for Palestinian Arabs seemingly was not an issue except in so far as injustice to them might harm American interests.

In a somewhat similar vein, Dean Rusk notes that Truman "agreed with Marshall that we needed a solution in the Middle East with which both sides could live, which would prevent a succession of wars between Arabs and Jews."[103] The Administration wanted peace; it seemed less interested in justice. Rusk writes: "We were looking for any plan that would work. If the

Jews and the Arabs had come up with one, we would have bought it."[104] Failure to inexorably link America's search for peace with an equally fervent search for true justice seemingly doomed the former.

Chapter Eleven

MORAL ISSUES IN AMERICA'S ROLE IN THE CONFLICT

This chapter reflects more fully on the morality of U.S. involvement in the Israeli-Palestinian conflict, particularly in the events which led up to and accompanied Israel's founding. The investigation is developed in the light of the history just examined. 1. The reflection briefly brings together some of the moral principles already treated separately in the historical chapters. 2. It expands on some of the moral principles and their applications which were touched on briefly in those chapters. 3. This chapter concludes by looking briefly at actions which fittingly stem from this reflection.

I. Reflections on What Took Place.

In order better to assess the morality of U.S. actions, the study first asked: Who has a greater moral right to the Holy Land? In response, Chapter One examined the issue of whether the Bible is a "deed of ownership" to the land of Canaan for today's Jewish people. It was noted that, except for Biblical literalists, most modern scripture scholars question the historical factualness of the pertinent passages. Therefore these passages are considered too flimsy as evidence to be used as a basis for a claim to a moral right to the land. Except for Biblical literalists, the Bible is not considered a "deed of ownership" to the Holy Land for today's Jewish people. Therefore American leaders who used the Bible as a basis for their own political actions which harmed the Palestinian Arabs were, at best, on theologically shaky ground. (The Church-State issue involved in U.S. officials taking a theological position based on their interpretation of the Bible is primarily a Constitutional issue.)

Chapter Two also responded to the question, who has a greater moral right to the Holy Land. It examined the *moral hereditary right* to it. The chapter showed that (a) most Jews did not choose to return to Palestine after the Babylonian Captivity ended; (b) in the succeeding centuries most Jews opted for life in the Diaspora rather than in Palestine, even when it was ruled by the Jewish Hasmonians; and (c) in the decades and centuries after the deportation by the Romans in A.D. 135 many Jews *freely* emigrated from Palestine, and most Diaspora Jews did not choose to immigrate to it. This gradually reduced to the vanishing point their descendants' moral hereditary right to Palestine. Therefore modern Diaspora Jews' historical relationship with *Eretz Israel* did not establish such a weighty moral hereditary right to its land that it outweighed the moral rights of the indigenous people, most of whom were Palestinian Arabs, to that same land.

Chapter Three treated the period from A.D. 1800 to 1914. It noted that Jews, *considered just as immigrants*, had at least as much moral right as other people to immigrate to Palestine. This right is limited; it must not violate the native people's moral right to their "common good rightly understood." Thus, no one has a moral right to move to a country intending to supplant its natives, prevent the exercise of their right to self-determination, or otherwise disrupt their common good. But many Zionist immigrants intended to establish an almost exclusively Jewish state or at least a specifically Jewish state in much or all of Palestine. Executing this intent would inevitably disrupt the natives' common good. Therefore it would seem that these Zionists *by their intent* forfeited whatever moral right they may have had to immigrate to Palestine.

The same onus, Chapter Three argued however, would not seem to fall on these immigrants' descendants who were born in Palestine. It would seem that ordinarily a person has a moral right to be a first-class citizen in the land of one's birth. Regardless of the moral legitimacy of one's parents' actions, it seems inappropriate to expel someone from the land of birth. A problem with this position is that one generation of aggressors can unjustly inundate a territory; then their children, enjoying the moral rights of first-class citizens, may be able to swamp the other natives. Like all other moral rights, this one must be weighed against competing moral rights. It thus seems difficult to delineate how substantial this birth right is, especially when applied to a large number of people in a limited time and space. Many Israelis were born in the Holy Land. Arabs should recognize that especially these Israelis may have a strong moral right to live there. Moreover, this moral right would seem to increase with the length of time that their *modern* ancestors have lived there.

If these moral rights apply to native Israelis they apply even more strongly to those Palestinians who have a longer *continuous* ancestry within the Holy Land. This includes refugees *and* those born away from their ancestral homes because their parents or grandparents were unjustly expelled or were unjustly barred from returning. Moreover, whatever moral rights to political self-determination might flow from birth in the Holy Land and from modern ancestral presence there, they would not establish a moral right to property confiscated as recently as 1948.

The conclusion of the first three chapters is that whatever moral claims Diaspora Jews may have had to the Holy Land prior to the Balfour Declaration of 1917, they were not great enough, even when combined, to outweigh the rights of the native people.

Chapters Four and Five showed how Britain, unjustly in terms of moral principles, deprived Palestine's natives of the exercise of their moral right to self-determination. Britain did this through its Balfour Declaration and its mandate over Palestine. For the reasons and moral principles set forth in the first five chapters it seems clear that one cannot objectively justify the actions of Presidents Wilson, Harding and Coolidge in their support of the Balfour Declaration and the British mandate. This is also true of the actions of both houses of the Sixty-seventh Congress, and of the Senate of the Sixty-eighth Congress, noted in Chapter Six. (The subjective aspects are, of course, beyond this investigation's purview.) At about the same time that the U.S. government was supporting Jewish immigration to Palestine it was restricting immigration to much less densely populated America.

Chapter Seven raised the question: Did the Holocaust create for those trying to escape death a moral right to immigrate to Palestine (a) in large numbers (b) with the intent of founding a Jewish state? The corresponding question was: Did Palestine's natives, and Britain as the mandate authority, knowing of the threat this presented to the natives, have a moral duty to accept Jewish refugees in large numbers? This moral issue was modified by the Zionist policy of opposing the settling of Jewish refugees in havens other than Palestine. It was thus never clear that Palestine was really the only haven to which refugees could have fled. Although this apparent victimization of Jewish refugees by Zionists seemingly increased the moral dilemma which the natives of Palestine faced, it is not clear that they had a moral obligation to accept the refugees as immigrants. For accepting them would foster the deprivation of their own moral rights to political self-determination, to their own culture, and to their own homes and land.

Chapter Seven noted that America itself accepted some refugees but rejected most. Their threat to America was presumably much less than their threat to the people of Palestine. President Roosevelt repeatedly tried to solve the Jewish refugee problem but was repeatedly thwarted by Zionists.

Chapter Eight dealt with Holocaust survivors, together with postwar Jewish refugees from eastern Europe. Many in these two groups reportedly chose Palestine as their preferred haven. This postwar Jewish refugee problem was also rendered less clear morally because of Zionist insistence that Palestine was its only solution. Again other possible havens were either rejected or not used to their full potential. Thus the refugees' plight was dragged on; this served the Zionist political goal of statehood in Palestine. Americans' guilt feelings and compassion regarding Jewish refugees were harnessed to support Zionist goals. Truman in effect adopted the Zionist position that Palestine was the refugee problem's only solution. However, he eventually also worked somewhat for Jewish refugees' admission to America. In time he allowed himself and America to become embroiled in the statehood issue itself.

Chapter Nine investigated America's role in partitioning Palestine. This role included the use of threats by federal officials to gain UNGA approval of partition. The chapter also dealt with the expulsion of Palestinian Arabs by the *yishuv*, and with Truman's recognition of the new state of Israel despite numerous atrocities committed by *yishuv* military. Truman had wide support within Congress and among American citizens for his actions. This seemingly increased America's moral involvement in the injustice.

Chapter Ten treated the new state's continuation of the policy of expulsion of Palestinian Arabs from their homeland. It also dealt with repeated truce violations in 1948 and 1949, through which Israel expanded the territory it controlled. America's implicit support of this expansion, in the UN and through financial assistance, deepened U.S. involvement, at least in a moral sense, as an accomplice in Israeli policies and actions.

II. Reflections on Moral Principles.

This section looks at (a) general moral principles which pertain to this investigation, (b) applied moral principles pointed to by international covenants, (c) moral principles regarding complicity in the unjust actions of other people, (d) certain moral rights of people involved in the conflict, (e) the moral responsibility to make reparation, and (f) Americans' corporate responsibility.

A. General Principles: The general moral principles used in this investigation do not reflect any one religious tradition but are widely accepted principles that cut across religious and cultural heritages. These include: do to others as you would have them do to you, help those in need, do not kill unjustly, and do not steal. The investigation asks whether a given situation or action is fair. It asks: If the roles were reversed so that what the *yishuv* or the Israelis did to the Palestinian Arabs were now done by the Arabs to the Israelis, how would one judge the morality of the action or situation? Conversely, if the policies of the Arabs toward Jewish refugees during World War II, for example, were reversed, how would one judge the morality of that situation? Or, for example, if the UN were to partition America to enable 500 million non-Americans to carve out a separate nation comprised of the seventeen contiguous states west of Kansas City (some 53 percent of U.S. territory), would Americans agree that this is fair? (Cf. Maps Two and Three.) One problem with this reverse-role method is that it tends to over-simplify complex issues. Many factors in a situation do not easily lend themselves to the reverse role. The method smacks of being *ad hominem*. However, it has great value in bringing home the principle of the golden rule.

B. Applied Principles: During the past century nations have enacted several covenants to make war more humane. These include (a) the Annex to the Fourth Hague Convention of October 18, 1907, signed by several major powers; (b) the Fourth Geneva Convention of August 12, 1949, which most nations eventually agreed to; and (c) the Universal Declaration of Human Rights (the scope of which was broader than warfare situations) which UNGA passed on December 10, 1948. These covenants are cited here not for their legal value but as attempts by nations with many different religious and cultural traditions to make life more truly human. It would seem that these agreements help guide people regarding what is widely considered moral or immoral in human-rights matters, particularly during warfare. As moral guidelines, or at least as rough approximations of moral guidelines, they seem to apply whether or not a nation or a group of people have formally embraced them. Thus, the policies and actions of both the Palestinian Arabs and the *yishuv*, even before achieving statehood, seemingly can be evaluated morally, partly in the light of the three covenants. (Again, this concerns objective, not subjective, morality.)

This line of reasoning seems particularly relevant to Americans. Americans were subject to the moral principles behind the covenants, especially after the development of the covenants made the moral principles behind them better known and understood. Or is this presuming too much? America voted for the Universal Declaration of Human Rights. America also eventually signed the Fourth Geneva Convention. Through these two actions it would seem that America added to its already-existing moral responsibility to observe the moral principles behind the covenants. It undertook an added moral responsibility not to be an accomplice in violating them. (Appendix Two has relevant excerpts from the two conventions.)

C. Complicity: From the viewpoint of objective morality, one is an accomplice in an unjust action if one cooperates in it in such a way that one's own action contributes to the injustice. Thus, if Wilson's approval of the proposed Balfour Declaration *helped* bring about its passage by the British war cabinet, Wilson was an accomplice in that injustice. This would be true even if Wilson's help was not crucial to the declaration's passage. The same would be true of America's much more vital role in the November 29, 1947, UN vote to partition Palestine. America's actions helped, and were probably crucial to, the passage of the partition proposal. America thus contributed to the injustice brought about by the partition.

To acquire more territory, Israel repeatedly broke various cease-fire agreements it entered into in 1948 and 1949. It seems clear that America was an accomplice in these actions because, through using its veto power in the SC and through other of its UN actions, it protected Israel in carrying out this policy. By these actions America also implicitly encouraged Israel to continue breaking its truce agreements. Both encouragement to perform unjust acts and protection afterward from their consequences are forms of complicity. (Cf. Appendix Three.)

Similarly, one may also be an accomplice after the fact if, for example, one helps maintain an injustice. America ran diplomatic interference for Israel and, after June 30, 1950, regularly gave it financial and eventually military aid. These U.S. actions directly helped Israel to continue barring the Palestinian Arab refugees from returning to their homes. This seemingly violates at least the spirit of Article 49 of the Fourth Geneva Convention. Yet America in August 1995 was still backing Israel in this.

D. Moral rights involved:

1. Regarding Palestinian *refugees* there are several moral-rights issues:

a. Their right to return to their ancestral homes. If their own property is not repossessable they have the right to just compensation for it and the right to live in their ancestral neighborhood or in some place nearby.

b. Their right either to repossess their property or, if they so wish, to be compensated for its value. If improvements have been made on the property by Israelis, the latter must be reimbursed for this by those Arabs who wish to repossess the property. (In Israel much of the land is held in trust for all Jewish people by the state, which leases it either directly or indirectly to individuals, who construct the buildings.)

c. Refugees' right to compensation for harm done to them as a result of their enforced exile.

d. Their right to be first-class citizens of Israel and to live anywhere in it. As noted above in Section I concerning Chapter Three, this right seemingly extends to refugees who were born outside of Israel because their ancestors were unjustly expelled or barred from returning to it.

2. Regarding the Arabs *living in Israel* the primary moral-rights issues are seemingly their *de facto* second-class citizenship and the fact that they have never been allowed to determine their own political life. Their lives were perhaps not as disrupted as were those of the refugees, although some were forced to relocate within Israel. Nevertheless, their common good and their other moral rights have also been seriously harmed by America's complicity in the *yishuv*/Israeli conflict with them. America's blatant disregard of human-rights violations in Israel, America's double standard by which it subsidizes a long list of discriminatory practices in Israel - all of this cries out for redress.[1]

3. Regarding the *non-refugee Palestinians in West Bank and Gaza*, the primary moral issue is seemingly their moral right to a fully independent state of their own. This assumes that all people are created equal, that they are endowed by their Creator with certain unalienable rights, and that among these is liberty.[2] One might also argue that non-refugee Palestinians in West Bank and Gaza have a moral right to some political participation in at least part of the territory that was taken from the Palestinians. This would seem to be more of a moral-rights issue for the Palestinian refugees from Israel than for the people whose roots are in West Bank and Gaza. However, it is not clear that the latter have no moral claim to political participation in at least some part of UN-allotted Israel. (When Israel's statehood was declared, its borders

were not defined. Its current frontiers are partly either truce or cease-fire lines, treaty lines with Egypt and Jordan, or the Lebanese border. (Cf. Map Five.) However, negotiations now taking place may soon change some of these situations.) To return to the Kansas City analogy, which parallels only the 53 percent allotted by the UN: If everything in the seventeen contiguous states west of Kansas City were taken from the Americans by the UN, would the Americans east of that line have a moral claim to regain all or part of that western area? If so, how long would that right last? Another analogy: In 1848, after America defeated Mexico in a war of aggression, Mexico was forced to cede its legal title to 40 percent of its territory. But a treaty unjustly forced on Mexico would not take away its *moral* right to its land. Does that right have any moral strength left in it for Mexico today, 147 years after the treaty? The analogy, though helpful, perhaps limps. The ceded land was part of Mexico when Mexico gained its independence from Spain in 1821. Spain had previously forced Spanish sovereignty on the indigenous tribes, and thus violated their political rights. These tribes' moral right to political self-determination would seemingly also need to be considered.

4. Regarding the Palestinian *refugees from Israel living in West Bank or Gaza*, and their descendants: They would seem to share in the issues mentioned in the previous paragraph. They also share in the issues that involve the refugees mentioned above.

5. Regarding Israeli frontiers: It might be argued that there are varying degrees of moral legitimacy to the areas now within Israel:

a. The most legitimate, morally, would seem to be the 5-6 percent of Palestine that Jews owned before the November 29, 1947, passage of the UN partition resolution. It would seem that the *yishuv* may have had a moral right to establish a Jewish state on at least the larger contiguous parcels of this territory. Such a basis for a moral claim has several weaknesses. It would allow any group who could purchase or gain political control over a parcel of territory to proclaim an independent state. This might violate the common good of the citizens of the rest of the state or area. The American Civil War was fought by the North to preserve the

Union. Northerners implicitly considered the Southern rebellion a violation of Northerners' common good. Southerners maintained that their right to self-determination included the right to secede. If the *yishuv* had a moral right to establish a state in the territory they owned, by the same token Arabs within Israel have an equal moral right today to form their own state. Arabs complain that Israel has effectively isolated Arab villages from each other by building intervening Jewish settlements and roads. This has cut up many large contiguous parcels of territory inhabited by Arabs.

b. Much less morally legitimate than the 5-6 percent owned by Jews before the November 1947 UN partition vote was the approximately 48 percent of Palestine that was then owned and inhabited by Arabs but allotted to the Jewish state by that UN resolution. This latter area arguably was gained through diplomatic aggression. Perhaps even less legitimate is the some 20 percent of Palestine taken by Israel through military aggression during the 1947-49 war or shortly thereafter. (The Golan Heights and the parts of West Bank incorporated into Jerusalem after the June 1967 war are outside the scope of this volume.)

E. Reparation: It would seem that the *yishuv*/Israel and Britain were the primary agents in the violation of Palestinian Arabs' rights. However, Britain's role virtually ceased in May 1948, shortly after America's role had become very significant. Ordinarily the primary agents rather than the accomplices have the first obligation to make restitution to the harmed party. However, if the primary agents do not make restitution, the obligation falls on the accomplices.

According to some theologians,[3] the moral obligation to make restitution is based not only on the harm done but also on the subjective guilt of those causing the harm. By this reasoning, if U.S. officials thought they were acting morally in supporting Israel the way they did, they have no moral obligation to make restitution. (However, if the action was also illegal, and a court ordered reparation, there would be a moral obligation to make the reparation.) A problem with this position is that unless a court requires reparation the harmed party is left without moral recourse. Meanwhile the accomplice of the one doing the harm, because of ignorance or some other faulty conscience, is completely free of a moral onus, at least in justice, to help the victim. This does not seem to meet the fairness criteria. It does not seem equitable. This conclusion seems helpful in evaluating America's role in the Israeli-Palestinian conflict. American leaders took it upon themselves to make decisions that would radically affect, for unforeseeable generations, the lives of millions of Palestinian Arabs. They therefore had a proportionately serious obligation to learn the facts that would enable them to make decisions based on justice, rather than on propaganda, guilt feelings, emotion or winning the next election. Can Americans just dismiss what seems at best irresponsible actions by some of their leaders and seemingly misguided support by many American citizens? Can Americans just say "Sorry about that!" and walk away?

F. Corporate Responsibility: What U.S. leaders have done regarding the Zionist/Israeli-Palestinian conflict has had either the approval or at least the acquiescence of most American citizens from Wilson's presidency to Bill Clinton's. Even Americans who now think that the Palestinians were treated unjustly, generally seem indifferent to, or at least reluctant about, changing U.S. policy. With regard to several American miscarriages of justice, including, as noted previously, the internment of Japanese-Americans during World War II, Americans have acknowledged corporate wrongdoing and made at least some sort of collective amends. Such acknowledgements do not require that judgement be passed on the subjective guilt or non-guilt of the persons involved in the act for which amends are being made. It would seem that in fairness, America, because it was an accomplice in various injustices against the Palestinian Arabs, especially the refugees and their descendants, should make reparations. These should be equal to the amount of harm done as a result of American actions.

III. Reflections on Actions Which Americans Might Take.

It is probably unrealistic to hope that Israel and Britain will make reparation for their acts. Waiting for them to do this would at least substantially delay correcting the injustice - which correction is already long overdue. Meanwhile, delaying justice is denying it. Although America should encourage both nations to make reparations, the demands of fairness in America's own relations with the Palestinians urge it to move ahead unilaterally. America could fund its reparations to the Palestinians, especially the refugees. Congress and the White House still send approximately three billion dollars in annual gifts to Israel. Except perhaps for commitments that America has already made to Israel, America does not owe it anything special in justice. In fact, it can easily be argued that U.S. gifts to Israel are perpetuating injustice and for that reason alone should be stopped. A strong case can be made that America owes the Palestinians a great deal. America has obviously exercised a long sponsorship of Israel and it should act in a manner that is appropriate to that relationship, as long as this does not require America to act immorally. This does not necessarily mean keeping Israel on the U.S. dole. America should make reparations for the wrongs America has done to Palestinians its second highest Mideast priority, surpassed only by true peace with justice. It should also serve notice that it will protect Israel from becoming a victim of injustice.

In addition to making financial restitution, America can make reparations in other ways. One way is to work not only for peace in the Holy Land, which it has already been doing, but to work for peace with true justice. If America seeks peace without also seeking true justice it will merely further institutionalize the injustices already committed. It is not the purpose of this investigation to try to solve the conflict but only to examine the morality of America's role in the conflict's beginnings and to urge correction of the injustices. But hopefully Americans will respond both by correcting the injustices and by working for true peace between Israelis and Palestinians. It will be a true peace only if it is a just peace for the people on both sides.

It must also be a peace with compassion. People on both sides have suffered horribly at one time or another since Hitler's rise in 1933. The residues of those traumas must be understood and cleansed in so far as this is possible if there is to be peace not only on paper but also in Israeli and Palestinian hearts and minds. Some Americans have wonderful insights into this dynamic. Hopefully they will contribute their skills as part of Americans' acts of reparation. For it is only through compassion, only through a loving entering into the suffering of the humans on the "other" side, that Israelis and Palestinians will be truly reconciled. But it must not end there. For true reconciliation should be only the beginning of a loving, neighborly friendship between these two peoples, both of whom may be children of Abraham, both of whom certainly are children of God.

Appendix One
Palestine's Jewish Population, A.D. 638-1800

This appendix expands on some historical points and population estimates for part of the period covered briefly in Chapter Two.

According to Israeli demographer Roberto Bachi, from the start of the Arab period in A.D. 638 until into the nineteenth century, Palestine's Jewish population was always less than ten thousand and in some periods was only a few thousand.[1]

I. Palestine Before the Crusades, 638-1099.

After Arabian Muslims conquered Palestine, the new rulers, primarily military leaders, left its civil service in native Byzantine hands. Greek remained the primary language. Palestine's conqueror, Caliph Omar I (582-644), was a devout, austere Moslem and personal friend of Mohammed. He treated Jews and Christians quite well. At the south end of the Temple Mount, Omar or a successor began to build a simple mosque, which was later replaced by the magnificent al Aqsa Mosque, which is still there.[2] Christian pilgrims were welcome in Palestine.

Under ensuing caliphs, treatment of Jews and Christians fluctuated. In about 688-91 Caliph Abd al-Malik (ruled 685-705), in a political move against his Muslim competitors in Arabia, erected the exquisite Dome of the Rock on the site of Solomon's temple. With it he hoped to divert Muslim pilgrims to Jerusalem and away from Mecca and Medina. Jews worked on the shrine's staff in lieu of paying taxes. Christian conversions to Islam under the harsh Caliph Omar II (ruled 717-720) plus continuing Muslim immigration from surrounding lands changed Palestine from a primarily Christian to a primarily Muslim area.[3] Caliph Harun al-Rashid (ruled 786-809) forced Christians to wear blue badges and Jews yellow ones. However, his son, Caliph al-Mamun (ruled 813-833), restored religious tolerance. In about 935, Jerusalem Jews were allowed to build a synagogue near the Wailing Wall.

During the tenth and eleventh centuries, as Fatimid power declined, Palestine was subject to raids by Seljuk Turks and

Bedouin tribes. In 1071 Seljuks captured Jerusalem and mistreated and overcharged Christian pilgrims. In 1076 Jerusalem revolted against the Seljuks but failed; many of its inhabitants were ordered killed. This deteriorating situation helped trigger the Crusades. In 1098 the Fatimids recaptured the city. The continuing havoc and resulting emigration also reduced Palestine's Jewish population to only a few thousand before the first Crusaders came.[4]

These mainly Frankish soldiers conquered Jerusalem in 1099 after a forty-day siege. Reportedly defying orders, they massacred its Jewish and Muslim inhabitants - almost forty thousand men, women and children. Some were tortured. This halted 461 years of Muslim rule over Palestine.

II. Palestine During the Crusader Era, 1099-1291.

Palestinian Jews experienced mixed fortunes under the Crusaders. Jerusalem's first Crusader ruler initially reinstated the ban against Jews living there; however, he or his successors exempted a few Jewish families. By 1110 the Crusaders, having gained military control throughout most of Palestine, relaxed their policies toward local populations and allowed them to remain. Jewish community life was centered in Acre, which had some two hundred Jewish families in 1167, in Ashkelon and some other cities. In about 1169 a Jewish traveler wrote that some two hundred Jewish families lived in the Tower of David area of Jerusalem. The Crusaders brought from Europe a rigid feudal system, to which Palestinian Jews had to conform.

In 1187 Saladin (ruled 1187-1193) defeated the Crusaders militarily, and most of Palestine returned to Muslim rule. He befriended Jerusalem's Jews and allowed other Jews to move into it, where they have been allowed to live ever since (except in the Old City while under Jordan's rule from 1948 to 1967).[5] Under Saladin Jews increased both in Jerusalem and elsewhere in Palestine.

In 1211 three hundred rabbis and other Jewish scholars fleeing persecution in France and England settled in Crusader Palestine and built new synagogues and schools. In 1229 Frederick II, the Holy Roman Emperor, negotiated a ten-year treaty that returned

Nazareth, Jerusalem and Bethlehem from Muslim to Christian rule. In 1244 Kwarizmian Turks invaded Jerusalem, plundered and destroyed it and massacred many of its inhabitants. However, in 1248 the Turks were driven out by Mamluks, a Muslim dynasty based in Egypt, which ruled the city until 1517. In 1260 Mongols invaded northern Palestine but were decisively defeated before reaching Jerusalem. The Mamluks also kept pounding away at the Crusaders in their increasingly few remaining fortresses along the coast. This frequent warfare played havoc with Palestine's inhabitants. In 1263 a traveler wrote that "only a handful" of Jews lived in Palestine. Virtually all of Jerusalem's Jews fled, many of them moving to Sechem, thirty miles north, in Samaria. At one point during that decade a visiting rabbi reported that Jerusalem had only two thousand Muslims, three hundred Christians, and one or two Jewish families. In 1267 Nahmanides, a Jewish visitor to Jerusalem, wrote that there were barely enough Jewish men there to form a minyan - ten men - to hold prayers in their house on the Sabbath. Nahmanides started a synagogue there but did not form a Jewish community.

Despite raids from the east and the gradual Mamluk advance from the south, Ashkenazi Jews from Europe immigrated to Palestine, especially to the fortified Crusader towns along the northern coast. The Jewish population in Acre, the Crusader capital from 1191 to 1291, grew considerably during the thirteenth century. Until this large influx of Ashkenazim, the majority of Palestine's Jewry had been Arabic-speaking "Eastern" Jews. Tensions developed between the two groups, who soon were declaring bans on each other.[6] In 1291 the Mamluks drove the Crusaders from Acre, their last Palestinian fort. The Sultan, avenging the slaughter by the Crusaders in Jerusalem 192 years earlier, ordered a massacre, which killed many Acre Jews.

III. Palestine Under the Mamluk Dynasty, 1291-1517.

Having ejected the Crusaders, the Mamluks wanted to prevent their return. They therefore destroyed the Crusader beachheads - Palestine's coastal cities. This forced these cities' people, including

Jews, to move inland. But destruction of the port cities deprived the inland cities of commercial access to the sea and to other international trade routes, causing a depression. Jewish emigration from Palestine exceeded immigration from Europe and North Africa; the Jewish population hit a new low which continued for several decades.[7] This trend was somewhat reversed during the mid 1300s as Jewish refugees increased, especially from France and Germany, where Jews were persecuted partly because of hysteria following the Black Death. In the early 1480s a visiting Christian reported that five hundred Jewish families lived in Palestine. However, a Jewish traveler at about that time said only about half that many lived there. Economic conditions were poor; Palestine shared with other lands in droughts, famines, earthquakes, epidemics, high taxes, high prices, government corruption, and attacks by Bedouins and bandits. In 1481 marauders attacked Jerusalem and plundered and burned nearby Ramla. A visiting rabbi that year reported that Palestinian Jews' primary income was donations from Diaspora Jews.[8] In the latter part of the 1400s the Mamluks forbade Jews and Christians to visit the Temple Mount or the Patriarchs' tombs in Hebron.

Spanish monarchs in 1492 expelled some 175,000 Jews from Spain and subsequently additional Jews from Spanish-ruled areas in the Mediterranean. This immense cruelty resulted in refugees settling in the four Palestinian cities holy to Jews - Jerusalem, Hebron, Safed, and Tiberias - during the late fifteenth and early sixteenth centuries. Estimates of Jewish population differ, but each of them indicates it was very low. One estimate in the early sixteenth century put Palestine's Jewish population at no more than five thousand.[9]

IV. Palestine Under the Ottoman Turks, 1517-1800.

In 1517 Ottoman Turks completed their conquest of Palestine. An estimated five hundred Jewish families lived in the entire country at the time, with less than half of them in Jerusalem. Sultan Suleiman the Magnificent (ruled 1520-1566) greatly enhanced the city by restoring and erecting Muslim shrines, including the Dome of the Rock, and by repairing the city wall and adding handsome gates, which still add to the city's charm. He was a great improvement over the Mamluks. Under Suleiman and the Turks generally, Jews were treated relatively well. They continued to have freedom of worship and freedom to administer their own marriage, divorce and inheritance laws.

By 1550 Palestine's total population was probably more than 200,000, of which 90 percent were Muslim, and 10 percent were non-Muslims, a substantial number of whom were Jews.[10] By that time Jerusalem had an estimated six thousand Muslims, three thousand Christians and one thousand Jews. A Jew who visited the city in about 1551 reported seeing a large school and two synagogues, the smaller for Ashkenazi Jews, and the larger for Sephardic Jews. The latter speak Ladino, a Judeo-Spanish dialect which soon became the common language of North African and Mideast Jews, later known as "Oriental" Jews. Safed, by then the main center of Jewish life in Palestine, had perhaps another one thousand or more Jewish families.

About 1560 Don Joseph Nasi (1524-1579), a Jew who was an Ottoman tax official and adviser to the Ottoman government, persuaded Suleiman and his son and successor, Prince Selim II, to deed over to him Tiberias and the surrounding region, including seven villages. This area was to be used as a homeland for Jewish refugees, especially from Spain, as well as from Portugal, which in 1498, under Spanish pressure, had also banished all Jews. The Tiberias project was under way by 1564 but increasing opposition from neighboring Arabs worked against building the new settlement. Moreover, Nasi was either too busy with his government duties in Istanbul (Constantinople renamed) or had lost interest in the project and it failed. However, Solomon Aben-Jaish (1520-1603) revived the plan and received government approval. His family moved to the Tiberias area and restarted the project but this too failed.[11]

Meanwhile, the Jews in Safed prospered and increased. It again was a thriving center for Jewish studies as well as for trade in grain and cloth, especially silk and wool fabrics. However, many Palestinian Jews, especially scholars, students, elderly and indigent, still depended primarily on donations from Diaspora Jews for their livelihood.

Toward the end of the sixteenth century Ottoman sultans began to lose their powerful hold on the empire. As generals vied for power, the role of Jews in the government in Istanbul shrank. Local officials squeezed high taxes out of their subjects, including Jews. Palestine became an increasingly neglected backwater of the hard-pressed empire - a condition that continued throughout the next three hundred years until the British and Arabs took it in 1917-18. By the late seventeenth century many Jews had abandoned smaller villages because of marauding nomads in search of grazing lands and plunder. Jews continued to live in Hebron and Gaza city; about twelve hundred lived in Jerusalem.

During the eighteenth century Palestine's Jews increased, especially through immigration of Hasidim from Poland and Russia. The Ottoman governor of northern Palestine rebuilt Tiberias; at his invitation Jews moved there in 1738. It soon became a center second only to Safed, which had a plague in 1742 and an earthquake in 1769. By 1776 a number of Russian Hasidim had moved to Safed.[12] Meanwhile, by the mid-1700s, the worldwide Jewish population stood at perhaps slightly more than two million.[13] About half lived in Poland, their ancestors having been welcomed there during persecutions in England, France, Germany and Spain.

Palestinian Jews, Samaritans and Christians alike had chafed under the harsh Roman-Byzantine imperial rule between A.D. 136 and 638. Yet this period often gave Palestine a peace and prosperity which supported a much larger population, including a much larger Jewish population, than did most or perhaps all of the Arab and Crusader periods between 638 and 1800. Not only was the Jewish population of Palestine very low between about A.D. 1000 and 1800, Palestine's total population was very low. After the Black Death in the fourteenth century its total population dipped to perhaps 150,000. Israeli demographer Bachi sums up much of the 800-year period:

As shown by an impressive quantity of historical records,

throughout the late Middle Ages and up to the 19th century, Jews immigrated...as individuals or in groups, prompted by the desire to be in the land of their fathers in order to pray, to study, and finally to be buried there. Sometimes they were inspired by Messianic hopes, and sometimes they sought asylum in the Holy Land during times of distress in the Diaspora.

However, statistically speaking, these movements were limited in size. It is also likely that poor economic conditions, lack of personal security and low health standards prevailing in the country were causes of substantial re-emigration and high mortality, which therefore greatly reduced the demographic influence of immigration.[14]

By 1800 perhaps 5,000-6,500 Jews and some 265,000-325,000 Arabs lived in Palestine.[15]

Appendix Two
Documents of International Agreements

International agreements have the nature of treaties and bind the signing nations.

The fourteen *Hague Conventions* of October 18, 1907, are agreements signed by several nations about war's conduct. The Fourth Convention dealt with treatment of civilians during war.

On December 10, 1948, UNGA passed the *Universal Declaration of Human Rights*. All UN members pledge to observe its thirty articles.

On August 12, 1949, seventeen nations signed four conventions in Geneva, including *The Fourth Geneva Convention, Relative to the Protection of Civilian Persons in Time of War*. By April 21, 1950, two nations ratified these conventions, which took effect between them six months later. By early 1956, fifty-two nations, including America and Israel, had ratified the Conventions.

Pertinent articles from two of these three documents follow:

"The Hague Convention Concerning the Laws and Customs of War on Land," 2nd Peace Conference, The Hague, October 18, 1907. Articles include:[1] Section II, Chapter I:

#23. It is especially forbidden:

c. To kill or wound an enemy who, having laid down his arms, or having no longer means of defence, has surrendered at discretion;

g. To destroy or seize the enemy's property, unless such destruction or seizure be imperatively demanded by the necessities of war.

#25. The attack or bombardment, by whatever means, of towns, villages, dwellings, or buildings which are undefended is prohibited.

#26. The officer in command of an attacking force must, before commencing a bombardment, except in cases of assault, do all in his power to warn the authorities.

#27. In sieges and bombardments all necessary steps must be taken to spare, as far as possible, buildings dedicated to religion, art, science, or charitable purposes, historic monuments, hospitals, and places where the sick and wounded are collected, provided they are not being used at the time for military purposes.

#28. The pillage of a town or place, even when taken by assault, is prohibited.

Chapter V:

#36. An armistice suspends military operations by mutual agreement between the belligerent parties. If its duration is not defined, the belligerent parties may resume operations at any time, provided always that the enemy is warned within the time agreed upon, in accordance with the terms of the armistice.

Section III:

#46. Family honour and rights, the lives of persons, and private property, as well as religious convictions and practice, must be respected. Private property cannot be confiscated.

#47. Pillage is formally forbidden.

#50. No general penalty, pecuniary or otherwise, shall be inflicted upon the population on account of the acts of individuals for which they cannot be regarded as jointly and severally responsible.

#56. The property of municipalities, that of institutions dedicated to religion, charity and education, the arts and sciences, even when State property, shall be treated as private property.

All seizure of, destruction or wilful damage done to institutions of this character, historic monuments, works of art and science, is forbidden, and should be made the subject of legal proceedings.

"The Fourth Geneva Convention Relative to the Protection of Civilian Persons in time of War," August 12, 1949, supplements Hague regarding civilians. Its 159 articles include:[2]

#29. The Party to the conflict in whose hands protected persons may be, is responsible for the treatment accorded to them by its agents, irrespective of any individual responsibility which may be incurred.

#32. The High Contracting Parties specifically agree that each of them is prohibited from taking any measure of such a character as to cause the physical suffering or extermination of protected persons in their hands. This prohibition applies not only to murder, torture, corporal punishments, mutilation and medical or scientific experiments not necessitated by the medical treatment of a protected person, but also to any other measures of brutality whether applied by civilian or military agents.

#33. No protected person may be punished for an offence he or she has not personally committed. Collective penalties and likewise all measures of intimidation or of terrorism are prohibited.

Pillage is prohibited.

Reprisals against protected persons and their property are prohibited.

#34. The taking of hostages is prohibited.

#41. Should the Power in whose hands protected persons may be consider the measures of control mentioned in the present Convention to be inadequate, it may not have recourse to any other measure of control more severe than that of assigned residence or internment, in accordance with the provisions of Articles 42 and 43.

In applying the provisions of Article 39, second paragraph, to the cases of persons required to leave their usual places of residence by virtue of a decision placing them in assigned residence elsewhere, the Detaining Power shall be guided as closely as possible by the standards of welfare set forth in Part III, Section IV of this Convention.

#42. The internment or placing in assigned residence of protected persons may be ordered only if the security of the Detaining Power makes it absolutely necessary....

#43. Any protected person who has been interned or placed in assigned residence shall be entitled to have such action reconsidered as soon as possible by an appropriate court or administrative board designated by the Detaining Power for that purpose. If the internment or placing in assigned residence is maintained, the court or administrative board shall periodically, and at least twice yearly, give consideration to his or her case, with a view to the favourable amendment of the initial decision, if circumstances permit....

#46. In so far as they have not been previously withdrawn, restrictive measures taken regarding protected persons shall be cancelled as soon as possible after the close of hostilities.

Restrictive measures affecting their property shall be cancelled, in accordance with the law of the Detaining Power, as soon as possible after the close of hostilities.

#47. Protected persons who are in occupied territory shall not be deprived, in any case or in any manner whatsoever, of the benefits of the present Convention by any change introduced, as the result of the occupation of a territory, into the institutions or government of the said territory, nor by any agreement concluded between the authorities of the occupied territories and the Occupying Power, nor by any annexation by the latter of the whole or part of the occupied territory.

#49. Individual or mass forcible transfers, as well as deportations of protected persons from occupied territory to the territory of the Occupying Power or to that of any other country, occupied or not, are prohibited, regardless of their motive.

Nevertheless, the Occupying Power may undertake total or partial evacuation of a given area if the security of the population or imperative military reasons so demand. Such evacuations may not involve the displacement of protected persons outside the bounds of the occupied territory except when for material reasons it is impossible to avoid such displacement. Persons thus evacuated shall be transferred back to their homes as soon as hostilities in the area in question have ceased.

The Occupying Power undertaking such transfers or evacuations shall ensure, to the greatest practicable extent, that proper accommodation is provided to receive the protected persons, that the removals are effected in satisfactory conditions of hygiene, health, safety and nutrition, and that members of the same family are not separated.

The Protecting Power shall be informed of any transfers and evacuations as soon as they have taken place.

The Occupying Power shall not detain protected persons in an area particularly exposed to the dangers of war unless the security of the population or imperative military reasons so demand.

The Occupying Power shall not deport or transfer parts of its own civilian population into the territory it occupies.

#53: Any destruction by the Occupying Power of real or personal property belonging individually or collectively to private persons, or to the State, or to other public authorities, or to social or co-operative organizations, is prohibited, except where such destruction is rendered absolutely necessary by military operations.

#78: If the Occupying Power considers it necessary, for imperative reasons of security, to take safety measures concerning protected persons, it may, at the most, subject them to assigned residence or to internment.

Decisions regarding such assigned residence or internment shall be made according to a regular procedure to be prescribed by the Occupying Power in accordance with the provisions of the present Convention. This procedure shall include the right of appeal for the parties concerned. Appeals shall be decided with the least possible delay. In the event of the decision being upheld, it shall be subject to periodical review, if possible every six months, by a competent body set up by the said Power.

Protected persons made subject to assigned residence and thus required to leave their homes shall enjoy the full benefit of Article 39 [re employment] of the present Convention.

#114. Detaining Power shall afford internees all facilities to enable them to manage their property, provided this is not incompatible with the conditions of internment and the law which is applicable. For this purpose, the said Power may give them permission to leave the place of internment in urgent cases and if circumstances allow.

#130. The detaining authorities shall ensure that internees who die while interned are honourably buried, if possible according to the rites of the religion to which they belonged and that their graves are respected, properly maintained, and marked in such a way that they can always be recognized.

#139. Each national Information Bureau shall, furthermore, be responsible for collecting all personal valuables left by protected persons mentioned in Article 136, in particular those who have been repatriated or released, or who have escaped or died; it shall forward the said valuables to those concerned, either direct, or, if necessary, through the Central Agency. Such articles shall be sent by the Bureau in sealed packets which shall be accompanied by statements giving clear and full identity particulars of the person to whom the articles belonged, and by a complete list of the contents of the parcel. Detailed records shall be maintained of the receipt and despatch of all such valuables.

#147. Grave breaches to which the preceding Article relates shall be those involving any of the following acts, if committed against persons or property protected by the present Convention: wilful killing, torture or inhuman treatment, including biological experiments, wilfully causing great suffering or serious injury to body and health, unlawful deportation or transfer or unlawful confinement of a protected person, compelling a protected person to serve in the forces of a hostile Power, or wilfully depriving a protected person of the rights of fair and regular trial prescribed in the present Convention, taking of hostages and extensive destruction and appropriation of property, not justified by military necessity and carried out unlawfully and wantonly.

#148. No High Contracting Party shall be allowed to absolve itself or any other High Contracting Party of any liability incurred by itself or by another High Contracting Party in respect of breaches referred to in the preceding Article.

#158. Each of the High Contracting Parties shall be at liberty to denounce the present Convention....The denunciation shall have effect only in respect of the denouncing Power. It shall in no way impair the obligations which the Parties to the conflict shall remain bound to fulfil by virtue of the principles of the law of nations, as they result from the usages established among civilized peoples, from the laws of humanity and the dictates of the public conscience.

UNGA passed the **Universal Declaration of Human Rights** on December 10, 1948. Ten articles are given in Chapter Ten, Section V.

Appendix Three
Moral Principles Regarding Ownership and Reparation

These are some of the moral principles that apply to aspects of Americans' responsibility toward Palestinian refugees:[1]

1. **OWNERSHIP** is the right freely to possess, use and dispose of a thing as one's own unless otherwise hindered. Civil laws and others' rights, such as eminent domain, squatters' rights, and easements, limit owners' rights.

2. Nature is the primary source of owners' rights. Experience teaches that human nature being what it is, common ownership of property for production or individual use is impractical and more harmful than helpful.

3. Sustaining human life is the first priority of earth's resources. Thus one in *extreme need* may take barely enough of another's goods to relieve it. But there must be no other way of getting what is needed. One may not take from one in an equally extreme need.

4. Civil law is a secondary source of owners' rights because the natural law does not specify these rights in detail. If the civil law is moral, it helps specify not only the legal right to property but also the moral right to it. If a particular civil law is immoral it is not a true law regarding its immoral aspects. In *those* aspects, that civil law is invalid because contradicted by a higher law of nature.

5. Property such as roads and village grazing lands, held in common, that is, by a moral (legal) person, ordinarily belong morally and ultimately to those for whose use they were primarily meant, even if held legally by the state.

6. The true owner of a property has a moral right to it regardless of who possesses it. The owner has a right to its fruits; no one else has a right to gain from that property.

7. For property to be considered *abandoned* and thus unowned, it must be abandoned freely. Goods lost in disasters are not considered abandoned unless the owner, including heirs, can no longer be determined.

8. a. If one *in good faith* takes possession of another's property without buying it, then so improves it that *the work is more valuable* than the original object, the final product belongs to the one

221

doing the work. But the original owner, if found, must be paid for what the object was worth before the work began. If *the work is less valuable* than the original object it still belongs to the original owner, who must reimburse the finder for his work and costs.

b. If the object was *stolen*, civil law often states that it be returned to its original owner and denies the worker compensation. Moral law judges each case on its merits to be fair to both parties.

c. If one in good faith *builds* on another's land, the structure belongs to the landowner, who must reimburse the builder. If the builder builds in bad faith, civil law often denies compensation. Moral law judges each case on its own merits.

9. **INJUSTICE** violates one's strict, personal right. The gravity of injustice depends on both the personal and societal harm.

10. *Robbery* (theft or stealing) is taking a thing against its owner's will with the intent of keeping it for oneself or of passing it on to another.

11. *Unjust harm* results either from damaging someone's property or from hindering someone from gaining something that he/she has a right to, in an unjust way, even if one gains nothing from doing so. Unjust ways include force, fear, fraud, bribery, dishonest competition and criminal negligence.

If one in good faith does an act which could harm another, he would be unjust not to stop the harm when he learns of it, *if* he himself would not incur a proportionately serious harm by stopping it.

12. *Restitution* is returning goods which another lost by a violation of personal justice. It is due for both wrongful possession and unjust harm.

13. *Restitution for wrongful possession*: A possessor *in bad faith* must a) return stolen goods *and* their natural fruits, and b) repair all of the harm which he foresaw at least indistinctly would result from his acts. A possessor in bad faith may keep the fruits of his labor and deduct his necessary and truly useful expenses.

a. The object itself must be returned even if its value has greatly increased since the owner lost possession of it. Mere financial compensation is not enough unless the owner freely agrees.

b. Both stolen property *and* other losses incurred from

robbery must be reimbursed fully.

    c. Bad-faith possessors include whoever later gets the property, knowing it to be stolen.

    14. A possessor *in doubtful faith* - whoever seriously doubts his true ownership of an object - must make reasonable efforts to solve the doubt. These must be proportionate to the object's value, the doubt's seriousness, and the hope of solving it.

    15. *Restitution for unjust harm*: Reparation is required either because of *the act directly causing the harm* or because of *unjust cooperation*.

    16. *Reparation for direct causation*: Reparation is required if the act causing the harm was itself unjust in the strict sense. This includes using unjust means to prevent someone from gaining something that one may lawfully acquire. The act must be the harm's real and effective cause. Thus no duty of reparation flows from an act which is only a) the occasion of some harm, or b) even a necessary condition, or c) the accidental cause of the harm. Thus one is not obliged to reparation if money that he loaned in good faith is used to cheat others.

    a. If one is in doubt whether his act has caused harm he need not make reparation.

    b. The act must be consciously and willfully unjust. The unjust intent may consist either in the resolve to do harm or in willful neglect. Harm caused by one's work must be repaired if ordered by a court, even if the injustice was not willful.

    c. If the injustice is not deliberate but there is a legal fault, one is morally obliged to compensate if ordered to by a court, for example, for breaking safety codes. One is liable for the harm he voluntarily caused, even if he regrets this after he activated the cause and then could not stop its harmful effects. If one involuntarily causes harm while committing a morally wrong act, he is not morally liable for this harm.

    d. The *gravity* of the duty to make reparation: One has a morally serious duty to make reparation for doing grave harm *if* he realized that the act was seriously wrong morally and yet willfully did it. If he did not realize this, he still has a moral duty to make reparation but it is not as morally serious.

e. The amount of reparation: One must repair all of the harm he foresaw at least indistinctly.

17. *Reparation for unjust cooperation*: The duty requires that the act a) be unjust, b) actually cause the harm, and c) be willfully wrong morally.

a. Whoever *commands* another to do an injustice is morally obliged to repair all the harm.

b. Whoever *counsels* an injustice is morally obliged to repair the harm in as far as by one's counsel one effectively persuaded another to do the unjust act, or showed him how to do it. Thus there would be *no effective influence* and no duty to make reparation if the one counselled had already decided to act unjustly and acted on his own initiative. A counsellor is not responsible for damage caused beyond what he counselled.

c. Whoever by *consent* with another culpably does unjust harm is an effective abettor of injustice and morally bound to make reparation. It must be proportionate to the effect of his consent. Thus one consenting to *vote unjustly* owes reparation. But whoever consents to an unlawful act in order to avoid a greater evil which cannot otherwise be avoided is not bound to reparation.

d. Whoever by *praise or blame* moves someone to do an injustice or who deters someone from making obligatory reparation, has the same duty of reparation as an unjust counsellor.

e. Whoever *shelters a culprit* or *receives or hides stolen goods* is morally bound to reparation to the extent that he effectively aids the injustice. This is not the case if one shields a thief because of friendship or to avoid great harm otherwise.

f. Whoever *positively cooperates* in an unjust harmful act must repair its harm 1) if his effective cooperation is willful, or 2) if it is unwillful, that is, done despite the foreseen harm, but without sufficient reason. *Immediate* cooperation in harming *property* because of grave fear is justified 1) if one intends to make reparation and is able to do so, or 2) if the harm will be done without his help, or 3) if he himself would otherwise suffer very grave harm, such as death. *Mediate* cooperation in injustice is justified if a proportionately grave reason for the cooperation (proximate or remote) is present. Thus, remote necessary cooperation or proximate free cooperation is justifiable to avoid an equivalent harm; *remote* cooperation is lawful even to avoid small harm.

g. *Negative cooperation*: One is morally bound to make reparation who by his job is in justice obliged to prevent injustice, but instead is silent or offers no resistance to the evildoer, or does not denounce him although he could without great inconvenience. Thus a delegate who wrongfully abstains from voting and so does not avert an avoidable injustice is bound to make reparation.

18. *Reparation for harm to life and health*: Reparation must be made for temporal harm related to unjust loss of life and health. Thus, reparation must be made to a murder victim's family members for the harm done to them.

19. The *order of precedence* among those who must make reparation: First, whoever possesses another's property or its equivalent. The next one obliged is whoever commanded the injustice; then whoever executed the orders; then all positive cooperators (by counsel, consent, etc.), and finally the negative cooperators.

If whoever is primarily bound to make reparation does so, those secondarily obliged are free. If the primary agent is excused the secondaries are thereby also excused, but not vice versa. If the secondaries make reparation, the primary agent must compensate them. If several people owe reparation *in the same degree* and one pays it all, the others must pay him. If the one to whom reparation is due excuses one debtor from his *pro rata* duty, the rest are not thereby freed from their duty.

20. The *amount* to be restored if there are several cooperators:

a. The whole injustice must be repaired by whoever was the effective agent of the entire harm. He is absolutely obliged to repair the entire harm; that is, whoever alone is the principal cause of the entire harm, must, independently of others, repair all of it. This duty falls on whoever commanded or counselled for his own advantage. If he (or they) default, the other cooperators are bound in the order in #19. But they may require payment from whoever was primarily obliged.

b. Each cooperator has a *conditional duty* to repair *all* of the harm if the others who are coequal agents fail to make reparation for their share. (Agents are coequal if each one's part is sufficient to cause the entire harm.) If one makes reparation alone, he may demand payment from the others. One is judged a cause of all of the harm equally with others if it flows from a strict conspiracy or could have been done only with his help. This is not the case if his help was neither necessary nor of itself enough to cause the harm.

c. Whoever was the agent of only part of the harm is morally obliged to repair only that part. In case of doubt the agent can be held morally responsible only for the harm he certainly caused. Thus he cannot be morally obliged to make total restitution if it is uncertain that he was the sole agent of all of the injustice, or if there is reason to think that the other agents will pay their share.

21. Reparation must be so made that justice is restored *fully* and as soon as possible. "Justice delayed is justice denied."

22. Causes which *excuse* from reparation:

a. Voluntary renunciation by the victim or *voluntary settlement* between him and the debtor.

b. Physical or moral impossibility postpones the duty and remits it if the impossibility is perpetual. Reparation is morally impossible if it would put the debtor in very grave need.

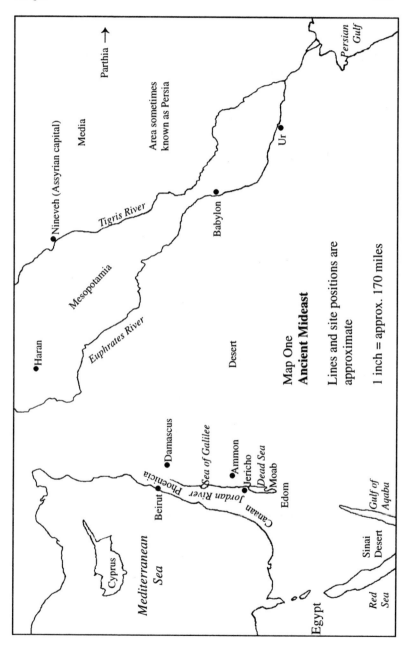

**Map One
Ancient Mideast**

Lines and site positions are approximate

1 inch = approx. 170 miles

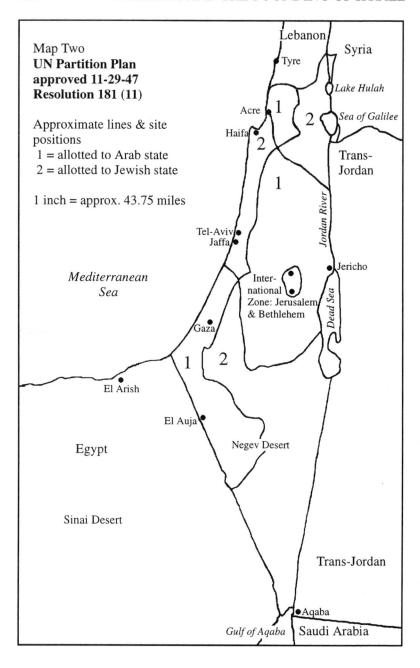

Map Two
UN Partition Plan
approved 11-29-47
Resolution 181 (11)

Approximate lines & site
positions
 1 = allotted to Arab state
 2 = allotted to Jewish state

1 inch = approx. 43.75 miles

Lebanon

Syria

Tyre

Lake Hulah

Acre   1

Haifa   2   2   Sea of Galilee

2   Trans-
         Jordan

1

Mediterranean
Sea

Tel-Aviv
Jaffa

Jordan River

Jericho

Inter-
national
Zone: Jerusalem
& Bethlehem

Dead Sea

Gaza

1   2

El Arish

El Auja

Egypt   Negev Desert

Sinai Desert

Trans-Jordan

Aqaba

Gulf of Aqaba   Saudi Arabia

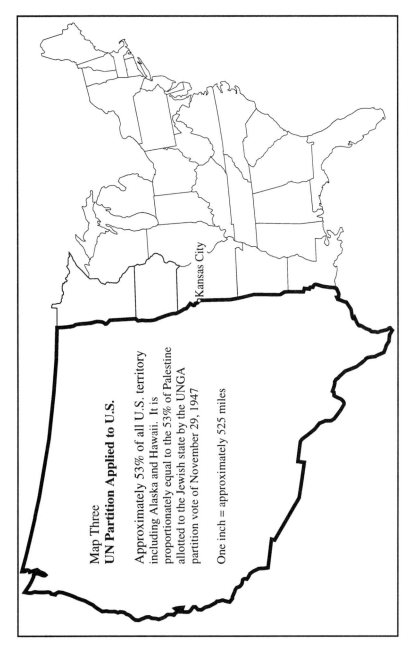

Map Three
UN Partition Applied to U.S.

Approximately 53% of all U.S. territory including Alaska and Hawaii. It is proportionately equal to the 53% of Palestine allotted to the Jewish state by the UNGA partition vote of November 29, 1947

One inch = approximately 525 miles

Kansas City

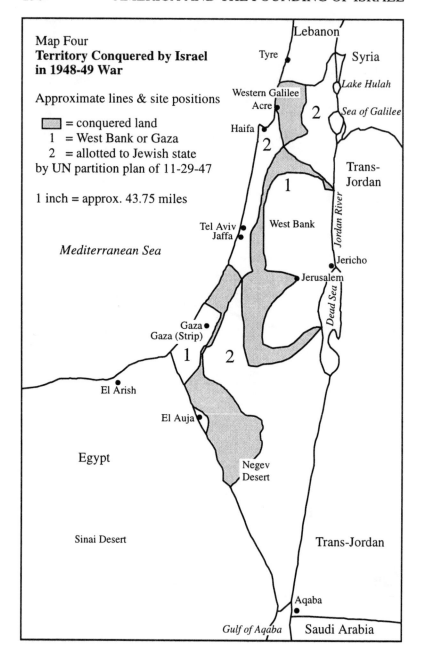

Map Four
Territory Conquered by Israel in 1948-49 War

Approximate lines & site positions

▨ = conquered land
1 = West Bank or Gaza
2 = allotted to Jewish state
by UN partition plan of 11-29-47

1 inch = approx. 43.75 miles

Mediterranean Sea

Lebanon
Tyre
Syria
Lake Hulah
Western Galilee
Acre
2
Sea of Galilee
Haifa
2
Trans-Jordan
1
Tel Aviv
Jaffa
West Bank
Jordan River
Jericho
Jerusalem
Dead Sea
Gaza
Gaza (Strip)
1
2
El Arish
El Auja
Egypt
Negev Desert
Sinai Desert
Trans-Jordan
Aqaba
Gulf of Aqaba
Saudi Arabia

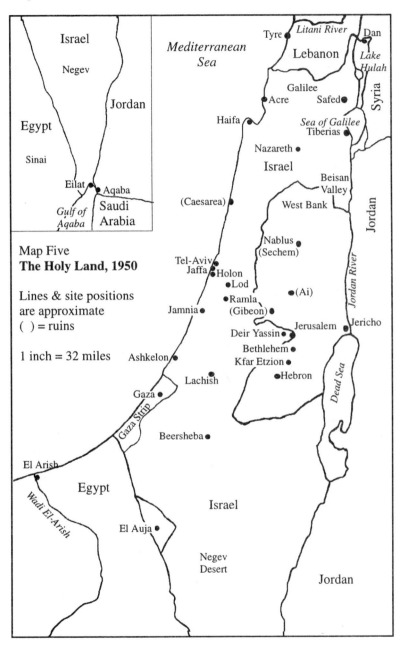

Map Five
The Holy Land, 1950

Lines & site positions
are approximate
( ) = ruins

1 inch = 32 miles

Notes

Ch. 1 The Bible: A "Deed of Ownership" to Canaan?

1. Cf. e.g., Elias Chacour, *Blood Brothers*; Rosemary Sayigh, *Palestinians: From Peasants to Revolutionaries*; & Sami Hadawi, *Bitter Harvest*, especially pp. 82-124.
2. The Jewish National Fund, *The Poetry of Achievement*, p. 12.
3. The terms "moderate historicalists" and "reductionists" are somewhat unsatisfactory terms to simplify the diverse positions of mainline scripture and related scholars. The two terms designate perhaps not so much two different schools of thought as two adjacent parts of a continuum.
4. Much of the information, though not the modern implications, in Sections II-VII is filtered from John Bright, *A History of Israel*, and Lawrence Boadt, C.S.P., *Reading the Old Testament*. For additional articles and bibliographical leads cf. Raymond E. Brown, S.S., Joseph A. Fitzmyer, S.J., & Roland E. Murphy, O. Carm., eds., *The New Jerome Biblical Commentary* (hereafter *NJBC*).

All biblical quotations are from *The Jerusalem Bible*.

5. Richard J. Clifford, S.J., "Genesis," *NJBC*, p. 9, favors the sixth century.
6. Cf. Boadt, pp. 92-103.
7. Clifford, "Genesis," p. 9.
8. Murphy, "Introduction to the Pentateuch," *NJBC*, p. 6.
9. Cf. Conrad E. L'Heureux, "Numbers," *NJBC*, p. 80. He observes that "this literature [about the flight from Egypt and entry into Canaan]...is much more concerned with later problems of theology and community organization than with presenting objective history." Moderate historicalists apply similar observations to Genesis' portrayal of the Patriarchs as well.
10. "Yahweh said to Abram, 'Leave your country [Haran]...for the land I will show you [Canaan]. I will make you a great nation.'" Gen. 12:1-2. Later God is portrayed as telling Abram, "'I am Yahweh who brought you out of Ur...to make you heir to this land.'...That day Yahweh made a covenant with Abram in these terms: 'To your descendants I give this land, from the wadi of Egypt to the Great River, the river Euphrates.'" Gen. 15:7,18. On a third occasion God is portrayed as saying to Abram, "'Here now is my covenant with you: you shall become the father of a multitude of nations. You shall no longer be called Abram; your name shall be Abraham....I will establish my Covenant between myself and you, and your descendants after you, generation after generation, a Covenant in perpetuity, to be your God and the God of your descendants after you. I will give to you and to your descendants after you the land you are living in, the whole land of Canaan, to own in perpetuity, and I will be your God....You on your part shall maintain my Covenant, yourself and your descendants after you, generation after generation.'" Gen. 17:3-5, 7-9.
11. Cf. Gen. 12-26, & Boadt, p. 135.

12. Cf. Gen. 27-37.

13. Genesis says that after God promised He would give Abraham's descendants land in Canaan, Abraham's wife, Sarah, remained childless. In accord with a custom of that time and area, Abraham had a son, Ishmael, by Sarah's slave, Hagar. Abraham asked God, "'let Ishmael live in your presence!' But God replied, 'No, but your wife Sarah shall bear you a son whom you are to name Isaac. With him I will establish my Covenant...in perpetuity, to be his God and the God of his descendants after him. For Ishmael too I grant you your request: I bless him and I will make him fruitful and will make him into a great nation. But my Covenant I will establish with Isaac.'" Gen. 17:18-21.

A few years after Sarah bore Isaac she told Abraham: "'Drive away that slave-girl and her son; he is not to share the inheritance with my son Isaac.' This greatly distressed Abraham...but God said to him...'Grant Sarah all she asks of you, for it is through Isaac that your name will be carried on. But the slave-girl's son I will also make into a nation, for he is your child too.'" Abraham "put the child on her shoulder and sent her away...God was with the boy. He grew up and made his home in the wilderness...and his mother chose him a wife from the land of Egypt." Gen. 21:10-14, 20-21.

14. During a famine Isaac planned to go to Egypt but God told him: "'Do not go down into Egypt; stay in the land I shall tell you of. Remain for the present here in this land, and I will be with you and bless you. For it is to you and your descendants that I will give all these lands, and I will fulfill the oath I swore to your father Abraham. I will make your descendants as many as the stars of heaven, and I will give them all these lands.'" Gen. 26:2-4.

15. Esau, the first born, had priority over his twin regarding inheritance rights. Through deception Jacob extracted these rights from his blind father while Esau was away: "Jacob said to his father, 'I am Esau your first-born.' Jacob came close to his father Isaac, who touched him and said...'Are you really my son Esau?' And he replied, 'I am.'...Isaac blessed him saying, '...May God give you dew from heaven, and the richness of the earth, abundance of grain and wine! May nations serve you and peoples bow down before you! Be master of your brothers; may the sons of your mother bow down before you! Cursed be he who curses you; blessed be he who blesses you!'" Gen. 27:19-29.

When Esau returned to his father, the latter realized he had been lied to; but he told Esau, "'I blessed him and blessed he will remain! When Esau heard his father's words he cried out loudly and bitterly, 'Father, bless me too!' But he replied, 'Your brother came by fraud and took your blessing....I have made him your master; I have given him all his brothers as servants, I have provided him with grain and wine. What can I do for you, my son?...Far from the richness of the earth shall be your dwelling-place, far from the dew that falls from heaven. You shall live by your sword, and you shall serve your brother. But when you win your freedom, you shall shake his yoke from your neck.' Esau hated Jacob because of the blessing his father had given him." Gen. 27:33-41.

On a later occasion Genesis portrays Isaac as repeating his blessing of Jacob:

"'May El Shaddai (God) bless you; may he make you fruitful and make you multiply so that you become a group of nations. May he grant you the blessing of Abraham, and your descendants after you, so that you may take possession of the land in which you live now, which God gave to Abraham.'" Gen. 28:3-4.

16. L'Heureux, p. 82, states: "Critical scholars are unanimous in viewing the numbers...as impossibly high."

17. Bright, p. 134; & A. Lucas, "The Number of Israelites at the Exodus," *Palestine Exploration Quarterly*, Jan.-April, 1944, p. 167.

18. Bright, p. 119.

19. Michael D. Coogan, "Joshua," *NJBC*, p. 112.

20. Cf. Judges 3:5.

21. Cf. Boadt, pp. 62 & 134.

22. Judges 1:27-36; 3:1-6.

23. Source books give slightly varying dates for the same events. This book uses a frequently used variant.

24. Trude and Moshe Dothan, *People of the Sea*, pp. 187f., 254; & Michael Grant, *A History of Ancient Israel*, p. 188.

25. Cf. e.g. Judges 1.

26. Places and people have varying spellings; this book uses a common one.

27. Boadt, pp. 207-209.

28. *Ibid.*, p. 209.

29. *Ibid.*, pp. 195f.

30. Cf. 2 Sam. 5-21; 1 Chron. 14, 18-19.

31. Cf. e.g. the introductory parts of these articles in *NJBC*: Murphy; Clifford, "Genesis" & "Exodus"; L'Heureux; & Coogan.

32. Cf. Niels Peter Lemche, *Early Israel*, pp. 377-379 & 383; pp. 384-435 deal with several issues treated in this chapter.

33. Cf. Thomas L. Thompson, *Early History of the Israelite People*; he develops these points throughout his book. Cf. also J.M. Miller & J.H. Hayes, *A History of Ancient Israel and Judah*.

34. Miller, pp. 159, 179-185, 214-6.

35. Cf. Hassan Haddad & Donald Wagner, eds., *All in the Name of the Bible*; & Grace Halsell, *Prophecy and Politics*.

36. The two books cited in the preceding note address the issue of literalism in the Holy Land conflict.

37. Interview, March 26, 1991, in Jerusalem.

38. Cf. e.g., Amos Oz, *In the Land of Israel*; Meron Benvenisti, *Conflicts and Contradictions*; & Deena Hurwitz, ed., *Walking the Red Line*.

Ch. 2 The Moral Hereditary Right to Return

1. Cf. Melvin I. Urofsky, *American Zionism from Herzl to the Holocaust*, pp. 241f.

2. Much of the narrative in Sections I and II of this chapter is based on Bright and Boadt.
3. Variant: 722 B.C. Cf. 2 Kings 17 for episode.
4. Cf. Prem Doss Swami Doss Yehudi, *The Samaritans of Israel*, p. 96.
5. Wm. F. Albright, *The Biblical Period from Abraham to Ezra*, pp. 87, 110f.
6. Ezra 2:64-65.
7. Boadt, p. 436.
8. Cf. Josephine Bacon, *Atlas of Jewish Civilization*, p. 31; & Bright, pp. 362, 365.
9. Bright, p. 409.
10. Variant: 167.
11. "Diaspora," *Encyclopaedia Britannica (Micropaedia)* (15th ed., 1992) vol. 4, p. 68. Bacon, p. 36, states that in the first century B.C. the Jews just in Cyprus and Alexandria exceeded those in Palestine. In 1930 A. Ruppin, in *Soziologie der Juden*, Berlin, *Juedischer Verlag*, 1930, vol. 1, p. 69, cited in Roberto Bachi, *Population Trends of World Jewry*, p. 25, estimated that in A.D. 65 there were some 4.5 million Jews worldwide, with some two million in Palestine. Even according to this more conservative worldwide estimate, most Jews were in the Diaspora.
12. Werner Keller, *Diaspora, Post Biblical History of the Jews*, p. 59. Cf. Shmuel Safrai, "History" section of "Israel, Land of," *Encyclopaedia Judaica*, vol. 9, p. 237.
13. Bacon, p. 47.
14. According to Eliyahu Ashtor & Haim Z'ew Hirschberg, "Arab Period" section of "Jerusalem," *Encyclopaedia Judaica*, vol. 9, p. 1410, there is some evidence that Jews may have lived in Jerusalem during the late Byzantine period.
15. Cf. e.g., Sumner Welles, *We Need Not Fail*, pp. 1-3; & Raphael Patai, "History of Zionism," *Encyclopedia of Zionism and Israel* (hereafter *EZI*), vol. 2, p. 1262.
16. Isaiah Gafni, "Judah ha-Nasi and his Era," *Ency. of Jewish History*, p. 56.
17. Keller, p. 82.
18. Michael Grant, *The Jews in the Roman World*, p. 275.
19. Cf. Mina C. & H. Arthur Klein, *Israel, Land of the Jews*, pp. 119f. Unfortunately we do not know what "its former level" was, or what the total population of northern Palestine was at that time.
20. Bachi, *The Population of Israel*, p. 19.
21. *Ibid.*, p. 19; cf. pp. 358, 360.
22. Grant, *Jews*, p. 288; Safrai, p. 261, gives a somewhat different version.
23. G.M. Watson, *The Story of Jerusalem*, pp. 128f.
24. Bacon, pp. 55f.
25. The profile of the Jewish population in Palestine between 638 and 1800 is treated more fully in Appendix One.

26. Paul Johnson, *A History of the Jews*, p. 171. Bachi, *Population Trends of World Jewry*, p. 25, states that a strong decline in the size of the Jewish population was due to the losses in the Roman-Judean wars. At the end of what he terms "the ancient era," probably the late Byzantine and early Arab eras, "losses to Jewish population may have been due...to conversions and persecutions." Later, "in the early middle ages," he believes, the causes which reduced the general population of Europe and the Middle East probably also decreased the Jewish population.

27. Klein, p. 145.

28. Nabih A. Faris, "From the Arab Conquest to A.D. 1900" section of "Palestine," *Encyclopaedia Britannica*, (14th ed., 1972), vol. 17, p. 167.

29. Cf. Justin McCarthy, *The Population of Palestine*, p. 1.

Ch. 3 The Right to Immigrate; the Start of Political Zionism

1. Some narrative in this chapter is adapted from Sami Hadawi, *Bitter Harvest*. All requotes in my book taken from *Bitter Harvest: A Modern History of Palestine* (4th ed.), Copyright © Sami Hadawi 1991, published by Olive Branch Press, an imprint of Interlink Publishing Group, Inc., are reprinted by permission.

2. Cf. McCarthy, pp. 10, 13; & Roberto Bachi, "Immigration to Palestine and Israel," *EZI*, vol. 1, p. 534.

3. Proto-Zionist writers are given in Isaiah Friedman, *From Precursors of Zionism to Herzl*, pp. 1-153.

4. Moshe Leshem, *Balaam's Curse*, p. 55.

5. The lower figure is given by demographer McCarthy from figures supplied by the Ottoman government and then corrected. However, he stresses, actual figures are unknown. Cf. McCarthy, pp. 10, 23f. The higher figure is from Y'huda Slutsky, "First Aliya," *EZI*, vol. 1, p. 325. It seems virtually impossible to reconcile Slutsky's figure with McCarthy's studies.

6. Cf. Conor Cruise O'Brien, *The Siege: the Saga of Israel and Zionism*, p. 109.

7. Ahad Ha'am, "Emmet me- Erez Israel," *Kol Kitvei*, p. 24, quoted in David Vital, *The Origins of Zionism*, p. 196. Reprinted by permission of Oxford University Press.

8. O'Brien, p. 109.

9. *Ibid.*, p. 84.

10. Ahad Ha'am: *Essays, Letters, Memoirs*, tr. & ed. Leon Simon, p. 282.

11. Ze'ev Dubnov to his brother, Shim'on, 10-20/11-1-1882, Druyanov, iii, no. 1163, cols. 495f, quoted in Vital, p. 85.

12. *Ibid.*

13. *Ibid.*

14. Cf. Alex Bein, "Herzl, Theodor," *EZI*, vol. 1, p. 491.

15. Walter Zeev Laqueur, *A History of Zionism*, p. 96.

16. Cf. Leonard Stein, *Zionism*, p. 62.

17. Theodor Herzl, entry for 9-3-1897, *The Complete Diaries of Theodor Herzl*, Raphael Patai, ed., translated from German by Harry Zohn, vol. 2, p. 581.

18. In 1897 (and usually today) "Palestine" referred to the area W of the Jordan R. and the Dead Sea from the northern border of biblical Galilee south into the Negev with its inverted apex at the northern tip of the Gulf of Aqaba. Its total area of 10,435 square miles is slightly larger than Vermont's; the land area is 10,163 square miles; the water area of 272 square miles includes L. Huleh, L. Tiberias (Sea of Galilee) and half of the Dead Sea. Areas E of the Jordan R. have been referred to as part of Palestine but these areas are more frequently referred to either as part of Trans-Jordan, which since 1950 has been called Jordan, or as part of Syria. In this book modern Palestine refers to the area of mandate Palestine. This was W of the river/Dead Sea, plus a small area N of the Yarmuk R.

19. Cf. McCarthy, p. 10. My Arab figure combines all Muslims and 80 percent of the Christians. McCarthy stresses that figures are not exact.

20. Neville J. Mandel, *The Arabs and Zionism Before World War I*, p. 45.

21. O'Brien, p. 111, adapted from Mandel, p. 46.

22. Mandel, p. 48.

23. O'Brien, p. 113.

24. Herzl, entry for 6-12-1895, *Complete Diaries*, vol. 1, p. 88.

25. Herzl to al-Khalidi, 3-19-99; quoted in *Igrot Herzl*, iii, no. 809, pp. 309f.; requoted in David Vital, *Zionism: The Formative Years*, p. 381, quoted here by permission of Oxford University Press.

26. O'Brien, p. 113.

27. Emanuel Neumann, *Theodor Herzl - Excerpts From His Diaries*, p. xx.

28. Laqueur, pp. 132f.

29. Joseph M.N. Jeffries, *Palestine: the Reality*, p. 40.

30. From *A History of Zionism* by Walter Laqueur, p. 210. Copyright © 1972 by Walter Laqueur. This and all subsequent quotes reprinted by permission of Henry Holt and Co., Inc.

31. Bein, p. 493, & Laqueur, p. 121.

32. Joseph Adler, "El-'Arish Scheme," *EZI*, vol. 1, p. 284.

33. Cf. Desmond Stewart, *Theodor Herzl*, pp. 316-322; Bein, *Theodore Herzl - a Biography*, pp. 453-461; & Gertrude Hirschler, "East Africa Scheme," *EZI*, vol. 1, pp. 263f.

34. Cf. Urofsky, p. 27.

35. O'Brien, p. 103; no further source given.

36. *Ibid.*

37. Hirschler, "East Africa," *EZI*, vol. 1, p. 264.

38. Gertrude Hirschler, "Jewish Territorial Organization," *EZI*, vol. 1, p. 636.

39. Bachi, *Population of Israel*, p. 43. Variants: 43-49 settlements & 13,000 occupants.

40. Laqueur, pp. 214, 79. Cf. also several chapters in Ruth Kark, ed., *The Land that Became Israel*.

41. According to Bachi, *Population of Israel*, pp. 42f., "Detailed research on the number of Arab peasant families [who] *remained landless* due to Jewish land purchases during seventy years is estimated by Porath* to less than four thousand." (Emphasis added; other families presumably may have been dispossessed but found other land to work on.) *Y. Porath, "The Land Problem in Mandatory Palestine," *The Jerusalem Quarterly*, n. 1, fall 1976, pp. 18-27. I have not found comparable estimates from Arab sources. For a detailed map of lands in Jewish possession, see Government of Palestine, *A Survey of Palestine*, Jerusalem: 1946, map 4.

42. Haim Hillel Ben-Sasson, "History," *Encyclopaedia Judaica*, vol. 8, col. 752.

43. Laqueur, pp. 218f., citing P. A. Alsberg, "The Arab Question in the Policy of the Zionist Executive before the First World War," in *Shivat Zion*, 4, Jerusalem 1956, p. 163.

44. Laqueur, p. 227.

45. Richard Lichtheim, report to Zionist Greater Actions Committee, 11-20-13, quoted in Yaacov Ro'i, "The Zionist Attitude to the Arabs 1908-1914," *Middle Eastern Studies*, vol. 4, n. 3, April 1968, pp. 214f.

46. Laqueur, p. 229, citing Lichtheim, *Ruckkehr*, (Stuttgart, 1970) p. 228.

47. Cf. Laqueur, p. 212.

48. Quoted in *Judische Rundschau*, Berlin: 11-27-31, quoted in Laqueur, p. 210.

49. Laqueur, p. 210.

50. *Ibid.*

51. Arab figures combine all Muslims and 80 percent of Christians. Cf. McCarthy, pp. 10 & 16-24, where he also discusses the disputed size of Palestine's 1914 Jewish population.

52. Bachi, *Population of Israel*, p. 35.

53. *Ibid.*

54. John XXIII, *Pacem in Terris*, Paragraphs 25, 106.

55. *Ibid.*, Paragraph 106.

Ch. 4 Wilson 1; the Balfour Declaration

1. Cf. Hadawi, pp. 9f., citing J. M. N. Jeffries, pp. 237f.

2. Laqueur, p. 190.

3. British government documents refer to itself in the plural.

4. Quoted in Hadawi, p. 11.

5. "The Inter-Allied Agreement of 1916," Para. 2, quoted in Roger Adelson, *Mark Sykes, Portrait of an Amateur*, p. 302.

6. *Ibid.*, Para. 3; & Hadawi, p. 11.

7. David Lloyd George, *Memoirs of the Peace Conference*, vol. 2, p. 664.

8. Palestine Royal Commission, *Report*, p. 17.

9. Letter, Arthur Balfour to Lord Rothschild, 11-2-17 photostated in Ibrahim Abu-Lughod, ed., *The Transformation of Palestine*, p. 60.

10. O'Brien, pp. 122f.

11. Quoted in Leonard Stein, *The Balfour Declaration*, p. 505.
12. *Ibid.*
13. *Ibid.*, p. 509, quoting House.
14. O'Brien, p. 129.
15. L. Stein, *Balfour*, p. 507.
16. O'Brien, p. 177.
17. L. Stein, *Balfour*, p. 530.
18. Laqueur, pp. 197f.
19. Quoted in L. Stein, *Balfour*, p. 545.
20. Michael J. Cohen, *The Origins and Evolution of the Arab-Zionist Conflict*, p. 48.
21. O'Brien, p. 130.
22. Laqueur, p. 181.
23. Urofsky, p. 241.
24. Cohen, *Origins*, pp. 53f.
25. John XXIII, Para. 106.
26. Tovia Preschel, "Balfour Declaration," *EZI*, vol. 1, p. 106, emphasis added.
27. Neil Caplan, *Palestine Jewry and the Arab Question, 1917-1925*, p. 29.

Ch. 5 Wilson 2; the British Mandate over Palestine

1. Quoted in George Antonius, *The Arab Awakening*, p. 268.
2. Hadawi, p. 14.
3. Quoted in Hadawi, p. 14.
4. Antonius, p. 434. Elie Kedourie, *England and the Middle East*, p. 113, dates the declaration in July.
5. The Anglo-French Joint Declaration, 11-7-18, quoted in Palestine Royal Commission, *Report* ("Peel Report"), Chapter II, Para. 23.
6. "Fourteen Points," *New Columbia Encyclopedia*, p. 989.
7. Hadawi, p. 10.
8. Herbert Hoover, *Ordeal of Woodrow Wilson*, p. 23.
9. *Ibid.*, p. 25.
10. *Ibid.*, p. 19.
11. Quoted in House Com. on Foreign Affairs, Report #1038 regarding House Joint Res. No. 322., *Congressional Record*, vol. 62, pt. 10, pp. 9799f.
12. Chaim Gvati, *A Hundred Years of Settlements*, p. 62.
13. Laqueur, p. 452.
14. Cohen, *Origins*, p. 67.
15. Urofsky, p. 232.
16. *Ibid.*
17. *Ibid.*, pp. 217f.
18. *Ibid.*, p. 231.
19. Quoted in *Ibid.*, pp. 231f., citing Wm. L. Westermann to Wm. C. Bullitt, 3-27-19, and other citations.

20. Urofsky, p. 232.
21. *Ibid.*, p. 241.
22. *Ibid.*
23. *Ibid.*
24. King-Crane Commission, "Final Report of the King-Crane Commission," *Foreign Relations of the United States* 1919, vol. 12, p. 769.
25. *Ibid.*, pp. 787, 806.
26. This statement was adapted from the Anglo-French Joint Declaration, issued on 11-9-18 (variants: 11-7 & 8), quoted in Jeffries, p. 238. The statement could also be a reference to Britain's pledge in its Declaration to the Seven. Similar British statements are also quoted in Hadawi, pp. 14f. Cf. Fred J. Khouri, *The Arab-Israeli Dilemma*, pp. 9f., & Kedourie, pp. 113-117.
27. King-Crane Commission, "Report," p. 792.
28. *Ibid.*
29. *Ibid.*
30. *Ibid.*
31. *Ibid.* Emphasis added.
32. *Ibid.*, p. 793.
33. *Ibid.*, p. 794.
34. *Ibid.*
35. *Ibid.*, p. 795.
36. *Ibid.*, p. 794.
37. Urofski, p. 237.
38. "Memorandum of Mr. Balfour respecting Syria, Palestine, and Mesopotamia," 8-11-19, *Documents on British Foreign Policy* (1919-1939), ser. 1, vol. 4, p. 345.
39. Doreen Ingrams, *Palestine Papers, 1917-1922: Seeds of Conflict*, pp. 96f., quoting Pro-FO, 371/5199.
40. *Ibid.*
41. *Ibid.*
42. Cohen, p. 68.
43. Urofsky, p. 238.
44. *Ibid.*, pp. 238f.
45. *Ibid.*, p. 240.
46. *Ibid.*, p. 471.
47. Cf. Laqueur, p. 450.
48. Tovia Preschel, "Balfour Declaration," *EZI*, vol. 1, p. 106.
49. O'Brien, p. 146.
50. Cohen, *Origins*, p. 68.
51. O'Brien, p. 147.
52. Jabotinsky to Zionist Actions Committee, July 1921, quoted in O'Brien, p. 175, & in Caplan, p. 113.
53. *Ibid.*
54. Urofsky, pp. 241f.

55. Ahad Ha'am, *Am Scheidewege* (Berlin, 1923) *Erster Band*, p. 87, cited in Walid Khalidi, *From Haven to Conquest: Readings in Zionism and the Palestine Problem until 1948*, p. 116.

56. Laurence Oliphant, *Haifa, or Life in Modern Palestine*, p. 59.

57. Frances E. Newton, *Fifty Years in Palestine* (London, 1948), p. 47, cited in Khalidi, *From Haven to Conquest*, p. 116.

58. S. Tolkowsky, *The Gateway of Palestine* (London, 1924), p. 144, cited in Khalidi, *From Haven to Conquest*, p. 116.

Ch. 6 Harding, Coolidge; U.S. Support of Mandate

1. Urofsky, p. 244.

2. Quoted in House Committee on Foreign Affairs, *Congressional Record*, 67 th Cong., 2nd sess., 1922, vol. 62, pt. 10, p. 9800.

3. United Kingdom, *1922 White Paper*, Cmd. 1700, June 3, 1922, photostated in *Great Britain and Palestine, 1920-1925*, vol. 13 in *The Rise of Israel* series, Howard M. Sachar, gen. ed., p. 284.

4. L. Stein, *Balfour*, p. 556.

5. O'Brien, p. 149.

6. Cohen, *Origins*, p. 83.

7. Quoted in House Com. on For. Affairs, *Congressional Record*, p. 9800.

8. *Congressional Record*, p. 9799.

9. Walter M. Chandler, Extension of Remarks, *Congressional Record*, 67th Cong., 2nd sess., 1922, vol. 62, pt. 10, p. 9810.

10. *Ibid.*

11. *Ibid.*, p. 9811.

12. *Ibid.*, p. 9805.

13. Laqueur, p. 247.

14. *Ibid.*, citing "Jews and Arabs in Palestine," *Socialist Review*, March, 1922.

15. Taken from two articles, "About the Iron Wall" & "The Ethic of the Iron Wall," in Jabotinsky's newspaper, *Razsvyet*, on Nov. 4 & 11, 1923, quoted in O'Brien, p. 175.

16. *Ibid.*

17. Cf. Laqueur, p. 246.

18. *Ibid.*, p. 468.

19. *Ibid.*

20. O'Brien, p. 174.

21. John Russell, *Report on Visit to Palestine, April, 1928*, pp. 9, 11.

22. O'Brien, p. 176; & McCarthy, p. 35. Their figures vary; McCarthy's reflect more recent studies, which this book uses.

23. O'Brien, pp. 185f.

24. Laqueur, p. 245.

25. *Ibid.*, pp. 245f.

26. Commission on the Palestine Disturbances of August, 1929, *Report of the Commission on...*, p. 159.
27. *Ibid.*, pp. 158f.
28. *Ibid.*, p. 165.
29. Laqueur, p. 189.
30. Cohen, *Origins*, p. 86.
31. *Ibid.*, p. 87.
32. Cf. Laqueur, 227.
33. O'Brien, pp. 189-192.
34. Laqueur, pp. 247f.
35. *Ibid.*
36. *Ibid.*, p. 474.
37. *Ibid.*, pp. 494f.
38. O'Brien, p. 187.

Ch. 7 Roosevelt; Americans' Balking over Added Refugees

1. Laqueur, pp. 508f.
2. Cohen, *Origins*, p. 90.
3. The Palestine Royal Commission, *Report* ("Peel Report"), p. 90.
4. *Ibid.*
5. McCarthy, p. 33.
6. Richard Breitman & Alan M. Kraut, *American Refugee Policy and European Jewry, 1933-1945*, p. 99.
7. *Ibid.*
8. Kenneth Stein, who researched Palestine land sales, stated: "If we assume that Jews purchased all of the Arab absentee-owned land, and there is no confirmation of this fact, then no less than 65 percent of the land sold legally to Jews in Palestine between 1932 and 1945 came from nonabsentee landlords, or exclusively from landlords and owner-occupants living in Palestine." Kenneth W. Stein, *The Land Question in Palestine, 1917-1939*, p. 178. For a discussion of Jews' positive and negative impact on Palestinian Arab economy and social services see Palestine Royal Commission's *Report* ("Peel Report"), pp. 90-94.
9. Also known as the Higher Arab Committee.
10. Laqueur, pp. 513f.
11. *Ibid.*, pp. 514f.
12. Apparently "at that time" refers primarily to the 1st Zionist Congress in 1897 and perhaps also to the time of the Balfour Declaration. Laqueur relates it to the latter. Cf. *ibid.* & next note.
13. David Ben-Gurion, quoted in Palestine Royal Commission, *Minutes of Evidence Heard at Public Sessions*, London, 1937, Colonial No. 134, p. 289; requoted in ESCO Foundation for Palestine, Inc., *Palestine, a Study of Jewish, Arab and British Policies*, vol. 2, pp. 801f.; cf. Laqueur, p. 515.

14. Cf. Yemima Rosenthal, ed., *Letters and Papers of Chaim Weizmann*, ser. A, vol. 17, Aug. 1935-Dec. 1936, pp. xxiif. & 380f., Barnet Litvinoff, gen. ed. Cf. also Jewish Agency for Palestine, *Memorandum to the Palestine Royal Commission*, London: JAP, 1936.
15. Chaim Weizmann, *The Jewish People and Palestine*, statement made before the Palestinian Royal Commission in Jerusalem 11-25-36, 2nd ed. p. 6. Cf. also his *Trial and Error*, p. 384; & Laqueur, p. 516.
16. Weizmann, Forward to 2nd ed., his *The Jewish People and Palestine*, p. 3.
17. Laqueur, p. 515.
18. Breitman, p. 228.
19. Cf. Jordan A. Schwarz, *The Speculator: Bernard M. Baruch in Washington, 1917-1965*, p. 564; & Margaret L. Coit, *Mr. Baruch*, p. 672.
20. Breitman, p. 102.
21. *Ibid.*, p. 103.
22. *Sunday Express*, 6-19-38, quoted in Laqueur, p. 508.
23. Laqueur, pp. 507f.; & Mark Wischnitzer, *Visas to Freedom*, pp. 152-4.
24. Weizmann, 2nd ed. of his *The Jewish People and Palestine*, p. 3.
25. Laqueur, p. 528.
26. *Ibid.*
27. *Ibid.*
28. *Ibid.*, p. 556.
29. O'Brien, p. 243.
30. Laqueur, p. 539.
31. *Ibid.*, p. 550.
32. Michael J. Cohen, *Truman and Israel*, p. 85.
33. American Palestine Committee, *Seventy Senators Back* "Restoration of Jews in Palestine," [sic] 4-20-41 news release, quoted in Richard P. Stevens, *American Zionism and U.S. Foreign Policy 1942-1947*, p. 27.
34. *Ibid.*, quoted in Stevens, p. 28.
35. *Ibid.* (emphasis added).
36. Cohen, *Truman*, p. 86, indicates an earlier date. Stevens, p. 29, says it started at the end of 1942. Samuel Halperin, *The Political World of American Zionism* (Silver Spring: Information Dynamics, 1985) p. 184, says it began 12-14-42.
37. Stevens, p. 29.
38. *Jewish Frontier*, June, 1942, p. 14, quoted in ESCO, pp. 1084f.
39. *Ibid.*
40. *Ibid.*
41. Laqueur, p. 548.
42. Yehuda Bauer, *From Diplomacy to Resistance*, p. 243.
43. Stevens, p. 206.
44. Breitman, p. 241.
45. Morris L. Ernst, *So Far So Good*, pp. 175f.

46. Quoted in the book *What Price Israel* by Alfred M. Lilienthal, p. 32. Copyright © 1953 by Regnery Publishing, Inc. All rights reserved. Reprinted by special permission of Regnery Publishing, Inc., Washington, D.C.

47. ZOA, *47th Annual Report*, p. 60, quoted in Stevens, p. 31.

48. Stevens, p. 31.

49. Abba H. Silver, *A Year's Advance: A Political Report Submitted to the Convention of the Zionist Organization of America, October 15, 1944*, NY: ZOA, 1944, p. 13, quoted in Stevens, p. 31.

50. Silver, *Ibid.*, quoted in Stevens, pp. 31f.

51. Stevens, p. 34, citing AZEC, *An Outline of Activities for Local American Emergency Committees*, p. 3.

52. Cohen, *Truman*, pp. 46-48.

53. The Republican Party 1944 plank: "In order to give refuge to millions of distressed Jewish men, women and children driven from their homes by tyranny, we call for the opening of Palestine to their unrestricted immigration and land ownership, so that in accordance with the full intent and purpose of the Balfour Declaration of 1917, and the resolution of a Republican Congress in 1922, Palestine may be constituted as a free and democratic Commonwealth. We condemn the failure of the President to insist that the mandatory of Palestine carry out the provision of the Balfour Declaration and of the mandate while he pretends to support them." The Democratic Party 1944 plank: "We favor the opening of Palestine to unrestricted Jewish immigration and colonization, and such a policy as to result in the establishment there of a free and democratic commonwealth."

54. Eddy, William A., *F.D.R. Meets Ibn Saud*, p. 36.

55. Cohen, *Origins*, pp. 99f.

56. Laqueur, p. 555.

57. *Ibid.*, p. 554.

Ch. 8 Truman 1; Settling Postwar Jewish Refugees

1. Statistical estimates vary widely due to rapidly changing, chaotic post-war conditions. Cf. Malcolm J. Proudfoot, *European Refugees 1939-52*, pp. 318ff.

2. Michael Checinski, *Poland, Communism, Nationalism, Anti-Semitism*, p. 17, citing Lucjan Dobroszycki, "Restoring Jewish Life in Post-War Poland," *Soviet Jewish Affairs*, n. 2, 1973, p. 59.

3. *Yiddish Bulletin*, 5-19-50, quoted in *What Price Israel* by Alfred M. Lilienthal, p. 36. Copyright © 1953 by Regnery Publishing, Inc. All rights reserved. Reprinted by special permission of Regnery Publishing, Inc., Washington, D.C.

4. Proskauer to Truman, 7-6-45, box 19 II, American Jewish Archives, quoted in Cohen, *Truman*, pp. 52f.

5. Menahem Kaufman, *An Ambiguous Partnership: Non-Zionists and Zionists in America, 1939-1948*, p. 195.

6. Harry S. Truman, *Memoirs*, vol. 1, p. 69.

7. Letter, Truman to Weizmann, 11-29-48, quoted in Truman, vol. 2, p. 169.

8. Weizmann to Moshe Shertok, 8-23-45, *The Letters and Papers of Chaim Weizmann* 1945-1947, ser. A, vol. 22, ed. Joseph Heller, pp. 37f. This and subsequent quote with permission, Weizmann Archives.

9. For full text of Harrison Report see 9-30-45 *NY Times* & *NY Herald Tribune*. Cf. also Leonard Dinnerstein, *America and the Survivors of the Holocaust*, p. 42; & Proudfoot, pp. 325-334.

10. Laqueur, p. 565.

11. Cohen, *Truman*, p. 53.

12. *Ibid.*

13. *Ibid.*

14. Blaustein notes, 9-29-45, Blaustein Papers, quoted in Zvi Ganin, *Truman, American Jewry and Israel*, p. 197.

15. Cf. Cohen, *Truman*, pp. 122f.

16. Virginia Gildersleeve, *Many a Good Crusade*, p. 185.

17. *Ibid.*, pp. 185f.

18. Laqueur, p. 566.

19. Cohen, *Truman*, p. 123, quoting Bevin to Ambassador Halifax, 10-12-45, E7757, FO 371/45381, PRO.

20. Stevens, pp. 140f.

21. Cf. Laqueur, p. 570.

22. Cohen, *Truman*, pp. 53-56.

23. Cf. Laqueur, p. 570.

24. Chaim Weizmann, *The Letters and Papers of Chaim Weizmann*, ser. B., vol. 2, ed. Barnet Litvinoff, p. 595. Text of his lengthy speech is given therein. Cf. Ch. 8, Endnote 8, above.

25. Cf. Cohen, *Truman*, p. 112.

26. Laqueur, pp. 570f.

27. Cohen, *Truman*, p. 129, quoting Niles to Matt Connelly, 5-1-46, Niles Papers, Harry S. Truman Library. (In July 1995 a HSTL archivist could not find a document with this quote. This is not to say that it was not there when Cohen did his research.)

28. Laqueur, p. 571, quoting Central Zionist Archives, meeting of 5-21-46, File S 25/1804.

29. Cohen, *Truman*, p. 127.

30. Laqueur, p. 572.

31. Cohen, *Origins*, p. 113.

32. Cohen, *Truman*, pp. 135f.

33. Cf. Laqueur, p. 573.

34. Cohen, *Truman*, p. 132, citing Benjamin Akzin to Rabbi Silver, 9-10-48, Benjamin Akzin Files, 70/9, Israel State Archives.

35. Cohen, *Truman*, p. 113.

36. Cf. Stevens, p. 154.

37. Cohen, *Truman*, pp. 113-115.
38. *Ibid.*, p. 59.
39. *Ibid.*, p. 78.
40. *Ibid.*, p. 83.
41. *Ibid.*, p. 86.
42. *Ibid.*
43. Phillip J. Baram, *The Department of State in the Middle East, 1919-1945.* p. 322.
44. Cf. Cohen, *Truman*, p. 89.
45. Dean Acheson, *Present at the Creation: My Years in the State Department,* p. 169.
46. Ad in *NY Herald Tribune*, 9-30-46.
47. Abraham Feinberg, interview, New York, 8-23-73, #041 384, Oral History Collection, Harry S. Truman Library.
48. Truman, "Statement by the President Following the Adjournment of the Palestine Conference in London," 10-4-46, reprinted in *Public Papers of the Presidents of the United States: Harry S. Truman, 1946*, pp. 443f.
49. Acheson, p. 176.
50. Cohen, *Truman*, pp. 144f.
51. William A. Eddy, *F.D.R. Meets Ibn Saud*, p. 37. Cohen, *Truman*, p. 295, states: "This quotation does *not* appear in the official State Department record of the meeting."
52. Loy Henderson to Dean Rusk, 11-20-77, box 11, Henderson Papers, quoted in Cohen, *Truman*, p. 90.
53. Cohen, *Truman*, pp. 145f.
54. Laqueur, pp. 573f.
55. Cohen, *Truman*, pp. 145f.
56. Laqueur, pp. 576f.
57. Stephen Wise, "My Report on the World Zionist Congress," photostated in *The Zionist Political Program 1940-1947*, ed. Michael J. Cohen, vol. 31 in *The Rise of Israel* series, p. 294.

Ch. 9 Truman 2; Palestine's Partition, Israel's Statehood

1. Cohen, *Truman*, p. 115.
2. Catholics of the Melkite Rite comprise one of the larger Christian groups in Palestine.
3. Elias Chacour, *Blood Brothers*, pp. 20-63.
4. Cohen, *Truman*, p. 117.
5. Dinnerstein, *America*, p. 156.
6. Lilienthal, *What Price Israel*, pp. 34f.
7. Quoted in Dinnerstein, p. 158.
8. Laqueur, p. 580.
9. Cohen, *Truman*, pp. 155f.

10. Laqueur, pp. 581f.

11. Cf. Stevens, pp. 172, 175.

12. Cohen, *Truman*, p. 156, where Cohen also describes other pressures put on Truman, & pp. 158f., quoting 2266/10, Israel State Archives.

13. Yehuda Karmon, "Negev," *EZI*, vol. 2, p. 829.

14. Bachi, *The Population of Israel*, pp. 47, 49, 337, 401.

15. Cf. Robert J. Donovan, *Conflict and Crisis: The Presidency of Harry S. Truman, 1945-1948*, pp. 327f.

16. Minutes of the 12-11-47 AZEC meeting, quoted in Ganin, p. 145.

17. Comay to Gering, chairman, South African Zionist Federation, 12-3-47, 2266/15, Israel State Archives, quoted in Cohen, *Truman*, p. 164.

18. Cohen, *Origins*, p. 126.

19. Cf. Stevens, p. 181, who mentions a telegram from 26 pro-Zionist senators, not 10. He states that it was also sent to 12 other delegations. Donovan states that 10 senators signed a cable sent to the president of the Philippines. Cf. Donovan, pp. 328-331, for his account of some of the intrigue surrounding the vote.

20. Cohen, *Truman*, p. 169.

21. *Ibid.*

22. Stevens, p. 179.

23. *Ibid.*, p. 182.

24. Harry S. Truman, *Memoirs*, vol. 2, pp. 158f.

25. Sumner Welles, *We Need Not Fail*, p. 63.

26. Dean Rusk as told to Richard Rusk, *As I Saw It*, p. 146.

27. *Ibid.*, p. 153.

28. Stevens, pp. 178f.

29. Cohen, *Truman*, pp. 169f.

30. *Ibid.*, p. 179.

31. Cf. Nafez Nazzal, "The Zionist Occupation of Western Galilee, 1948," *Journal of Palestine Studies*, vol. 3, n. 3, spring 1974, p. 58. Joseph Schechtman, "United Nations and Palestine-Israel," *EZI*, vol. 2, p. 1145, says that 397,000 Arabs, "46.46% of the total population there" were in the area allotted to the Jewish state. This probably excludes an estimated 66,000 to 105,000 Bedouin. Britain's official estimate of Palestine's population in December 1946 had 1,288,399 Moslems and Christians, most of whom were Arabs.

32. UN, *Official Records of the Second Session of the General Assembly: Plenary Meetings of the General Assembly*, 16 Sept.-29 Nov., 1947, p. 1637.

33. Cf. Cohen, *Palestine and the Great Powers*, p. 300.

34. Larry Collins & Dominic Lapierre, *O Jerusalem!*, p. 112.

35. Cf. Cohen, *Palestine*, p. 304.

36. *Ibid.*, p. 308; & Netanel Lorch, *The Edge of the Sword*, p. 58.

37. Cf. Collins, pp. 129-133.

38. *Ibid.*

39. Cohen, *Truman*, p. 118.

40. *Ibid.*, pp. 118f., quoting Marshall-Bevin conversation, 9-24-48, E12523, FO 371/68589, PRO.
41. Cohen, *Truman*, p. 192.
42. Quoted in *Foreign Relations of the United States, 1948*, vol. 5, pt. 2, p. 653.
43. Cohen, *Truman*, pp. 187, 190f.
44. *Ibid.*, pp. 194f.
45. Cohen, *Palestine*, p. 337.
46. Rosemary Sayigh, *Palestinians: From Peasants to Revolutionaries*, p. 75.
47. According to Collins, p. 279, Palestine's "High Commissioner Sir Alan Cunningham...had had enough contacts with the Haganah to know that the organization was incapable of such an action."
48. Jacques de Reynier, private diary, quoted in Collins, p. 278. Cf. also Reynier, *1948 a Jerusalem*, pp. 69-78.
49. *Ibid.* quoted in Collins, p. 278.
50. Quoted in Collins, p. 279.
51. Quoted in Sayigh, p. 76, & in Collins, p. 276.
52. Collins, p. 275.
53. Sayigh, p. 76.
54. *Ibid.*
55. *Ibid.*, p. 75.
56. Nazzal, "Zionist Occupation," p. 62.
57. Cf. summary of report of Col. Pa'el in *Yediot Aharonet*, 4-4-72, printed in *Journal of Palestine Studies*, vol. 1, n. 4, summer 1972, pp. 143f.
58. Cf. Sayigh, p. 75.
59. *Ibid.*, p. 76.
60. Menachem Begin, *The Revolt*, NY: Henry Schuman, 1951, p. 164, quoted in I. F. Stone, *Underground to Palestine*, p. 259.
61. Seth P. Tillman, *The United States in the Middle East: Interests and Obstacles*, p. 190.
62. Nazzal, "Zionist Occupation," p. 65.
63. Benny Morris, "The Causes and Character of the Arab Exodus from Palestine: The Israeli Defense Forces Intelligence Branch Analysis of June 1948," *Middle Eastern Studies*, vol. 22, n. 1, Jan. 1986, pp. 6-11.
64. Collins, pp. 135-138.
65. *Ibid.*, pp. 283-291.
66. *Ibid.*, pp. 347f.
67. *Ibid.*, pp. 349, 362f.
68. *Ibid.*, pp. 363f.
69. *Ibid.*, p. 364.
70. Sayigh, pp. 74f., 81.
71. Nazzal, "Zionist Occupation," p. 67, quoting interview on 3-4-73 with two residents of the village at the time it fell: Hussein Assad Khalil's uncle and aunt, who requested anonymity.

72. "Convention Concerning the Laws and Customs of War on Land - Annex to the Convention," *Conventions and Declarations Between the Powers Concerning War, Arbitration, and Neutrality*, no pagination. This and all subsequent quotes from this source are reprinted by permission of Kluwer Academic Publishers.
73. *Ibid.*
74. *Ibid.*
75. *Ibid.*
76. Cohen, *Truman*, p. 209.
77. *Ibid.*, pp. 204, 209f.
78. Hadawi, p. 131.
79. Rusk, p. 151.
80. Cf. *Ibid.*, pp. 150f.; & Truman, vol. 2. p. 164.
81. Cohen, *Truman*, pp. 218-220.
82. Austin to Marshall, 5-19-48, *Foreign Relations of the United States, 1948*, vol. 5, pt. 2, pp. 1013f.
83. *Ibid.*
84. Cohen, *Truman*, p. 221.
85. Stevens, p. 208, citing Arthur Koestler, *Promise and Fulfilment*, NY: Macmillan, 1949, p. 22.

Ch. 10 Truman 3; First Israeli-Arab War and Refugees

1. *Time*, 8-16-48, p. 25, emphasis added.
2. Cf. Khouri, pp. 69f.
3. *Ibid.*, p. 71.
4. Cf. e.g., Joan Peters, *From Time Immemorial*, p. 13.
5. Sayigh, p. 92.
6. Erskine B. Childers, "The Other Exodus," *The Spectator*, London, 5-12-61, p. 672.
7. Sayigh, p. 66. Cf. Walid Khalidi, *What Made the Palestinians Leave?* Middle East Forum, Beirut, 1959; Arab Office of Information, London, 1963.
8. Childers, p. 672.
9. Sayigh, p. 66.
10. *Ibid.*, p. 64.
11. Lt. Col. Rabbi Abraham Avidan (Zemel), "An Army Rabbi Calls for the Killing of Civilians," an IDF booklet, quoted in Israel Shahak, ed., *Begin and Co. As They Really Are*, requoted in Hadawi, pp. 89f.
12. *Ibid.*
13. *The Journal of Palestine Studies*, vol. 1, n. 4, summer 1972, p. 144, citing *Yediot Aharonot*, 4-4-72.
14. *Ibid.*, pp. 144f.
15. Nazzal, "Zionist Occupation," pp. 71f., based on an interview on 2-23-73 with Hussein Shehada, a resident of the village at the time of the attack.

16. *Journal of Palestine Studies*, vol. 1, n. 4, p. 145, citing *Yediot Aharonot*, 4-4-72.

17. Cf. Hadawi, p. 89; & Noam Chomsky, Introduction to Sayigh, p. 3, & Sayigh herself, pp. 75 & 95.

18. Hadawi, p. 89.

19. Sayigh, p. 75.

20. Sayigh, pp. 76f., quoting Khalidi, *What Made the Palistinians Leave?*, p. 42, quoting Yigal Allon, *The Book of the Palmach*, vol. 2, p. 286.

21. Yosef Tabenkin, "Doctrine of Raids," quoted in Yigal Allon, *The Making of Israel's Army*, pp. 193f.

22. Nazzal, "Zionist Occupation," pp. 70f. This article contains many such accounts, some of which are reproduced in Sayigh, pp. 83-91.

23. Nazzal, "Zionist Occupation," pp. 72f., quoting Hassam Ahmad Abdullatif, interviewed 2-13-73.

24. Sayigh, p. 84.

25. Nazzal, "Zionist Occupation," p. 90, citing interview with Nimir Ayub, 3-11-73.

26. N.a., "The Arab Refugees," *The Economist*, 10-2-48, p. 540.

27. Folke Bernadotte, *To Jerusalem*, p. 200.

28. Collins, p. 561.

29. Quoted by Hirst, p. 130, citing *Davar*, 9-29-67.

30. Joseph Weitz, *The Struggle for the Land*, p. 6, emphasis added.

31. Collins, p. 561.

32. Edgar O'Ballance, *The Arab-Israeli War 1948*, p. 63, emphasis added.

33. *Ibid.*

34. *Ibid.*

35. *Ibid.*, p. 64, emphasis added.

36. *Ibid.*

37. Quoted in Laqueur, p. 551.

38. Sayigh, p. 83.

39. Nazzal, "Zionist Occupation," p. 65.

40. Sayigh, p. 84. Cf. e.g., the case of R.M., p. 86.

41. Nathan Chofshi, in *Jewish Newsletter*, 2-9-59, quoted in Hadawi, pp. 94f.

42. Erick Fromm, in *Jewish Newsletter*, 5-19-58, quoted in Hadawi, p. 95.

43. *Ibid.*

44. Sayigh, p. 82.

45. *Ibid.*, p. 65.

46. Bachi, *The Population of Israel*, p. 402.

47. These did not include perhaps 66,000 to 105,000 Bedouin Arabs, who were not included in the first Israeli census. *Ibid.*, p. 381.

48. Quoted by Nazzal, "Zionist Occupation," p. 76, from his 2-4-73 interview with 'Ali Fayyad.

49. Cf. Truman, vol. 1, p. 69, & vol. 2, pp. 132-169.

50. Collins, p. 561.

51. Cf. Folke Bernadotte, *Progress Report of the United Nations Mediator on Palestine* 9-16-48 (A/648), p. 43.

52. Hadawi, p. 109.

53. *NY Times*, 1-2-53.

54. F. Bernadotte, "Report of Mediator to Security Council," 8-12-48 (S/961), *Yearbook of the United Nations, 1947-48* (hereafter *YUN...*), p. 443. Copyright © United Nations. All United Nations rights reserved.

55. Bernadotte, *Progress Report of the United Nations Mediator on Palestine* 9-16-48 (A/648), pp. 39f.

56. *Ibid.*, p. 14.

57. *Ibid.*

58. *Ibid.*

59. UN, summary of statement by Israeli representative Abba Eban to UNGA Political and Security Committee, 11-29-48, *Official Records of the Third Session of the General Assembly, Part I, First Committee*, Sept.-Dec., 1948, p. 805.

60. Khouri, *The Arab-Israeli Dilemma*, p. 85.

61. *Ibid.*, p. 87.

62. Ralph Bunche, Report to the [UN] Secretary-General concerning the Negeb situation 10-18-48 (S/1042), *Security Council Official Records Supplement for October 1948*, p. 61; also quoted in *NY Times*, 10-19-48, p. 4.

63. Khouri, p. 88.

64. *Ibid.*, pp. 89-91, citing *NY Times*, Oct. 28-31, 1948.

65. Khouri, pp. 91f.

66. Truman, vol. 2, p. 132.

67. Letter, Truman to Weizmann, 11-29-48, quoted in Truman, vol. 1, p. 169.

68. Bunche, Report to president of the Security Council concerning fighting in the Negeb 12-25-48 (S/1152), *Security Council Official Records Third Year, Supplement for December 1948*, p. 303.

69. Khouri, pp. 93f.

70. UN, "Universal Declaration of Human Rights," *Human Rights*, pp. 1-3; emphasis added.

71. UN, *YUN, 1948-49*, p. 175.

72. *Ibid.*

73. UN, summary of testimony of Israeli representative Michael Comay at 433rd Meeting of Special Political Committee, 10-15-65, *Official Records of the General Assembly Twentieth Session Special Political Committee*, p. 2.

74. Khouri, p. 96.

75. Cf. *YUN, 1948-49*, p. 184f.

76. Hadawi, pp. 98f.

77. O'Brien, p. 299.

78. UN, *Official Records of Third Session of General Assembly*, Part II, 191st PM, 4-13-49, pp. 38ff.; & UN General Assembly *Ad Hoc* Political Committee, *Summary Records & Annexes, Session Three*, 42nd Mtg., 5-3-49, p. 186f.; 45th

Mtg., 5-5-49, pp. 219ff.; quote *re* testimony of Abba Eban: p. 230.

79. UN, testimony of Columbian delegate Francisco Urrutia to the 46th Mtg. of the *Ad Hoc* Political Committee, 11-26-48, *Official Records of the Fourth Session of the General Assembly Ad Hoc Political Committee, 1949*, p. 276.

80. UNGA Resolution 273 (III), *YUN, 1948-49*, p. 405; also quoted in Hadawi, p. 131; & Khouri, p. 105.

81. Quoted in Khouri, p. 107.

82. Khouri, pp. 107-110.

83. Hadawi, p. 128.

84. Israel, *Government Yearbook 1950*, p. 143.

85. UN Conciliation Commission for Palestine, *Third Progress Report* (for 9 April through 8 June 1949) 6-21-49 (A/927), p. 8.

86. Cf. Note 60.

87. UN Conciliation Commission for Palestine, *Third Progress Report* (for 9 April through 8 June, 1949) 6-21-49 (A/927), p. 3.

88. Cf. Jean S. Pictet, ed. *Commentary IV Geneva Convention Relative to the Protection of Civilian Persons in Time of War*, pp. 3-9.

89. S. Tolkowsky, ed., *The Israel Yearbook, 1950/51*, p. 291.

90. *Ibid.*

91. Bachi, "Preface" to Statistical Abstract, State of Israel, *Government Yearbook 1950*, p. 323.

92. Cheryl Rubenberg, *Israel and the American National Interest*, p. 67.

93. Hadawi, pp. 100 & 103.

94. UNGA Resolution 394, *YUN, 1950*, p. 334.

95. Cf. Hadawi, p. 127.

96. Gen. Vagn Bennike, "Report of the Chief of Staff on the Implementation of the Security Council's Resolution of 18 May" 7-8-51 (S/2234), cited in *YUN, 1951*, p. 291.

97. UNSC Resolution 2157, 5-18-51, *YUN, 1951*, p. 291.

98. *Ibid.*

99. Rubenberg, p. 67.

100. *Ibid.*

101. Truman, vol. 2, p. 132.

102. David McCullough, *Truman*, p. 597.

103. Rusk, p. 147.

104. *Ibid.*, p. 153.

Ch. 11 Moral Issues in America's Role in the Conflict

1. These are expected to be included in another volume.

2. Cf. American *Declaration of Independence*.

3. Cf. Heribert Jone, *Moral Theology*, p. 233.

Appendix 1 Palestine's Jewish Population, A.D. 638-1800

1. Bachi, *Population Trends of World Jewry*, pp. 64f.
2. Klein, pp. 131-3, 135.
3. Nabih A. Faris, "From the Arab Conquest to A.D. 1900" section of "Palestine," *Encyclopaedia Britannica*, 14th ed., 1972, vol. 17, p. 167.
4. Editors, "Erez Israel Under Arab Rule," *Ency. of Jewish History*, p. 65.
5. Klein, p. 156.
6. Yael Katzir, "Jews and Crusaders in Erez Israel," *Encyclopedia of Jewish History*, p. 75.
7. *Ibid.*
8. Cf. Klein, pp. 164-6.
9. Bachi, "Immigration to Palestine and Israel," *EZI*, vol. 1, p. 534.
10. Cf. McCarthy, p. 1.
11. Keller, pp. 275f.
12. Klein, p. 178.
13. Bachi, *Population Trends of World Jewry*, p. 26.
14. Bachi, *The Population of Israel*, pp. 77, 362.
15. Cf. McCarthy, p. 1.

Appendix 2 Documents of International Agreements

1. All articles are direct quotes from *Conventions and Declarations Between the Powers Concerning War, Arbitration and Neutrality*, no author or pages. Reprinted by permission of Kluwer Academic Publishers.
2. All articles are direct quotes from Jean S. Pictet, ed. *Commentary IV Geneva Convention Relative to the Protection of Civilian Persons in Time of War*: #29 p. 209, #32 p. 221, #33 pp. 224-25, #34 p. 229, #41 p. 255, #42 p. 257, #43 pp. 259-60, #46 p. 270, #47 p. 272, #49 pp. 277-78, #53 p. 300, #78 p. 367, #114 p. 473, #130 p. 505, #139 p. 537, #147 pp. 596-97, #148 p. 602, #153 p. 611, #154 p. 613, #158 pp. 623-24, & #159 p. 628.

Appendix 3 Moral Principles of Ownership and Reparation

1. This appendix is based in large part on Rev. Heribert Jone, O.F.M. Cap., *Moral Theology*, translated and adapted by Rev. Urban Adelman, O.F.M. Cap.

GLOSSARY OF TERMS AND PEOPLE

I. Terms.

Aliyah: Jewish immigration to Palestine or Israel; an immigration wave
Amorites: ethnic group including perhaps the Aramean subgroup
Arameans: Abram's immediate ethnic group
Diaspora: Jewish life, especially in groups, outside of Palestine
Eretz Israel: "the Land of Israel"
Hagana: *yishuv's* official underground military forces
IDF: Israeli Defense Forces; succeeded the Hagana
Irgun: 1931-48, unofficial *yishuv* underground military-terrorist organization led by Menachem Begin 1940-48
Lehi: 1940-48, unofficial *yishuv* military-terrorist organization aka Stern Gang
Moral right: either a) inherent: possessor has it independently of any human law or decree, e.g., the right to life or to religion; or b) semi-inherent: it may flow partly from one or more primary moral rights and partly from human law or other type of legal action, e.g., some inheritance rights & political rights
Objective morality: moral rightness or wrongness of an act considered just in itself, regardless of what the one doing the act thinks of its morality
Palmach: full-time, elite core of the Hagana
Pogrom: organized persecution, especially of Russian Jews
Subjective morality: the moral rightness or wrongness of an act as perceived by the one doing it
Yishuv: the Jewish community in Palestine, especially Zionists

II. People who are less well-known but repeatedly mentioned in the book.

Abdullah ibn-Hussein 1882-1951 Trans-Jordan's emir 1921-46, king 1946-51
Attlee, Clement 1883-1967 Br. prime minister 1945-51
Austin, Warren 1877-1963 US ambassador to UN under Truman
Balfour, Arthur 1848-1930 Br. foreign secretary under Lloyd George
Baruch, Bernard 1870-1965 Roosevelt adviser, devised plan to settle Jewish refugees in Africa
Ben-Gurion, David 1886-1973 headed Jewish workers in Palestine, & Palestine Executive of Jewish Agency, Israeli prime minister 1948-53, 1955-63
Begin, Menachem 1913-92 headed *yishuv* revisionists & Irgun, Israeli prime minister 1977-84
Bevin, Ernest 1884-1951 Br. foreign secretary under Attlee
Blaustein, Jacob 1892-1970 led AJC Executive Com., Truman era
Boadt, Lawrence 1942- Old Testament scholar
Brandeis, Louis 1856-1941 US Supreme Court justice, Zionist leader
Byrnes, James 1879-1972 US secretary of state 1945-47

Clifford, Clark 1906- Truman adviser

Curzon, George 1859-1925 chairperson of British cabinet committee on Middle East acquisitions 1917, foreign secretary 1919-24

Feisal ibn-Hussein 1885-1933 allegedly signed two pledges to support Jewish home in Palestine, king briefly of Syria, then of Iraq

Frankfurter, Felix 1882-1965 US Supreme Court justice, Zionist leader

Haj Amin al-Husseini 1893-1974 grand mufti of Jerusalem, Palestine political leader, staunch opponent of Zionism

Hussein Ibn Ali (Sherif) 1856-1931 Arab leader in Ottoman Empire, negotiated with British; cf. two sons, Abdullah & Feisal

Jabotinsky, Vladimir 1880-1940 leader of revisionists, once Zionism's most militant wing

Laqueur, Walter Zeev 1921- historian

Lloyd-George, David 1863-1945 British prime minister 1916-22

Lovett, Robert 1895-1986 undersecretary of state under Truman

Lowenthal, Max 1888-1971 Clifford's adviser on Palestine 1947-48, crucial White House advocate of Zionism

Marshall, George C. 1880-1959 secretary of state during Truman's 1st term, strongly questioned his Mideast policy

Neumann, Emanuel 1893-1980 organized Zionist fronts in Washington

Niles, David 1890-1952 Roosevelt/Truman aide, Truman's liaison with Jewish community

O'Brien, Conor C. 1917- wrote *The Siege: The Saga of Israel and Zionism*

Proskauer, Joseph 1877-1971 president of American Jewish Committee (AJC), which was anti-Zionist to November, 1947

Roosevelt, Eleanor 1884-1962 US delegate to UN, FDR's wife

Rusk, Dean 1909-94 State Department's head of Washington UN desk

Silver, Abba 1893-1963 rabbi, headed aggressive wing of US Zionism

Taft, Robert 1889-1953 senator from Ohio, strong Zionist supporter in Roosevelt/Truman eras

Urofsky, Melvin 1939- historian of Zionism

Wagner, Robert 1877-1953 senator from NY, lent name, support to Zionist lobby in Roosevelt/Truman eras

Weizmann, Chaim 1874-1952 usually Zionism's world leader from WWI to Israel's founding, Israeli president, 1949-52

Wilson, Woodrow 1856-1924 US president 1913-21

Wise, Stephen 1874-1949 rabbi, US Zionist leader

BIBLIOGRAPHY

Abu-Lughod, Ibrahim. *The Transformation of Palestine*. Evanston: Northwestern University, 1971.

Acheson, Dean. *Present at the Creation: My Years in the State Department*. New York: Norton, 1969; © by author.

Adelson, Roger. *Mark Sykes: Portrait of an Amateur*. London: Cape, 1975.

Adler, Joseph. "El-'Arish Scheme." *Encyclopedia of Zionism and Israel* (hereafter *EZI*). Ed. Raphael Patai. NY: Herzl/McGraw-Hill, 1971.

Albright, Wm. *The Biblical Period from Abraham to Ezra*. NY: Harper, 1963.

Allon, Yigal. *The Making of Israel's Army*. NY: Vallentine, Mitchell, 1970.

Antonius, George. *The Arab Awakening: The Story of the Arab National Movement*. Philadelphia: Lippincott, 1939; © now HarperCollins.

N.a. "The Arab Refugees." *The Economist*, Oct. 2, 1948.

Ashtor, Eliyahu, & Haim Z'ew Hirschberg. "Arab Period" section of "Jerusalem." *Ency. Judaica*. NY: Macmillan, & Jerusalem: Keter, 1971.

Ateek, Naim S. *Justice and Only Justice*. Maryknoll, NY: Orbis, 1989.

Austin, Warren. UNSC speech, 2-24-48. *For. Rel. US* 5, pt. 2 (1948).

Bachi, Roberto. "Immigration to Palestine and Israel." *EZI*.

---. *Population of Israel*. Jerusalem: No publisher given; sponsored by The Institute of Contemporary Jewry at Hebrew U. of Jerusalem and by the Demographic Center of the Prime Minister's Office, 1974; produced by S.T.I. Scientific Translations International, Ltd.

---. *Population Trends of World Jewry*. Jerusalem: Hebrew U., 1976.

---. "Preface" to Statistical Abstract. Israel. *Government Yearbook 1950*. Jerusalem: Government Printer, 1950.

Bacon, Josephine. *Atlas of Jewish Civilization*. Lon.: A. Deutsch, 1990.

Balfour, Arthur. "Memorandum of Mr. Balfour respecting Syria, Palestine, and Mesopotamia." *Documents on British Foreign Policy* (1919-1939). 1st ser., vol. 4. London: His Majesty's Stationery Office, 1952.

Baram, Phillip J. *The Department of State in the Middle East, 1919-1945*. Philadelphia: University of Pennsylvania, 1978.

Bauer, Yehuda. *From Diplomacy to Resistance*. Philadelphia: Jewish Publication Society of America (hereafter JPSA), 1970.

Begin, Menachem. *The Revolt*. NY: Henry Schuman, 1951.

Bein, Alex. "Herzl, Theodor." *EZI*.

---. *Theodore Herzl - a Biography*. Tr. Maurice Samuel. Phila.: JPSA, 1940.

Bennike, Vagn. "Report of the Chief of Staff on the Implementation of the Security Council's Resolution of 18 May," 7-8-51 (S/2234). *Yearbook of the United Nations, 1951* (hereafter *YUN...*). NY: UN.

Ben-Sasson, Haim Hillel. "[Jewish] History." *Ency. Judaica*.

Benvenisti, Meron. *Conflicts and Contradictions*. NY: Villard, 1986.

Bernadotte, Folke. *Progress Report of the United Nations Mediator on*

Palestine. 9-16-48 (A/648). Paris: UN, 1948.

---. "Report of Mediator to Security Council," 8-12-48 (S/961). *YUN, 1947-48*. NY: UN.

---. *To Jerusalem*. Tr. Joan Bulman. Lon.: Hodder & Stoughton, 1951.

Boadt, Lawrence. *Reading the Old Testament*. Mahwah: Paulist, 1984; © The Missionary Society of St. Paul the Apostle in the State of New York.

Breitman, Richard, & Alan Kraut. *American Refugee Policy and European Jewry, 1933-1945*. Bloomington: Indiana Univ., 1987.

Bright, John. *A History of Israel*, 3rd ed. Phila.: Westminster, 1981.

Brown, Raymond E., Joseph A. Fitzmyer & Roland E. Murphy, eds. *New Jerome Biblical Commentary*. Englewood Cl.: Prentice-Hall, 1988.

Bunche, Ralph. "Report to the President of the "Security Council Concerning Fighting in the Negeb," 12-25-48 (S/1152). *Security Council Official Records Third Year, Sup. for Dec., 1948*. NY: UN.

---. "Report to the Secretary-General Concerning the Negeb Situation," 10-18-48 (S/1042). *Security Council Official Records Third Year, Supplmnt. for Oct. 1948*. NY: UN.

Caplan, Neil. *Palestinian Jewry and the Arab Question, 1917-1925*. Totowa, NJ: Cass, 1978.

Chacour, Elias, & David Hazard. *Blood Brothers*. Grand Rapids: Zondervan, 1984.

Checinski, Michael. *Poland, Communism, Nationalism, Anti-Semitism*. New York: Karz-Cohl, 1982.

Childers, Erskine B. "The Other Exodus." *The Spectator*, May 12, 1961.

Clifford, Richard J. "Genesis" & "Exodus." *The New Jerome Biblical Commentary*. Cf. Brown.

Cohen, Michael J. *The Origins and Evolution of the Arab-Zionist Conflict*. Berkeley: Univ. of California, 1987; © the Regents of the Univ. of Calif.

---. *Palestine and the Great Powers, 1945-1948*. Princeton: Pr. U., 1982.

---. *Truman and Israel*, Berkeley: Univ. of Calif., 1990; © Regents, U.C.

Coit, Margaret L. *Mr. Baruch*. Cambridge: Riverside, 1957.

Collins, Larry, & Dominique Lapierre. *O Jerusalem!* NY: Simon, 1972.

Comm. on the Pal. Disturbances of 8-29. *Report of the Commission on the Palestine Disturbances of August, 1929*. London: His Majesty's Stationery Office, 1930.

Comptroller General of the U.S. *U.S. Assistance to the State of Israel*. Gaithersburg, Md.: GAO, 1983.

Cong. Record 67th Cong., 2nd sess., 1922, vol. 62, pt. 10: 9799-9811.

Conventions and Declarations Between the Powers Concerning War, Arbitration and Neutrality. The Hague: M. Nijhoff, 1915. Reprinted by permission of Kluwer Academic Publishers.

Coogan, Michael D. "Joshua." *NJBC*. Cf. Brown.

Democratic Party. National platform. Washington: 1944.

"Diaspora." *Ency. Britannica.* 15th ed., 1992.

Dinnerstein, Leonard. *America and the Survivors of the Holocaust.* NY: Columbia Univ., 1982.

Donovan, Robert J. *Conflict and Crisis: The Presidency of Harry S. Truman, 1945-1948.* NY: Norton, 1977.

Doss, Prem Doss Swami Doss Yehudi. *The Samaritans of Israel.* Vanchiyoor, Thiruvananthapuram, Kerela, India: Sachetuana, 1991.

Dothan, Moshe, & Trude Dothan. *People of the Sea.* NY: Macmillan, 1992.

Eddy, William A. *F.D.R. Meets Ibn Saud.* NY: American Friends of the Middle East, 1954.

Elon, Amos. *The Israelis: Founders and Sons.* NY: Holt, Rinehart, 1971.

"Erez Israel Under Arab Rule." *Ency. of Jewish History.* English ed. Eds. Ilana Shamir & Shlomo Shavit. NY: Facts on File, 1986.

Ernst, Morris L. *So Far So Good.* NY: Harper, 1948 © Joan Ernst; © now HarperCollins.

ESCO Foundation for Palestine. *Palestine, a Study of Jewish, Arab and British Policies.* New Haven: Yale Univ., 1947.

EZI: Cf. *Encyclopedia of Zionism and Israel.*

Faris, Nabih A. "From the Arab Conquest to A.D. 1900" section of "Palestine." *Ency. Britannica,* 14th ed.

Feinberg, Abraham. Interview, #041 384, Oral History Collection. Independence, MO: Harry S. Truman Library, 1973.

Flapan, Simha. *The Birth of Israel: Myths and Realities.* NY: Pantheon, 1987.

"Fourteen Points." *New Columbia Encyclopedia.* Ed. Wm. H. Harris *et al.* NY: Columbia Univ., 1975.

Friedman, Isaiah, ed. *From Precursors of Zionism to Herzl.* Vol. 1 of *The Rise of Israel.* Gen. ed. Howard M. Sacher. NY: Garland, 1987.

Gafni, Isaiah. "Judah ha-Nasi and his Era." *Ency. of Jewish History.*

Ganin, Zvi. *Truman, American Jewry and Israel, 1945-1948.* NY: Holmes & Meier, 1979.

Gildersleeve, Virginia. *Many a Good Crusade.* NY: Macmillan, 1954.

Grant, Michael. *A History of Ancient Israel.* NY: Ch. Scribner's Sons, 1984.

---. *The Jews in the Roman World.* London: Weidenfeld & Nicolson, 1973.

Gvati, Chaim. *A Hundred Years of Settlements.* Tr. Fred Skolnik. Jerusalem: Keter, 1985.

Ha'am, Ahad [A. Ginsberg]. *Essays, Letters, Memoirs.* Tr. & ed. Leon Simon. Oxford: Phaidon, 1946.

Hadawi, Sami. *Bitter Harvest: a Modern History of Palestine.* NY: Olive Branch Press, an imprint of Interlink Publishing Group, Inc., 1991.

Haddad, Hassam, & Donald Wagner, eds. *All in the Name of the Bible.* Brattleboro, Vt.: Amana, 1986.

Halperin, Samuel. *The Political World of American Zionism.* Silver Spring, Md.: Information Dynamics, 1985.

Halsell, Grace. *Prophecy and Politics*. Chicago: Lawrence Hill, 1986.

Hertzberg, Arthur. *Jewish Polemics*. NY: Columbia Univ., 1992.

Herzl, Theodor. *The Complete Diaries of Theodor Herzl*. Ed. Raphael Patai, trans. Harry Zohn. NY: Herzl & Thomas Yoseloff, 1960.

Hirschler, Gertrude. "East Africa Scheme." *EZI*.

---. "Jewish Territorial Organization." *EZI*.

Hirst, David. *The Gun and the Olive Branch: The Roots of Violence in the Middle East*. NY: Harcourt Brace Jovanovich, 1977.

Hoover, Herbert. *Ordeal of Woodrow Wilson*. NY: McGraw-Hill, 1958.

Howard, Harry. *The King-Crane Commission*. Beirut: Khayat, 1963.

Hurwitz, Deena. *Walking the Red Line: Israelis in Search of Justice for Palestine*. Philadelphia: New Society, 1992.

Ingrams, Doreen. *Palestine Papers, 1917-1922: Seeds of Conflict*. London: John Murray (Publishers) Ltd., 1972.

Israel. *Government Yearbook 1950*. Jerusalem: Government Printer, 1950.

Jeffries, Joseph M.N. *Palestine: the Reality*. London: Longmans, 1939.

The Jerusalem Bible.

Jewish Agency for Palestine. *Memorandum to the Royal Commission* (Peel). London: Jewish Agency for Palestine, 1936.

Jewish National Fund. *The Poetry of Achievement*. Jerusalem: Keren Kayemeth LeIsrael, 1988.

John XXIII. *Pacem in Terris*. Vatican City: Vatican, 1963. Rpt. in Joseph Gremillion, ed., *The Gospel of Justice and Peace*. Maryknoll, NY: Orbis, 1976.

Johnson, Paul. *A History of the Jews*. NY: Harper & Row, 1987.

Jone, Heribert. *Moral Theology*. Tr. & adapted by Urban Adelman. Westminster, Md.: Newman, 1953.

Kark, Ruth, ed. *The Land That Became Israel*. NH: Yale Univ., 1989.

Karmon, Yehuda. "Negev." *EZI*.

Katzir, Yael. "Jews and Crusaders in Erez Israel." *Ency. of Jewish History*.

Kaufman, Menahem. *An Ambiguous Partnership: Non-Zionists and Zionists in America, 1939-1948*. Jerusalem: Magnes Press, 1991.

Kedourie, Elie. *England and the Middle East*. Boulder: Westview, 1987.

Keller, Werner. *Diaspora: The Post-Biblical History of the Jews*. Trans. Richard & Clara Winston. NY: Harcourt, Brace & World, 1969.

Khalidi, Walid A. *From Haven to Conquest: Readings in Zionism and the Palestine Problem Until 1948*. Beirut: Institute for Palestine Studies, 1971.

---. *What Made the Palestinians Leave?* Beirut: Middle East Forum, 1959, & London: Arab Office of Information, 1963.

Khouri, Fred. *Arab-Israeli Dilemma*. 3rd ed. Syracuse: Syracuse U., 1985.

King-Crane Commission. "Final Report of the King-Crane Commission." *Foreign Relations of the United States* 12 (1919).

Klein, Mina C., & H. Arthur Klein. *Israel, Land of the Jews: a Survey of Forty-three Centuries*. Indianapolis: Bobbs-Merrill, 1972.

Kraut, Alan M. Cf. Breitman.

Laqueur, Walter Zeev. *A History of Zionism.* NY: Holt, Rinehart, 1972.

Lemche, Niels Peter. *Early Israel: Anthropological and Historical Studies on the Israelite Society Before the Monarchy.* Leiden: Brill, 1985.

Leshem, Moshe. *Balaam's Curse.* NY: Simon & Schuster, 1989.

L'Heureux, Conrad. "Numbers." *NJBC.* Cf. Brown.

Lilienthal, Alfred M. *What Price Israel.* Chicago: Henry Regnery, 1953.

Lloyd George, David. *Memoirs of the Peace Conference.* NH: Yale U., 1939.

Lorch, Netanel. *The Edge of the Sword: Israel's War of Independence, 1947-1949.* NY: G.P. Putnam's Sons, 1961.

Lucas, A. "Number of Israelites at the Exodus." *Palestine Exploration Quarterly* (Jan.-Apr., 1944).

Mandel, Neville J. *The Arabs and Zionism Before World War I.* Berkeley: Univ. of California, 1976.

McCarthy, Justin. *The Population of Palestine.* NY: Columbia U., 1990.

Miller, J. Maxwell, & John H. Hayes. *A History of Ancient Israel and Judah.* Philadelphia: Westminster, 1986.

Morris, Benny. "The Causes and Character of the Arab Exodus from Palestine: The Israeli Defense Forces Intelligence Branch Analysis of June 1948." *Middle Eastern Studies* 22 (Jan. 1986).

Murphy, Roland E. "Introduction to the Pentateuch." *New Jerome Biblical Commentary.* Cf. Brown.

Nazzal, Nafez. *Palestinian Exodus from Galilee, 1948.* Beirut: Institute for Palestine Studies, 1978.

---. "The Zionist Occupation of Western Galilee, 1948." *Journal of Palestine Studies* vol. 3, n. 3 (spring 1974).

Neumann, Emanuel. *Theodor Herzl - Excerpts From His Diary.* NY: Scopus, 1941.

New Jerome Biblical Commentary (NJBC): cf. Brown.

O'Ballance, Edgar. *The Arab-Israeli War 1948.* London: Faber, 1956.

O'Brien, Conor. *The Siege: The Saga of Israel and Zionism.* NY: Simon, 1986.

Oliphant, Laurence. *Haifa, or Life in Modern Palestine.* Ed. with Introduction and © by Charles A. Dana; NY: Harper, 1887; © now HarperCollins.

Oz, Amos. *In the Land of Israel.* NY: Random House, 1984.

Pa'el, Meir. Report. *Yediot Aharonet.* Apr. 4, 1972. Summary printed in *Journal of Palestine Studies* 1, n. 4 (summer 1972).

---. "History of Zionism." *EZI.*

Peel Commission Report: cf. UK. *Palestine Royal Commission Report.*

Peters, Joan. *From Time Immemorial.* NY: Harper & Row, 1985.

Pictet, Jean S., ed. *Commentary IV Geneva Convention Relative to the Protection of Civilian Persons in Time of War.* Geneva: International Committee of the Red Cross, 1958.

Preschel, Tovia. "Balfour Declaration." *Ency. of Zionism and Israel.*

Proudfoot, Malcolm J. *European Refugees 1939-52*. London: Faber, 1957.

Rabie, Mohammed. "U.S. Aid to Israel." *The Link* 22 (May-Jn. 1989).

Republican Party. National platform. Washington: 1944.

Reynier, Jacques de. *1948 a Jerusalem*. 2nd ed. Neuchatel, Switz., Editions de la Baconniere, 1969.

Ro'i, Yaacov. "The Zionist Attitude to the Arabs 1908-1914." *Middle Eastern Studies* (1968).

Rubenberg, Cheryl A. *Israel and the American National Interest: A Critical Examination*. Urbana: Univ. of Illinois, 1986.

Rubinstein, Amnon. *The Zionist Dream Revisited: From Herzl to Gush Emunim and Back*. NY: Schocken, 1984.

Rusk, Dean, as told to Richard Rusk, ed. Daniel Papp. *As I Saw It*. NY: Norton, 1990; © Richard Rusk.

Russell, John. *Report on Visit to Palestine, April, 1928*. London: Zionist Organization, 1929.

Safrai, Shmuel. "History" section of "Israel, Land of." *Ency. Judaica*.

Sayigh, Rosemary. *Palestinians: From Peasants to Revolutionaries*. London: Zed, 1979.

Schechtman, Joseph. "United Nations and Palestine-Israel." *EZI*.

Schwarz, Jordan A. *The Speculator: Bernard M. Baruch in Washington, 1917-1965*. Chapel Hill: Univ. of No. Carolina, 1981.

Slutsky, Y'huda. "First Aliya." *EZI*.

Stein, Kenneth W. *The Land Question in Palestine, 1917-1939*. Chapel Hill: Univ. of No. Carolina, 1984.

Stein, Leonard. *Balfour Declaration*. London: Vallentine, Mitchell, 1961.

---. *Zionism*. London: Kegan Paul, Trench, Trubner, 1932.

Stevens, Richard P. *American Zionism and U.S. Foreign Policy 1942-1947*. NY: Pageant, 1962.

Stewart, Desmond. *Theodor Herzl: Artist and Politician*. Garden City, NY: Doubleday, 1974.

Stone, I.F. *Underground to Palestine*. NY: Pantheon, 1978.

Telders (Professor) Study Group. *United Nations Textbook*. Leiden: U. of Leiden, 1954.

Thompson, Thomas L. *Early History of the Israelite People*. Leiden: Brill, 1992.

Tillman, Seth P. *The United States in the Middle East: Interests and Obstacles*. Bloomington: Indiana Univ., 1982.

Tolkowsky, S., ed. *The Israel Yearbook, 1950/51*. NY: Zionist Organization of America, n.d.

Truman, Harry S. *Memoirs*. 2 vols. Garden City: Doubleday, 1956.

---. *Public Papers of the Presidents of the United States: Harry S. Truman, 1946*. Washington: Office of the Federal Register National Archives and Records Service, 1962.

UK. *1922 White Paper*. Cmd. 1700. London: His Majesty's Stationery Office (1922). Photostated in *Great Britain and Palestine, 1920-1925*. Vol. 13, *The Rise of Israel*. NY: Garland, 1987.

UK, Government of Palestine. *A Survey of Palestine*. Jerusalem: 1946.

UK, Palestine Royal Commission (Peel Comm.). *Palestine Royal Commission Report*. London: His Majesty's Stationery Office, 1937. Reprinted 1945.

UN. *Official Records of the General Assembly Twentieth Session Special Political Committee*. NY: UN, 1966.

---. *Security Council Official Records* Third Year, Supplements for Oct., Dec. 1948. NY: UN. Cf. Bunche.

---. "Universal Declaration of Human Rights." NY: UN, 1948. Reprinted in UN. *Human Rights: a Compilation of International Instruments of the United Nations*. NY: UN, 1967.

---. *Yearbook of the UN, 1947-8, 1950, 1951*. NY: UN Office of Public Information; 1948-49 & 1950 eds. pub. by Columbia U. with UN.

UN Conciliation Commission for Palestine. *Third Progress Report* (A/927). NY: UN, 1949.

UNGA. *Plenary meetings of General Assembly*, 1947-1949. NY: UN.

UNGA *Ad Hoc* Political Committee. *Summary Records and Annexes*, Session 3, 1948-1949, Part 1. Paris: UN.

UNGA Political and Security Committee. *Official Records*, several years including Session 3, Part 1, 1948. NY: UN.

U.S. Gov't. *Foreign Relations of the United States, 1948*. Wash.: GPO, 1976.

U.S. King-Crane Commission. "Final Report of the King-Crane Commission." Reprinted in *Foreign Relations of the United States* 12 (1919).

Urofsky, Melvin I. *American Zionism from Herzl to the Holocaust*. Garden City, NY: Doubleday, 1975.

Vital, David. *The Origins of Zionism*. Oxford: Clarendon, 1975.

---. *Zionism: the Formative Years*. NY: Oxford U. Press, 1982.

Watson, G.M. *The Story of Jerusalem*. London: Dent, 1918.

Weitz, Joseph. *The Struggle for the Land*. Tel Aviv: Lion, 1950.

Weizmann, Chaim. *The Jewish People and Palestine*, statement before Pal. Royal Comm., Jerusalem, 11-25-36, 2nd ed. London: Zionist Org., 1939.

---. *Letters and Papers of Chaim Weizmann*. Vol. 17, ser. A. (8-35 - 12-36), ed. Y. Rosenthal. Vol. 22, ser. A, (1945-1947) ed. J. Heller. Vol. 2, ser. B, ed. B. Litvinoff. New Brunswick: Transaction Publishers, Rutgers U., 1968-80.

---. *Trial and Error*. NY: Harper, 1949.

Welles, Sumner. *We Need Not Fail*. Boston: Houghton Mifflin, 1948.

Wischnitzer, Mark. *Visas to Freedom*. Cleveland: World, 1956.

Wise, Stephen. "My Report on the World Zionist Congress." Reproduced in *Zionist Political Program 1940-1947*. Ed. Michael J. Cohen, vol. 31, *The Rise of Israel*. NY: Garland, 1987.

INDEX

("City" and "vil." are Holy Land sites. BrG, USG, etc. are British, U.S., etc. government personnel. "Throughout" indicates references that are throughout all or part of book. Role refers to role in book.)